A life on Gorge River

A life on Gorge River

New Zealand's remotest family

ROBERT LONG

RANDOM HOUSE
NEW ZEALAND

This book is dedicated to my wife, Catherine, and our children, Christan and Robin, to sustain them into the future.

A RANDOM HOUSE BOOK published by Random House New Zealand
18 Poland Road, Glenfield, Auckland, New Zealand

For more information about our titles go to www.randomhouse.co.nz
A catalogue record for this book is available from the National Library of New Zealand

Random House New Zealand is part of the Random House Group
New York   London   Sydney   Auckland   Delhi   Johannesburg

First published 2010. Reprinted 2010 (twice)

Cover: Laura Forlong
Text design: Sarah Elworthy and Pieta Brenton
Map: Janet Hunt
Printed in Australia by Griffin Press an Accredited ISO AS/ NZS 14001:2004 Environmental Management System printer.

contents

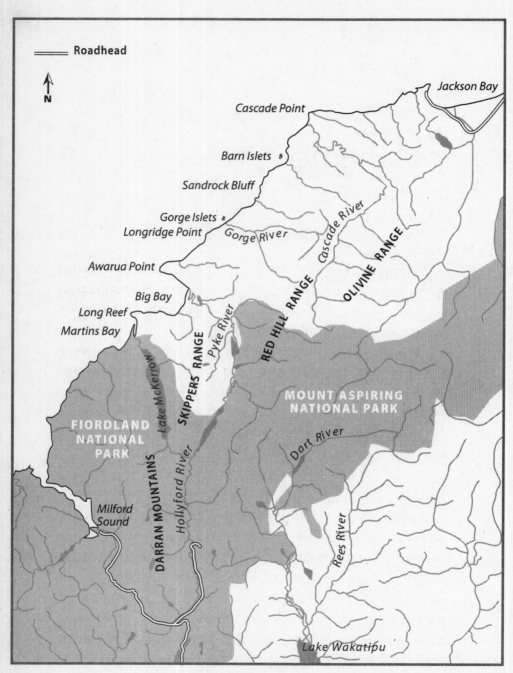

N

Jackson Bay

Cascade Point

Barn Islets   8

Sandrock Bluff

Gorge Islets   8
Longridge Point

Gorge River

Cascade River

OLIVINE RANGE

RED HILL RANGE

Awarua Point

Big Bay

Long Reef

Martins Bay

Pyke River

SKIPPERS RANGE

Lake McKerrow

MOUNT ASPIRING
NATIONAL PARK

FIORDLAND
NATIONAL
PARK

DARRAN MOUNTAINS

Hollyford River

Dart River

Rees River

Milford
Sound

Lake Wakatipu

South Westland, showing Gorge River and surrounds

prologue

Sometimes I lie awake at night thinking about how we are going to cross the Cascade. This mighty river separates us from the rest of humanity — we are living in the never-nevers and the Cascade is the border.

We try to choose a window of opportunity between weather systems to give us enough time to walk from Gorge River up the coast, across the Spoon and Hope Rivers to Barn Bay. After a night's rest we head up the north bank of the Hope for two kilometres, then along the bottom of the foothills above Cascade's Hermitage Swamp. Eventually we arrive at the middle Cascade flats and look for a suitable place to ford.

By the time our children, Christan and Robin, reached the age of about three and a half they had become too heavy to carry over long distances, but they were also becoming mobile enough to travel the terrain under their own steam. But a journey that in earlier years had taken one day on the shortest day of the year would now take us five days, allowing them to walk the 45-kilometre distance. We would break the walk to Barn Bay by staying a night at the Spoon River, where we left tents stashed on both sides of the river mouth. Then between Barn Bay and the Cascade Homestead we would stay at the Hope Hut, and then at Maurice Nolan's beautiful rimu-lined musterers' hut just south of the Cascade River.

Patience was the key as our children adapted readily to this adventure. When they were young either Catherine or I would hold their hands as they walked the long, sandy beaches or hopped across endless stretches of cobblestones and boulders. We would watch over them like falcons to ensure their welfare and safety. Mind over matter is a factor in any physical challenge, and the sooner you learn this, the easier the task will be.

On most occasions when we walk out, we make a point of not having a deadline to keep, otherwise we run the risk of pushing our luck with regard to the weather and the state of the river flows. It's important to be flexible. But occasionally we can't avoid having a time constraint, such as when there's a plane to catch.

In November 1996 we headed out to fly to Australia to celebrate my father's seventieth birthday. Christan was five and Robin was just two, so she was still being carried in our backpacks. We needed two fine days to walk to Barn Bay. As we set off from Gorge River the water was dropping rapidly after the latest rain. We rowed the dinghy across the river, setting off at about midday to allow Christan time to walk the eight kilometres up to the Spoon. Once there we forded the river, found our tent stash and set up camp for the night. In the evening we lit a small campfire on the beach head, cooked up a meal and watched the waves rolling in. As we were making our way to bed the cloud began to thicken, then it turned to rain which persisted all night. We always carry a sheet of black plastic in case we need an emergency shelter, and this night we snuggled up warm and dry in our tent with the sheet of plastic acting as a tent fly.

By the next morning the Spoon was flooded, and we knew we would not be able to ford the Hope and reach Barn Bay. We would have to sit tight. We only had enough food to reach Barn Bay, so to conserve energy I lay in the tent until the afternoon when the tide was out and I was able to forage for mussels. We fed Christan and Robin as usual but Catherine and I were on rations. After eating the mussels we also drank the mussel water to help keep us going.

When we awoke the next morning, hoping for a fine sunny day of course, it sounded as if there was a light rain outside. Luckily this just turned out to be the movement of thousands of persistent sandflies between the tent and the fly. When we peered out the sun was blazing away and the streams were dropping. We were soon packed up and on the way to Barn Bay.

This was a big day for us all, especially Christan, since we had to climb up over a large sea bluff and then boulder-hop for the rest of the day. Bluff Creek was still running high, but by the afternoon the Hope had subsided enough for us to ford it. We settled into Barn Bay for the night.

We had food stashed at Barn Bay, so we stocked up and headed off in the afternoon, aiming for the Hope Hut. This was just two kilometres upriver, but it meant the next day's tramp would be that much shorter. We spent most of the following day dodging muddy puddles and windfalls before finally reaching the safety of Maurice Nolan's hut.

I always love the walk out. The journey culminates in the fording of the Cascade River, but the whole journey is a memorable adventure for all of us. It is always fascinating when first walking inland from the ocean up the Hope River from Barn Bay then tramping through the forest for the rest of the day. At this point we have usually been by the sea constantly for about five months, with the continual sound of the ocean rolling in. Once deep within the forest the silence is almost tangible. Bird songs are much clearer while the base drone of the mountains can be heard. As we near the Cascade, the deep blue pools between powerful rapids emanate an awesome energy, drawing a deep respect from my inner being.

On this particular occasion, three days had elapsed since the latest rains. All my attention became focused on this water flow. The shape and position of the ford is forever changing, so I studied the tracks leading through the grass and gravel along the river bank and flats where people and vehicles had recently travelled. We finally recognised the place. The river had widened so that it was maybe a hundred metres across; the deeper water had gradually become shallower and quicker. Below the ford, the river narrowed once again to form a swift, strong rapid, a place to be avoided.

As we prepared for the crossing I changed into shorts and stowed my trousers in my pack. Luckily the ford appeared quite even, so Catherine, Robin and I started out, leaving Christan behind for the second trip. We stayed well above the rapid, entering where the water was a little deeper and going slightly with the current rather than fighting it. The swirling water was up to about the top of my thighs. Robin was perched in my pack, and Catherine was downstream of me, holding my hand. We kept up a steady momentum, leaning slightly upstream, our legs and knees in constant motion. As the current and riverbed slipped beneath us the fluid motion almost mesmerised me, but the numbing, clear water ensured a sense of place and kept us focused as we reached the intensity and depths midstream, sensing that the northern bank was eventually going to be won.

As the shallows welcomed us, I breathed a sigh of relief. I quickly headed up to the edge of the grassy flats and unpacked the padding around Robin, then removed her and all the other gear from my pack. I then headed straight back across the river to Christan, waiting patiently on the southern side. He climbed into my pack, I hoisted it to my shoulders and we forded once again.

As we strode out along the northern river bank towards the Martyr Homestead, our circulation revved up to ward off the cooling effect of the crossing. The journey now opened up in front of us. We had left the never-nevers once again, for the land of roads and bridges.

As the sands of time drift by we watch our children grow, finding their way in the wider world. The story of my own search, of how I found my true home in the southwest corner of the South Island of New Zealand, begins a long time ago. Memories always lead me back to my first beginnings, to the inner child we all know well.

chapter 1 the early days

I remember sitting on our back porch at the age of three, gazing up into the endless, dazzling night sky. Countless millions of stars, seen with a single glance, part of our realm and a place to explore. My first conscious thought was a perception of endless space and time. It's a concept I have carried with me throughout my life.

What wonders and potential lay ahead, to be explored within the vast reaches of time and space? My existence was an integral part of all this, and I felt that my essence would survive to continue the search even beyond this earthly realm.

Sometimes I would lie on my sisters' beds when they weren't there, and I could see the hijinks still lingering and floating in the room from Susan and Annette's playful antics. I could see toys, fruit and lollies floating, and taste the colours as they swirled about the walls and ceiling.

When I was very young I used to rock instinctively. If I was sitting in a chair my body would sway gently to a rhythm as real as my heartbeat and breathing. At night I would always rock for an hour or so before lying down to restful sleep.

I loved exploring, and I used to wear out my clothes so quickly that Mum became tired of having to make new ones, so she sewed my shorts out of leather to make them last. One day when we were visiting the Huka Falls on the Waikato River near Taupo, I disappeared, much to my parents' horror. I had explored my way into the back of a cave, then suddenly found myself at the bottom of a deep, rocky shaft, after shaving my eyebrows off.

Another time, when I was four, I remember having a skiing holiday up Mt Ruapehu. We stayed at the Chateau Tongariro and had skiing lessons with a Swiss ski instructor. I spent most of the time building snowmen and having snowball fights with Annette and Sue, but one day we walked over to Mt Ngauruhoe, passing through dripping rainforest and fluffy tussock, past waterfalls and beautiful stands of ponga.

Another day, when it was fine and clear, Dad and I travelled to the top of the ski-lifts on Mt Ruapehu, walked up past a higher section of unused ski-lift towers, then kept climbing up to the top of the mountain where we looked down onto the steaming crater lake. We could see forever in all directions, across distant plains that disappeared into a purple-blue haze.

My parents, and my sisters, Susan, Annette and later Vivienne, provided me with a loving, friendly environment where I felt safe and cherished. I quickly developed confidence as I gained experience of the world, knowing I had the support of my family.

We lived in Auckland when I was young, and when I reached school age off I went to Holy Cross Convent where my sisters were already studying. The nuns who ran the school — the Sisters of Mercy — dressed in full habits, and all you could see of them were their hands and faces, never a strand of hair, ears or neck. I wore a school uniform of navy-blue shorts, a grey shirt and blue tie. We had to wear shoes in winter and sandals during the summer months. In class we always wore slippers, and bare feet during playtime.

In the mornings Sue, Annette and I would walk up to the shops, then catch the bus to school, and later we'd catch the bus home again — until one day I took my last bus ride. As we neared the second-to-last stop someone pulled the buzzer for the bus to stop, but no one stood up to get off. The bus took off again, and as we neared our stop at Kautami Avenue, Great South Road, I pulled the buzzer.

'Who pulled the buzzer?' roared the bus driver. Then, as I began to move to the front of the bus he began to abuse me verbally. Though I was innocent I was speechless, and I nearly peed myself with fright. From then on I walked home every day, much to my enjoyment since the journey only took 20 minutes via a shortcut across a picturesque little creek, and I had sixpence to save or spend. I usually bought a twopenny chocolate-coated caramel bar halfway home, then saved the rest with the other one shilling and sixpence pocket money I got from Mum and, after I turned seven, the two shillings and sixpence I got from Dad for mowing the lawns.

I'd been made aware of the power of saving when Dad took me to the stock-car races and Grand Prix at Pukekohe, south of Auckland. Someone handed me an empty soft-drink bottle and told me to go and claim the refund. I couldn't believe it. After I handed the empty bottle in to a nearby Coca-Cola pie cart, the cashier gave me back a twopenny coin. In amazement I looked about the surrounding landscape where there were empty Coke and Fanta bottles lying strewn everywhere.

For the remainder of the day I hardly saw any racing cars flying by. I still heard their roar and smelt their fuming exhausts, but my focus was on finding every empty soft-drink bottle I could. Most people were happy enough to let some small kid pick up the bottles that were lying untidily about their picnic umbrellas, tables and car underbellies. By day's end a new dimension had opened for me, and I left reluctantly after Dad had endured enough of the dust and noise. I showed him the 10 shillings I had accumulated. This was a small fortune in those days, and I kept adding to it until I had enough to buy a white metal Dinky Toys ambulance, with an opening rear door and stretcher inside, for 19 shillings and sixpence. From then on I collected toy cars for the remainder of my boyhood.

In the Christmas holidays we would go and stay on our grandfather's farm near Kawhia, a sleepy town that lay on the west coast of the North Island near Te Awamutu. The 500-hectare farm was on the high land of the peninsula between Kawhia and Aotea Harbour to the north. Green pastures turned into rolling sandhills that eventually met a wild, isolated ocean beach.

The farm was owned by Mum's father, Harry Lawrence Smith. His father, also Harry Smith, with his wife Emily Lawrence, had migrated from Gloucestershire in England in the 1890s and had joined the coastal militia, protecting the flat-bottomed scows that carried goods up and down the coast. Later Harry took up the post of constable at Kawhia, and settled on the land.

Grandad had grown up in this area alongside the local Maori, and he spoke the Maori language fluently. He had also been a sergeant in the New Zealand police force, and on one occasion had led a contingent of 40 New Zealand policemen who were sent to the Cook Islands to quell a rebellion. During the Royal Tour of New Zealand in 1935 he had acted as bodyguard and escort for the Duchess of York.

I remember my grandfather as a stern, upright man who carried an aura of authority. He wasn't afraid of his own company, and in later years spent much of his time alone at Kawhia. My grandmother had died before I was born. Grandad employed a Maori family, the Hohuas, to manage the sheep, beef cattle and horses stocking the pastureland. The old farmhouse was divided into two living quarters, one for Grandad, and one for Tua and his wife, their sons Monty, Freddie and Happy, and their daughter Eva. Grandad's half was where we stayed. Each night we would hear Monty, Freddie and Happy singing and playing their guitars at all hours of the night as we fell asleep. Their bedroom walls were covered in Elvis Presley posters.

During the day we would venture forth down the green pastures, past a large U-shaped lake surrounded by giant pohutukawa, to the sandhills. We'd spend hours climbing up the steep faces of the sandhills, then running off the top terraces and rolling all the way to the bottom again. We'd also explore them, finding old Maori middens with shells, obsidian and basalt implements. Grandad had a drawer full of basalt and pounamu adzes in his wooden sideboard, all found on the farm. Part of the farm is Maori land, and during the Land Wars this had been a place of refuge.

Sometimes Freddie, Monty and Happy would muster and saddle up the horses so we could ride out to the mouth of the Aotea Harbour where we would dive for mussels. Mum and Dad would often drive us down to Kawhia township, to fish, dive and swim off the old fishermen's wharf, or buy fresh crayfish off the boats there. The old pohutukawa where the *Tainui* canoe first anchored is still growing beside the harbour, and the canoe is buried at the local Maketu marae. We'd sometimes visit the marae, and would enjoy partaking of the large hangi feasts they would put down.

Today Mum's brother Laurie owns the farm, though he has a manager running it since he works as a surgeon. At Christmas 2008, which would have been Mum's eightieth birthday, 21 of us came together at Kawhia for a family reunion. Laurie unveiled a memorial statue beneath the pohutukawa on the peninsula overlooking the lake, to commemorate his sister, my mother, Ngaire Constance Long; our grandmother, Susan Smith; and our great-grandmother, Emily Smith. My sisters Susan and Annette, Vivienne's son Nicholas and I each planted a kowhai tree there.

My great-great-grandfathers on my father's side were Robert Long and Walter Baskerville, who were both members of the Irish Regiment of the British Army, and part of a contingent of 700 men who were sent to defend the young settlement of Auckland, which in the 1840s was the capital of New Zealand.

Robert Long was born at Pullock, King's County, Ireland in 1809, and served with the 19th Irish Regiment in the West Indies and Mediterranean. He sailed from the Irish port of Galway aboard the sailing ship *Clifton* on 26 September 1847, with his wife Ellen (née Spillane) and their two children, arriving in Auckland harbour on 23 January 1848.

Walter Baskerville was born in 1807 in County Mayo, Ireland. He joined the 17th Regiment, and sailed from Portland on 28 January 1852 with his wife Ann (née McFaul) and their daughter. Walter served as schoolmaster for the length of the voyage on board the *Inchinnan*, which arrived in Auckland on 27 May 1852.

The *Clifton* and the *Inchinnan* were two of the 10 Fencible ships that set sail for Auckland between 1847 and 1852, forming settlements at Howick, Panmure, Otahuhu, Onehunga and Auckland Central. Their job was to build highways to link these settlements, so that troops could be mobilised when needed.

The Longs and the Baskervilles settled on one-acre sections in Panmure on opposite sides of the same street, now Allenby Road. After seven years of service they received further grants of the very fertile land beside the Tamaki River. Robert Long received another four acres and Walter Baskerville six acres at Mt Wellington, which was later cultivated as market gardens. They also grazed cattle on other common land. It was on this land at Mt Wellington that Dad, much later, built his first home.

In 1863 Robert Long was elected as a representative on the Auckland Provincial Council, and in 1868 Walter Baskerville became chairman of the Mt Wellington Highway District Trust. Their children, Robert Long and Margaret Baskerville, married, and in 1887 my grandfather, Robert Baskerville Long, was born.

He was a lucky man. In time he inherited the six acres of land at Mt Wellington, plus a building in the main street of Toowoomba, in Queensland, from his uncle John, who had no children. He served as a Company Sergeant-Major during the First World War, fighting in Gallipoli and France, and received three medals for valour and bravery after being wounded in battle. Of his company of 200 men only 28 survived. All the officers were dead.

After the war Robert married his sweetheart, Mabel

Johnstone, who bore two sons, Jack Robert and Robert Baskerville (better known as Bob), my father. Mabel's grandmother, Sarah Wallace, had first arrived in New Zealand around 1842 on the *Louisa Campbell*.

My father grew up in Auckland and, after leaving college, joined the Royal New Zealand Air force, serving during the occupation of Japan, based at Hiroshima. When he left to travel overseas with J Force he asked his father for some words of advice: Dad's father replied that after all his years at war and under siege, his greatest fear was that he would get drunk one night and wake up with a tattoo.

Dad was involved in weighing gear and organising the loading of freight aircraft. He always carried a slide rule in his top pocket, which added to his air of expertise. His photograph albums from those days always sent a chill up and down my spine, showing as they do the total devastation caused by the nuclear explosions in Nagasaki and Hiroshima.

On his return from the war Dad worked for the National Airways Corporation as an administrator, organising flights between Fiji, Samoa, Tonga and New Zealand. Later he worked very successfully for Colonial Mutual Life — in 1962 he sold more business for the company than any other agent in New Zealand, Australia, Britain, Canada or South Africa — receiving a variety of awards, including silver trays and coffee sets, electric frypans and toasters, along with a silver cup that I have at home.

My parents married in 1951, and my eldest sister, Susan, was born in 1952. Annette followed in 1953 and I was born on 17 November 1955 in Tauranga. My father owned a milkbar on the beach there for a while, but we moved back to Papatoetoe soon after I was born. My youngest sister Vivienne arrived in August 1958.

My father was a keen fisherman and gatherer of shellfish, and we often used to fish for snapper out in the Waitemata Harbour and fossick for rock oysters in the Hauraki Gulf. At low tide we'd find scallops in the Manukau Harbour, where the runway of the international airport now lies.

One day a week I attended Scouts near the Papatoetoe velodrome, and we'd go away on camp each year to practise the navigation and survival skills we'd been taught, as well as learning discipline, bush cooking, Morse code and signals.

On Saturday and Sunday afternoons my mates and I would meet and head out past the edge of suburbia toward the rural wilderness, where farms, creeks, railway bridges, forest, mud and quicksand lay waiting to be explored.

Other times Mum would take us to the Auckland War Memorial Museum, where I was always intrigued by the carved Maori canoes, meeting houses and greenstone adzes. I was an enthusiastic student of Maori culture, and knew that with flax, stone, timber and fish I could settle this bounteous land as they had.

Our godparents, Milly, Polly and Walter Malone, still lived out at Panmure where their family had originally settled, and we used to love visiting them on a Sunday afternoon. Walter still market-gardened on the fertile volcanic soil, digging over his fields by the sweat of his brow. His gentle, resilient nature made him a favourite. Nasturtium flowers ran wild across the scoria stone walls along their boundaries, and the grassy fields seemed to run off to the horizon.

Milly was a saintly person, and a beautiful woman in her youth. She was my grandmother Mabel's best friend, and my grandfather had stayed with the Malones when he first returned from the war.

Milly and Polly always served us tea and scones when we visited, and they all spoke of the old times, back in the days when they travelled by horse and dray to Auckland town for supplies, and how the bishop used to come out for afternoon tea on Sundays.

These people were living history, and I listened to all they had to say, even though I'd heard much of it before.

chapter 2 off and away

O ne day as I was watching *Crusader Rabbit* on television, a couple of men in overalls came into the living room, switched off the television set and proceeded to carry it across the room and out the door. Our family was suddenly on the move to another country. Dad had been appointed manager of the Brisbane branch of a Sydney-based insurance company, Provident Life. He would also be managing Long's Building in Toowoomba on behalf of his brother Jack and their mother Mabel.

My father was drawn to Australia, seeing it as a land of opportunity. I had never left anywhere before, so I was unaware of what was really happening. I was nearly 10 years old in 1965 when our house was sold and we moved to Australia. Dad went on ahead, and in early November Mum, Sue, Annette, Viv and I boarded a TEAL Electra at Whenuapai airport and flew to Brisbane to join him.

What struck me most when we arrived in Australia was, of course, the heat, but also the abundant animal life. At first we lived in a rented house in the suburb of Toowong, with a creek running through the backyard and a vacant wild area next door that was overgrown with prickly lantana bushes among the eucalyptus trees. Large skinks, about 45 centimetres long, and blue-tongue lizards were common sights, along with large tortoises, eels, snakes, frilly lizards and goannas. The ground teemed with large biting green and bull ants, and there were shoulder-high clay termite nests scattered beneath the gum trees. Frogs abounded and the nights came alive with their continuous croaking and, of course, squadrons of mosquitoes. Whenever I light a mosquito coil today it takes me back to this time. There were no mozzy screens on the windows, so Mum would light a whole coil in each room every summer night so we could fall asleep.

During the long school holidays we spent three hours each morning at the local swimming pool, and within a week we could all swim like fish. Though we had had swimming lessons in Auckland, until now I couldn't swim to save myself. In the afternoons we'd watch TV — with the novelty of four channels to choose from I became a TV addict, and soon knew the schedules off by heart.

On Sundays Dad would often take us to Surfers Paradise on the Gold Coast. We used to love the 80-kilometre drive, anticipating the refreshing surf and golden, sandy beaches. Back then there were no buildings over two storeys high and the beaches had not yet been affected by the raging cyclones that later began to ravage this coastline, leaving undersea troughs and sandbars that created offshore rips.

Before heading for the beach we'd often try our hands at fishing and canoeing on the Nerang River estuary behind the Gold Coast, and Dad would love to show us around the canal estates, where we'd gawk at all the big flash houses built on their own little islands from sand pumped over the original mangrove swamps, where everyone possessed their own slice of beach.

Later, we would cruise down Cavell Avenue to visit the American donut shop, and maybe have a game of 10-pin bowls or attend the Hawaiian night beside the beautifully lit-up pool of the Beachcomber Hotel. Then there would be a long, slow haul back to Brisbane, the road clogged with traffic jams. We'd arrive home tired, sandy, and ready for a shower and a good night's sleep.

My first day at school brought me right back down to earth: new country, new school, new boy. It was hard. I had no friends and had to start from scratch. During breaks I'd look forward to going back into class rather than sitting around on my own watching all the other kids play.

I attended St Joseph's College, Nudgee Junior, an all-boys school with mainly boarders and a few day boys. I was a day pupil. The school was more like a prison, with the boarders as the inmates. They hailed from outback cattle stations, and a variety of countries, including New Guinea, Malaysia and Indonesia. Some were snake charmers, carrying snakes and frilly lizards into class down their shirts.

On my first day Roderick Trebrett, a boy from Sarawak in Malaysia, came and talked to me. He could understand how I was feeling, since he was five and a half thousand kilometres from his own family. This made me realise I was actually pretty well off, and I soon began to settle in.

I completed my last three years of primary school at Nudgee Junior, grades 5, 6 and 7. In grade 6 my classroom was right next to the library, and I began avidly reading novels, taking in half the story while waiting for other boys to complete their school work, then the other half at home once I had finished my homework. I continued reading nearly a book a day through grades 6 and 7 and came first in the class those two years. I also won the art prize in grade 6.

Sport also featured strongly. Nudgee was a very strong rugby union school, and we used to win most of our games in the interschool competition. We played sport after school four days a week, as well as interschool matches on Saturdays, and I participated enthusiastically in cricket, football and athletics.

The Christian Brothers could be very strict, often using leather straps for punishment. 'Six of the best' was often the order of the day. Sometimes they would even throw wooden chairs across the room, and look out if it was coming your way. They were a law unto themselves, and of course it was much worse for the boarders, who had it 24/7.

A year after we arrived in Australia my grandmother, Mabel Long, paid for a ticket for me to fly alone from Brisbane to Auckland. She wanted to see her grandson again, as she was missing me. At the age of 11, this was a great holiday for me since I loved staying with Nana. She and I were in harmony and never tired of each other's company. She usually called me 'Boy'. Her late husband, Robert Baskerville Long, was buried the day I was born.

Nana lived along Remuera Road opposite the Catholic Church, and the pealing of the church bells was always a highlight on Sunday mornings. It was also only a short walk down to Newmarket where my favourite hobby shop lay.

I stayed in Auckland for six weeks altogether, spending some time with friends and staying with my uncles and aunts before heading home for the start of the school year. My Uncle Lawrence and Aunty Sadie were living next to

Middlemore Hospital, where Laurie worked as a general and vascular surgeon, and I had a great time with their family. Dad's brother, my Uncle Jack, his wife Aunty Doreen and their family have always been superb hosts too. Jack and Doreen have always been my mentors, offering friendly wisdom and advice. Jack has been an electrician and builder all his life. Nana's unit was a house that Jack built, and he also constructed warehouses, flats and suburban shopping centres.

Two years after this visit Nana suffered from a stroke. She and Uncle Jack visited us in Brisbane after she recovered, but by then she was confined to a wheelchair and was becoming quite senile. This was more of a shock to me than when she died of another stroke not long after. Even so, I felt I had lost one of my very best friends.

In 1969, after Nana died, Dad and Jack took over ownership of Long's Building in Toowoomba. They had spent much of their working lives saving for the day when they would have to pay death duties to the tune of 50 per cent of the value of the property in order to keep it intact. Once this was all in order, my father retired at the age of 47. The funds from leasing out the shops, offices and parking spaces were sufficient to support him and Mum, and their main pastime became travelling the world. Together they travelled extensively throughout Europe, America, Russia, the Middle East, India and Asia, as well as making many other shorter journeys across the Pacific to Hawaii, the mainland US and New Zealand.

During our first two years in Brisbane we had lived in rented houses, until finally we moved into our own home, built on a bush block about 13 kilometres west of the centre of town at Brookfield. We had a section of around 1.4

hectares, and Dad had this thinned, initially felling every second eucalyptus tree to decrease the fire risk. He left the bush to regenerate from then on. We cleared an area of about half a hectare for the house and lawns but the rest was pretty much wild, as was the case for all our neighbours. Next door was a cattle farm with plenty of trees, which gave the place a park-like air. During the winter, when the westerly winds blew like fury for months on end, the trees sounded like ocean waves as they leaned and rustled in the wind.

A level terrace was bulldozed out of the gently sloping terrain, and on this a long colonial-style cavity brick house was constructed. We spent many hours toiling around the base of the terrace, stacking local shale rocks as a retaining wall to hold back the fill. This was our pioneering period. After years spent toiling, the house was landscaped with a long driveway, gardens, slate letterbox and pathways. A grassed terrace beside the house looked out over the trees and valley below.

It was great to sit out on the long verandah of an evening, when the tropical storms would set the bush alive, flickering with sheet lightning as the torrential rains began their deluge, cooling the stifling evening air. Friends would often come round for a barbecue on a Saturday or Sunday afternoon, and it became my regular job to cook the steaks and sausages.

One Friday afternoon Dad and his mate Don McDonald picked me up early from school and we headed out west, past Toowoomba, Dalby and Roma towards St George. We were off to go roo shooting.

After about 500 kilometres had drifted by we headed south off the main highway, speeding along dusty flat gravel roads heading straight to nowhere. As we flew along at 130–

150 kilometres per hour I sat in the back seat watching the gum trees and termite nests flash by. I felt as if my mind was expanding with the country as I took in the vastness of the outback. I gazed at the fence posts as they flickered past the window, and made up my mind to remember all of this — this striking country, its enormity, one tree after another gone, never to be seen again.

Later that night we camped in an empty old homestead, and the next morning we met up with a party of hunters. But it's not the hunting that I remember — I've never been a hunter myself — it was the experience of being out in the outback. Far away from the city, the outback had now become real to me.

At the end of my grade 7 year I was awarded a scholarship to attend Downlands, a secondary boarding school 130 kilometres west of Brisbane. But I didn't want to be away from home, so it was decided I would attend St Joseph's College, Gregory Terrace, as originally planned. St Joseph's was a boys' school with about a thousand pupils, situated near the heart of town.

Military Cadet training was compulsory at 'Terrace' from grades 9 to 11, unless you were exempted on medical grounds. For the school to receive funding for this, the Australian Army required each cadet to fire 20–30 rounds of live ammunition every year. We were basically being trained as potential soldiers should the need arise.

So in early February 1970 we boarded khaki buses and were taken to the Army Q stores at Enoggera, where we were each issued with two sets of khaki trousers and shirts, a woollen serge jumper, four pairs of woollen socks and a stout pair of leather combat boots. We were also given strong webbing belts with brass buckles and stays, felt slouch hats with brass badges, and Army insignia to be sewn onto the shoulders of our uniforms. All these brand-new items were stowed in a green Army duffel bag. We were in the Army now, and quickly made aware of the fact that we were merely grubby, snotty-nosed cadets, with basically zero mana, wanting for discipline and knowledge.

On the first of many parades, on a Friday afternoon after school, we were ordered into three ranks of 10, to make up a platoon. Corporals held authority over the rank and file, and orders were issued by a sergeant, under instructions from the Cadet Under Officer or CUO. There was no mucking around. Discipline was the order of the day. Chin up, chest out, eyes front. Stand at attention, stand at ease or easy. Orders snapped out required instant action in unison if you didn't want to have rank screaming down your earhole at point-blank range. Our platoon quickly became a unit, and pride began to emerge with each successfully accomplished drill. As we were marched — left, right, left, right, left from here to there and back again in step, left turn, right turn — we gradually became a team.

A platoon is part of a company; a company is part of a regiment. Terrace's Regiment consisted of 12 platoons in three companies, A, B and C, plus a company of Adventure Trainees similar to the SAS. First thing each Friday afternoon we filed through the school's basement Q store to be issued with Lee-Enfield .303 rifles. The school held roughly 300 such rifles, some of which had seen service in the Boer War of the 1890s, and many in the First World War. There were also Bren light machine guns which were used extensively in training and fired with live ammunition at the Army rifle range.

On Queen's Birthday weekend, in June, we were loaded into buses and headed southwest to the Beaudesert army base. Here we were issued with two pairs of old dungarees each, trousers and shirts, a woollen greatcoat, four woollen blankets, a groundsheet, poncho and a bivvy sheet. Then we headed bush until all signs of civilisation had vanished, leaving only thickets of trees and undergrowth. Next we were ordered to team up with a partner to make a hutchie. We clipped our bivvy sheets together, then tied a rope between two trees at waist height, laid the joined bivvy sheets across the rope, and fastened the sides to the ground to make a tidy A-frame shelter — this would provide shelter for two cadets, warding off the dew, cold rain and whatever else came our way.

This became our home for the long weekend. Our other home was soon a distant memory, a mirage, and despite some longing for its lost comforts we made the best of our situation and arranged our bedding as best we could.

At least, hopefully, they would eventually feed us, but first there was the 'Emu Bob'. This sounded interesting. As we were lined up I was anticipating some profound lesson from my commanding corporal, David Usasy. At last he gave the order: 'Now keep your eyes to the ground and move, picking up any rubbish you find.' A great way to start the training of a lifetime.

When the food finally arrived we were issued with one large cardboard box per section of seven cadets. Each box held enough food for a day's meals. As our corporal unfastened the box he revealed an array of unmarked tin cans, each with a colour coding on the lid; all the tins marked with red were for breakfast; the blue were for lunch, and the green for supper. It was very simple — canned potatoes, canned carrots, canned sausage, canned stew, even canned cake. Everything except toilet paper was canned, it seemed. Each meal was to be cooked over a fire in a large, low-sided, open, square cast-iron dish. We became adept at fire-lighting, with an ample supply of fallen branches and sticks all about us.

We also fuelled up another fire, beneath a half 44-gallon drum, split lengthwise and sitting up on four steel stakes hammered into the ground. Into the half drum we ladled water by the bucketful and brought it to the boil in order to sterilise the metal dixies from which our hot meal would be eaten. It's funny how every meal, regardless of the combination of ingredients, all became the same brown, stewed-up mush. But it filled the gap, followed by a boiling brew of tea and condensed milk to wash down the dust and ashes lining our throats.

That first hard day seemed to last a lifetime, but by the end of it we were all sitting around the campfire telling yarns, making new friends and seeing old acquaintances in a completely new light. There were always the comedians, keeping the rest of us entertained into the night, until weary heads rested upon makeshift pillows, tucked away but still under the brilliant stars of a black night.

The silence of the morning was broken by reveille and roll call. We were ordered out of slumber and into shuffling ranks, each cadet buried under his greatcoat, breathing warmth into his hands as the sergeant barked out each name from a list under the light of his torch. The dawning light was just beginning to breathe life into a new day.

The lessons came thick and fast, and we learnt quickly. Adapt or die, leave the pretences behind, together we stand, divided we fall.

I spent four years in the Army Cadets, working my way up the chain of command. Each year we attended an annual camp during the first week of the August holidays, then a promotion course took up the first two weeks of the Christmas break. Some of those training us were Vietnam veterans. Everything had to be 100 per cent right for inspections. A crease in a blanket or a speck of dust in the bore of a rifle was enough for them to take issue and get right up you. Any form of verbal abuse was acceptable, and you only made each mistake once.

During the sergeant's course I gained the second-best pass in southeast Queensland, so I was promoted to Company Sergeant-Major on my return to school, issuing orders to C Company with its four platoons. During my fourth year, when I was Cadet Under Officer, I commanded a platoon of 20 cadets and was responsible for their discipline and welfare on bivouac and annual camp. I found this very rewarding. The persistent emphasis on survival skills, navigation, discipline and responsibility meant these things became ingrained, but what I valued above all else was the teamwork and the real sense of camaraderie that developed.

Today I feel like my cadet training has been part of the keelstone that has helped keep me stable throughout life. To live in a remote area successfully a person needs to take hygiene, responsibility and safety seriously so I use these skills on a daily basis, and aim to pass them on to my children.

Rowing was another discipline that was a real test of both physical strength and character. Beside this everything else was easy.

In 1972 I rowed in the school's First Four, then the following year in the First Eight. Some days we rowed 58 kilometres up the Brisbane River and back, and that was on a Sunday which should have been our 'day of rest'. The last three or four kilometres would be rowed at maximum pace, with all eight blades working in unison, passing through the pain barrier until your body went numb.

During the week Mum would wake me at 4.30 with a cooked breakfast already on the table. Then she would drive me through the darkness to the nearest railway station at Indooroopilly, where I'd meet Joe Tooma, the School Captain and my best mate, and away we would travel through the city to Fortitude Valley Station. Here we hopped in the back seat of a car driven by our coach, Peter Cole, and by 6am we'd be on the mirror-flat water, not a breath of wind as we brought the sleek-sided racing eight into motion. During the next two hours we'd travel to hell and back, rowing through central Brisbane as the city rose from its sleep. Afterwards the lads would eat a rushed breakfast of fizzy drinks and cream buns at the local dairy, then we would taxi to school in time to be in class by 8.30.

During the lunch break we did 45 minutes of weights and circuit training, eating our lunch as we walked back into class. Then, after finishing my homework in the evenings, I would run six kilometres before showering and going to bed. Our hard work paid off when we won the odd race, but man to man we were outweighed by some of the colossuses in the other crews. But the whole experience toughened me up — there is a home on the other side of pain.

I was keen on sports, and in 1973, my last year at school, I received the Sportsman of the Year Award after becoming Queensland schoolboys high-jump champion. But sport wasn't the only emphasis during these years. I'd been secretary of the school's branch of Interact, a society sponsored by the Rotary Club, had taken part in interschool debates, and was awarded the Senior Christian Doctrine prize, receiving a silver cross and chain from the Archbishop of Brisbane, Francis

Rush. I was also chosen to be Deputy School Captain. Academically I had done well, especially in art, where I gained the best mark in my class for the state assessment exam in geometrical drawing and perspective.

But while all this was going on, and the school was busy pumping out lawyers, doctors and engineers, my real life was happening elsewhere, nearer to home.

chapter 3 brookfield years

The forested ranges west of Brisbane virtually sur-rounded our Brookfield home, and I used to love taking to the hills with my mates, climbing up the spurs to find the little-used 4WD timber tracks along the main ridges. The more you climbed and the further you walked, the deeper the forest became.

This was our place, where we could roam totally undisturbed. I can't remember a time when we came across anyone else during the many explorations we undertook amid the virtual jungle of eucalyptus and rainforest remnants.

One time when I was about 15 my friend Nicky Moore and I took off for several days during the school holidays. We walked almost to the end of Gold Creek Road, a dead end, then ascended a spur up to the main ridge track. From there we headed further west until we were far above the Gold Creek Reservoir, then we descended a gully until we were on the edge of a vast expanse of water.

We camped here in a little area surrounded by dense stands of rainforest trees, palms and ferns, and as the days drifted by we became totally in tune with the area. We had put layers of dried ferns on the ground to ward off the cool of the night, with a blanket or two and a campfire to keep our bodies warm. Day after day we sat around the smouldering flames, fire-hardening sticks and sharpening them to use as implements. I had decided to take some of the seedling plants home on our return, carefully removing them from the hard, compact soil so as not to disturb the roots. After a time the English language we normally spoke began to be replaced with what seemed more like an aboriginal dialect, which felt like a more effective way to communicate. We felt as if we were becoming more a part of the bush than the civilisation we had left behind.

Eventually our food ran out and hunger pangs drove us back to our homes. As we sauntered back along the tracks and out onto the road we knew we would never be the same again. There was another world out there, and the appreciation we had developed would stay with us forever. Nick later became a forestry ranger, looking after koalas and kangaroos at wildlife sanctuaries, and capturing snakes that had entered people's homes.

On a later journey up to the tracks, we purposely took along as little shelter as possible. I had decided that as long as we could find ample fields of dried grass among the trees we could use this to insulate us from the ground, and we could also place a layer between two cotton sheets to form a sort of eiderdown. Even though it was wintertime, we challenged ourselves by bringing only one cotton sheet each for our bedding. No groundsheets or waterproofing.

This time when we ascended the timber tracks we went much further back into the ranges, staying up high. Our journey eventually brought us out way above the Enoggera Dam, which feeds the thirst of Brisbane city, itself a glow far in the distance. We immediately built a framework of light dried sticks for a hutchie, covering an area about three metres by three metres and about one and a half metres high. We covered this with a dense layer of dried grasses, forming something similar to a grass igloo, then we insulated the ground and laid out our large 'eidergrass' bed cover.

We stayed up there for three or four days, each day exploring further along the ranges, seeing large pythons, frilled lizards, kookaburras and wallabies, and each evening coming back to our shelter.

On my thirteenth birthday Dad bought me a canoe made of canvas stretched across a wooden frame. After fibreglassing the bottom we headed for the nearest waterhole, a place called Reuben's. My sisters, Susan, Annette and Viv, helped me to portage the canoe the kilometre or so, with the help of Tim and Simon O'Donnell, who lived up our street.

This waterhole became a favourite place to cool off in, and Tim and I would return regularly during the heat of the day to jump off the Tarzan swing into the refreshing waters. As the years rolled by others came and went seeking refuge at the waterhole, to fend off the summer heat and above all have some fun plunging off the swing, which gradually became fastened higher and higher up the large silky oak tree.

One of the enterprising locals erected a large painter's trestle way up the creek bank so that as you launched yourself off the top your eyes were about five metres above water level. As you swung out on the 10-metre-long rope you would nearly brush the water, then be propelled back up to nearly five metres clear of the surface before you jumped or dived in. At midnight when there was a full moon this was a great experience — swinging out like a bob on a pendulum, holding on, head hanging down, then out at the top of your swing looking down at the moon's reflection in the water below, then letting go and falling head first into the moon image below. It was even more thrilling on a pitch-black night, since you would plunge into blackness until you hit the water, then sink deeper towards the shingly bottom to cool off from the heat and humidity of the muggy night.

Over time there emerged a hard core of Brookies, pilgrims who above all else loved coming and sharing the waters each day after school. Moby, Tim and I would jump off the bus at the top of Greentrees Avenue, head home to my place for a bite to eat, then head straight to the creek. Dave, Nick and George would be off at the next stop, Jacaranda Avenue, and eventually meet us at Reuben's. The waterhole was our rendezvous nearly every day of summer and part of winter for about 10 solid years. During the summer holidays we would only come home to eat and sleep.

These Brookie days influenced me a lot, helping to develop my idealism and sense of brother- and sisterhood, and a true sense of community. We loved each other and worked together as a team. The six of us were all born in different countries — the US, Scotland, England, Nigeria, Australia and New Zealand. We needed little money since we grew to realise that the best things in life were free — swimming, walking, running, food and girls. Suburbia lurked a couple of kilometres away, but we avoided pinball machines and shopping malls and made our own fun.

It was Dave who had diverted us away from watching TV. He began sitting next to the TV, staring at us and laughing, and telling us that we were just sitting there staring at a box on the wall for hours on end.

'So what should we do?' we asked him.

'Let's go out and have a bonfire at the top of the hill beside

Reuben's Creek and watch for satellites and UFOs and sing.'

So we swam all day and night, and from then on kept the night alive beside a bonfire until the early hours of each morning. We loved listening to music. Dave played bass guitar in a school rock band that practised on the weekends at Dave and Nick's house, so we hung out there when we weren't down at the creek. While listening to the music I'd study books on the great artists — Michelangelo, Constable, Gainsborough, Turner, Leonardo da Vinci, Raphael, van Gogh and the like.

During these years we happily grew under each other's skins. We trusted in our ability to hold our relationship above all else, so that it became a framework on which to build the rest of our lives.

We knew that between us we possessed the answer, the thing that all the people out there in the distant glow we could see from the top of the hill were trying to fathom — day on day, year on year, searching for success, satisfaction and, above all, some meaning to their lives. We had it, and in each other's glowing eyes that knowledge was sealed and never to be lost, whatever the changes and whatever the cost. The jewel that we shared was the key to all we could search for in this life.

We aspired to life without all the pretences that the world has to offer, just basic human relationships with the least possible fuss, with the wild and basic elements of nature thrown into the mix. Respect for the animals and plants too; their lives were just as important as ours.

If we had all been dressed in rags our feelings would have been no different. We imagined that if the world would just let us be, and wasn't pulling us in all different directions, then we could all settle here and raise our families together in this place. Basic people, living basic lives and doing our best to keep each other happy. This was the dream we shared; like a tribe with an instinct for survival and cohesion, we all felt confident and settled. If this world would let us be, and the landscape stay the same, then we would build our simple shelters here.

The dream has never faded but the hill is now covered in houses, hundreds and hundreds of them, with their fences and roads. Though the hill has changed those precious days can never be lost — they are the jewels that keep my life going, my keelstone. And I bet the Brookies have grown up in every generation and in every place upon the Earth throughout the ages. Their dreams hold the key to life — free of pretence, full of care and consideration — they know that together we stand, divided we fall.

The symbol of the Brookies is the Eternal Flame. We have each been presented with one in recent years by Timothy. The Eternal Flame is surrounded by a circlet of golden leaf and mounted on a wooden shield, with our names and nicknames engraved on it.

chapter 4 to the other side and back

When I was a young boy I had always been intrigued by the thought of how people lived on the other side of the world. Since the world is a sphere, I thought, they are actually upside down compared to us, and I wondered if they would be very different.

This fascination with how other people lived had never left me, and during my last year at school I convinced myself that I needed to take a journey to the other side of the planet, travelling as far away as possible without actually leaving the Earth. At last I could find out what made people tick over there. My journey was not to see landscapes, but to learn more about the people and their cultures.

I was planning to study medicine at university, and I decided that if I could save enough money then I could take a trip to London at the end of my first year. My plan was to save enough for the airfare over the summer holidays, before I started at university, then add to this by working weekends during the year. So after completing my last year of school I began my holidays looking for work.

Dad agreed to drive me around some building sites where

I could try to get work as a labourer, and at just the second site I was offered a job with a Yugoslavian immigrant by the name of Les Lubin. He was hanging doors, installing walk-in wardrobes and putting up handrails in a three-storey block of newly constructed units. He had a deadline to keep, and realised that he needed help to achieve this.

We quickly became a team as Les taught me all I needed to know to complete the same tasks as him. He trained me to use power saws, drills and planes, as well as a nail gun to secure timber to masonry. It was hard but enjoyable work, requiring a carpenter's skill. Building the wardrobes was interesting, and before long I was able to build them alone with Les checking up on me from time to time. The skills I developed doing this sort of work have served me well later in life, as living in South Westland has required me to be a jack of all trades.

By the end of that summer I had saved $750, the equivalent of a student's return airfare to London. In January 1974 I enrolled at Queensland University, and for the rest of that year I concentrated on my medical studies, still determined to travel to Europe at the end of it. Once Dad realised that I was serious about my travel plans he offered to pay half the cost, since he didn't want me working on weekends while I was doing my first year of medicine. The money I had saved sat in the bank all year, untouched, and in November my father bought me a return ticket to London. I would return in time for the start of my second year at university a few months later. The money I had earned would be my spending money.

My flight to London left from Sydney, so I farewelled my family and friends and climbed aboard a bus for the first leg of my journey. I was off on the adventure of a lifetime, alone but confident. I had turned 19 the month before, and I felt like the world was mine to explore. Two of my sisters were working in London at this time as well, and I was looking forward to seeing them.

In Sydney I caught a suburban train from Circular Quay to the airport, where a four-hour wait gave me time to relax and centre myself for the long flight ahead. Finally the time came to board the Thai Airways flight to Bangkok, where we would stop over for a day before continuing on to London.

Bangkok was a revelation — I was blown away by the hustle and bustle of the place. There were about five million people there, and all the buildings were covered in mosses and fungi since the air was so hot and humid. The air reeked of boiled cabbage and there was the constant sound of music and people 24 hours a day. The airline put us up in a hotel as part of the deal, and I teamed up with a roommate and spent the day touring the city and temples by taxi. Our hotel was often used by US soldiers on R&R from Vietnam, and fortunately it had a clean swimming pool where we could cool off. But the Thai culture was a stark contrast to what I was used to, and coming to Bangkok provided by far the biggest learning curve of my life up to this point.

The next day found us back at the bustling airport, where we boarded another Thai Airways flight and headed for Copenhagen and on to London. My sister Annette was there to greet me with open arms, and we loaded my gear into a Volkswagen Kombi van that she and her flatmates had earlier taken over to Europe and Morocco.

After Annette had negotiated the motorways, crowded streets and bustling traffic of London, we arrived and parked on the roadside in front of the large one-roomed flat she shared with Dave and Jimbo. I was offered a mattress on the floor next to the front bay window, and the cosy flat became my base for the next three months.

My only previous exposure to London's place names was on the Monopoly board, but now I was able to actually visit these places, making extensive use of the city's famous Underground system. During the six weeks I spent exploring this great city I only caught a bus once, mainly for the experience of riding a red double-decker.

One of the first places I visited was the National Gallery, near Trafalgar Square. I had read about many of the artists whose work was on show here, and seen reproductions of many of the great works that hung on the walls. I loved the works of Gainsborough, Constable and Turner, and studied these works and others with awe. Little did I realise at the time that my future profession would be linked to these works, now viewed at first hand. These landscape artists captured the essential countryside of Britain with its subtleties of light and colour and its distinctive culture. The works of others such as Titian, Monet, Rembrandt, van Gogh, da Vinci and Raphael were there too, many of them massive paintings hung in ornate gilded frames.

As the days went by, Piccadilly Circus, Bond Street, Oxford Street, Fleet Street, Park Lane and Mayfair became familiar places as I walked the streets of central London observing the architecture of the solid stone buildings and checking out the shops and stores. Sometimes I'd go to the theatre — *Jack the Ripper* was still playing in the same theatre after 70 years, and this was also the time of *Jesus Christ, Superstar*, *Oh, Calcutta*, and Michael Crawford's *Some Mothers Do 'ave 'em* — and there were often parties at the flat, with Annette's London friends or travellers who were passing through.

After a week or so I signed up with an employment agency to find a job to supplement my ever-shrinking bundle of traveller's cheques. I worked for about 10 days on a building site, earning £1 an hour carrying doors onto lifts and up to their destination many storeys above the hustle and bustle of the streets below. Luckily, Mum had made me a large woollen coat from two brand-new woollen blankets that she had purchased from a woollen mill. This coat, which I still have today, helped to ward off the severe winter cold, which could chill you to the bone.

I also spent a week working as an office clerk, sorting through customer competition documents for a car company. There was even a telephone on my work desk, so early one morning I tried ringing my girlfriend back in Brisbane, Wendy Bopp, and then Mum and Dad. There was no answer at either of those so I tried ringing Nick and Dave and reached their mother, Mrs Moore. She didn't believe I was in London so it wasn't much of a conversation. Anyway, it was a thrill to be speaking to someone on the other side of the Earth.

I hadn't been in London very long when Moby, one of my Brookfield mates, arrived from the US, where he had gone as part of a Rotary student exchange programme. He had been caught streaking down the main street of the conservative Pennsylvania town where he was billeted, and as a result had been sent home. His parents had decided to send him to stay with his London-based aunt until he was due back in Brisbane from his exchange trip, so we teamed up. We hatched a plan to go exploring over in Europe. Since we had limited funds we planned to travel on the cheap, hitchhiking and staying at youth hostels.

We left London on the 15th of December, hitching to Dover and catching the ferry across the English Channel to Calais, then taking a train to Paris, where we planned to spend a few days before heading south to Spain. After checking in to a youth hostel we walked down to Notre-Dame cathedral, a massive carved-stone structure shrouded in history and intrigue. Ugly gargoyles peered down at us. While I studied the cathedral Moby went off to find some food, coming back a couple of hours later with a handful of chocolates. He had discovered the exquisite food shops that ran the length of the Champs Elysée. I had been expecting a feed of bread and cheese — our appetites were becoming sharper each day since our budgets were not keeping up with our energy needs — but Moby was adamant that these expensive chocolates could not be passed up.

One of the highlights of our stay in Paris was a visit to the Louvre, which houses some of the greatest works of art in the world. Massive paintings the size of a wall in an average Kiwi house bedecked room after room throughout the many wings of this ornate old palace. We gazed upon the *Mona Lisa*, Leonardo da Vinci's greatest portrait, Michelangelo's statue of *David*, and the *Venus de Milo*. All the great artists of the Renaissance period are well represented here, and we were enthralled by many of these works. One that especially appealed to me depicted the survivors of a shipwreck on a raft out in a raging sea. I could sense the overwhelming power and foreboding of the ocean, and empathise with their ray of hope for rescue as a distant sail appeared above the cresting waves.

I loved this city and its people. Their culture seemed to express so much passion and emotion, and the people we met were friendly and helpful. The women were well dressed and looked beautiful in their fur coats, and they were not afraid to look you straight in the eye. Though French had been my worst subject at high school I was grateful now for my three years of study, since it meant I could hold a halting conversation with any French person patient enough to try to communicate with me.

Back at the hostel we met a lovely lady by the name of Giselle. She was from Toulouse in southern France, and she encouraged us to visit and stay with a friend of hers who lived there, a man by the name of Christian Pierre Bidel.

So we took Giselle's advice and headed south, hitchhiking out of Paris until the cold and threatening rain sent us to buy train tickets as far as Limoges, which was halfway to Toulouse. We were hoping the conductor wouldn't notice if we stayed on the train overnight as it travelled further south, but our carriage was uncoupled at Limoges. However, we were able to stay in the carriage for the rest of the night, before emerging onto the streets of Limoges. This is a beautiful town, and we spent a day and a night there, looked after by a university student who offered us space in his apartment and guided us through the museums where the famous Limoges pottery was on show.

The next morning we packed up and continued on our way to Toulouse, blessed with a lovely fine day. The cerulean-blue skies enhanced the rural beauty of the surrounding landscape, well established with trees, farming stock and traditional buildings.

Once in Toulouse we found our way out to Christian Pierre Bidel's home on the outskirts of the city, where he lived with his mother on a small farmlet. When we mentioned that Giselle had sent us to see him he welcomed us like long-lost brothers, and offered us lodgings in a large barn that had been converted into a house.

We cranked up the open fire to ward off the cold, and took the opportunity to rest up. Christian Pierre came over from time to time to ensure we were comfortable, then he asked us if we'd like to accompany him to a Christmas gathering up in a mountain village a couple of hours' drive away where he had inherited a 500-year-old cottage.

Soon after this a friend of Christian Pierre's, a French school teacher who was working in Morocco, arrived to drive us up to the village. We wound our way south towards the Pyrenees through farm and forest land, the towns and villages becoming sparser and the road becoming more narrow and twisting. We finally arrived at a tiny village surrounded by birch forest. All the houses had thatched roofs and were built of stone that was covered with clay then whitewashed. The walls of Christian Pierre's house were about a metre thick at the base. At one end of the main living room there was an enormous open fireplace from which hung massive cast-iron pots and camp ovens. These were being tended by a middle-aged lady who was dressed like a peasant, obviously a local villager.

We seemed to have entered a time warp. The cottage contained no modern conveniences. The water was drawn from a crystal-clear spring surrounded by large flat stones, at the end of a lane between the village houses. One cottage was continuous with the next until they merged back into the forest.

Other friends soon began to arrive, until there were about 15 of us. There were large hams and cheeses hanging from the roof near the chimney, which was more like a hole in the roof. Beautiful cakes and pastries were laid out on the table, like the ones Moby and I had often seen in bakeries but couldn't afford to buy. Our meagre budget had allowed us basic bread, cheese and a little ham.

After a while Christian Pierre's friend from Morocco stood up and began a lengthy speech, *en français*, of course, so we could understand only the odd word. Then he opened up a large suitcase that was sitting on a stool in front of him. It was filled with colourful glazed pottery bowls, each with the words 'Cercle d'Oc' printed on it. He handed each of us one of the bowls as a gift. Apparently we had just been made honorary members of this circle of friends in the region of Occitan. Just like the Brookies, this group of people were celebrating their togetherness, and the kind teacher had specially commissioned a Moroccan potter to create these beautiful bowls for them.

We partied on into the night, strumming guitars and singing ballads, and later joined in a dance and celebration at the village hall.

The next morning I wandered through the village, admiring the reed and stick thatching up on the roofs, until eventually I found myself in the nearby forest. As I walked through the glades of beautiful trees, the soft winter light dappling their branches, I felt an affinity with this place. As I thought about this I began to realise that my Baskerville family bloodline had its origins within this region of the world. We were near the Spanish–French border in the foothills of the Pyrenees where the Basque people live. My great-great-great-great-grandfather, a Captain Baskerville, was part of a contingent of 4000 Spanish soldiers who had left this region to support the Irish Catholics in their fight against the colonising English. I remembered how my godmother, Milly Malone, whose mother was a Baskerville, would comment on my life and spirit, look at me with a twinkle in her eye, and say, 'It's the Baskerville in you.'

I followed a clear, bubbling stream back towards the village, coming out just below the spring where I took a deep draught of thirst-quenching water as the significance of all this sank in.

But it was time for us to move on, so we farewelled Christian Pierre, thanking him for his great generosity and kindness, and caught the train for Barcelona. We stayed there long enough to celebrate New Year, exploring the beach and enjoying the high spirits of the Spanish people. By then our money was really starting to run out, though we both had more back in London, so it was time to head north again. With pleasant memories of Spain, and having learnt a few basic words of the language, we caught a train to Switzerland. After a night in Geneva it was back to Paris, where we found the train to Calais and the Channel had just left for the day, so we had another night to wait. By the time we had bought our tickets for the train to Calais, the ferry, and the train to London, our only option was to sleep the night in the waiting room of the railway station.

Moby and I took turns to stay with our gear while one of us wandered off for a look around and to rustle up some food. I was amazed to come across a shop that was selling mink coats for vast sums of money.

At first we were about the only people in the waiting room, but as the evening wore on more and more people moved in. We assumed they were all in transit like us, and it wasn't until the morning when the gendarmes came in and checked people for tickets that we realised they were actually homeless street people. The poverty of these unfortunate people was in sharp contrast to the fortunate ones who were browsing and buying apparel in the fur coat shop nearby. There were people of all ages, and Moby and I began to see the other side of life, the haves and the have-nots. These people didn't look very different from each other, but their fortunes had taken different pathways.

Back in London, I fell into my old routine of catching the

Underground and exploring the city. My eldest sister, Susan, was also living in London at this time, and together we took a tour down to Cornwall. After a couple of days in Plymouth we took a bus to Penzance, which is a stone's throw from Land's End. Here, in the far southwest of England, the waves roll in off the mighty Atlantic Ocean and crash into the bottom of the high rocky bluffs that line most of the Cornwall coastline. The ultramarine sea has shaped the hard granite cliffs into wild-looking forms, and it was an eerie feeling to peer down hundreds of feet to the white-crested waves below.

From Penzance we travelled north along narrow lanes and roadways lined with basalt- and granite-stacked stone walls. The lovely green farmlands would end abruptly as we neared small villages composed of terrace houses all lined up next to each other, then they too ended just as quickly as the countryside took over again. Sheep, beef and dairy cows were grazing on lush green grass interspersed with wind-breaks of oak, walnut, elm and birch trees.

Eventually we arrived in the ancient Roman town of Bath to stay with our English relatives, Tom and Grace Harper, who owned the Lark Hall Inn. Sue and I both thoroughly enjoyed our stay here, and spent much of the time working behind the bar. Before too long I had gained the skill of pouring a brown top, an ale or a cider with just the right amount of froth on top. The beer was all on tap, so the knack was in the right amount of lever action. We also heard the horrors and joys of the infamous Scrumpy Cider, which apparently needed the addition of a dead bat to help it to maturity.

Each morning Tom and I took long walks across the rolling hills and pathways between farms, and along canals that were still in service to transport goods from country to market. The long flat barges were often loaded with coal, and sometimes with people just cruising through England.

From Bath we returned to London, then in late January I once more set off for Kent, this time to the port town of Folkestone to catch the ferry for Ostend in Belgium. From there I travelled by train to the capital, Brussels. As I was leaving the railway station through an underground tunnel two guys walking along beside me asked if I knew where they could stay. I said, 'I don't know, but if you come with me we'll find somewhere,' and we did. They were from Brazil and also planned to travel to Amsterdam, so after a day exploring the city's modern architecture we caught the Trans-European Express for Holland. After arriving in Amsterdam we booked into a hotel just across the road from the station and ended up staying there a week. We met some interesting people there, including some who were smugglers, bringing their wares cross-country from Pakistan and Afghanistan to sell in Paris and Amsterdam. They were mainly Americans, and this is how they made their living and travelled the world. I listened to many of their stories of danger and intrigue.

One afternoon we all went to a big rock concert that went for two days and featured some well-known bands such as the Doobie Brothers, Graham Central Station, Montrose and Little Feat. As I made my way home in the early hours of the morning I stumbled upon the red-light district and was amazed to see naked women and girls lounging behind the shop-front windows and leaning out of doorways, obviously waiting for customers.

Before too long it was time to move on. This city was full of potential dangers and addictions, and while I had thoroughly enjoyed meeting some adventurous people, home beckoned me once more. I made my way back to London, where it was now time to prepare for my journey to Sydney.

My flight left Heathrow very early in the morning, so I farewelled Annette the night before then sat up until it was time to leave at about 4am. I flew to Bangkok, then via Singapore to Sydney. After arriving late at night in Sydney I made my way to the nearby Tempe Railway Station with a few other passengers, and we shared our overseas experiences until we could catch the first morning train to Central Sydney Station. Here I caught the train to Brisbane. This was the slowest train in existence. I hadn't slept for four nights, and the train spent as much of the journey stationary as it did moving, until eventually our destination was reached. I caught a bus to Kenmore and walked the last three kilometres to my home in Brookfield, totally exhausted but glad to be back.

Within two days I was walking back into the same university lecture hall I had left three months earlier, to begin my second year of medicine. After travelling 50,000 kilometres, my mind still felt stretched from one end of the world to the other. I sat down, but my body housed a different person as I gazed up at the lecturer, framed by his large blackboard. At times I noticed my lecture notes were being recorded backwards.

Within a couple of weeks I had settled back in, but there was a restlessness and awareness growing within me. My journey across the planet was leading me on to new and unknown pathways. By the year's end I had reached a threshold, and a new era was dawning.

chapter 5 a new beginning

O n the first day of my university studies, after I had sat down with 400 other medical students in the large auditorium, the professor had announced: 'Look at the person beside you. One of you will not be here next year, as there are only 200 places for second-year students.'

What a great way to start the year — stress, competition, and more stress.

Pretty much straight away everyone had knuckled down and we were working our way through subjects like physical chemistry, physics, zoology and psychology. An old school friend of mine, Peter Steinheure, helped me pick up any lecture points that I failed to grasp, and I spent numerous hours at home and in the university library studying and preparing for exams. Despite all this I managed to lead a fairly busy social life, the highlight of which was my friendship with Wendy Bopp. She was still in her last year of high school, but we spent most of our spare time together.

Luckily my grades had been good enough to get me into the second year. The sense of relief among the 200 fortunate students was palpable, and relations were much less strained than in the first year.

As we burrowed down into study again our core subjects of anatomy, physiology and biochemistry provided me with a wealth of knowledge and intrigue. We were undertaking an exploration of the entire human condition, involving the dissection of a whole and intact human body, following every muscle, vein, artery and nerve, and including all its organs, bones and special features.

Physiology involved the plumbing and pressure systems, while biochemistry led us to a better understanding of the chemical analysis of all the body's systems, including nerve impulses, blood, bones, protein, fat and carbohydrate absorption. Another subject, histology, took us on a microscopic journey through the body's tissue on a cellular level. I enjoyed this second year of study, and the company of my classmates, immensely. I had always had a strong desire to reach my full potential, and although during my last year of school I had considered becoming an engineer or an architect, medicine held the strongest lure. But I had always thought I would have a family too, and now I was beginning to wonder how I would ever have time to spend with my children. Perhaps I would have five minutes a day, if I was lucky. My life ahead seemed to be closing in like a tunnel. As I gazed along this tunnel, from the busy present into the even busier future, I could see my personal time being squeezed out until there was none left.

My sense of humanity was enriched by my friendship with my Brookfield companions, along with the intense love I felt for Wendy and later, Annette Holden. I felt a deep respect and love for mankind, but the world's preoccupation with material goods was at odds with the values my

Brookfield friends had instilled in me; that the best things in life are free. I thought deeply about the existence of mankind, and the effects people's actions had upon themselves and the world that supported them. Deep down I was searching for answers about the meaning of existence. But I never reached any conclusions or solutions.

Up to this point my life had been etched with the working knowledge of peaceful, meaningful coexistence with other people. Alongside this I felt the intense futility of war, feelings that stemmed from studying the effects of nuclear holocaust through my father's photographs of Hiroshima and Nagasaki. Meanwhile our rampant colonisation of racial cultures was creating incredibly stressful political situations.

I was aware, too, of the stresses we put on our own bodies. When I was at school Dad used to drive me each day into the centre of the city, where the smog enveloped the towering buildings in a shroud of exhaust fumes. We were supposed to breathe that stuff! I don't expect everyone to agree with my perspective, and over the years the intensity of my views has mellowed in a day-to-day sense, but as a species we were putting incredible pressure on our natural systems.

One of my early dreams, which you may well share, had been to go and live on a deserted island, to live off the bounty that nature would surely provide. So during the mid-year break my friend Duncan Lay and I headed off to Great Keppel Island on the Great Barrier Reef, our chosen wilderness. We caught the train from Brisbane to Rockhampton full of excitement and anticipation.

We purposely arrived under-supplied in the stores department, carrying a kilogram of rice to supplement our diet, most of which we planned to catch or find. The ferry dropped us near a tourist resort, where there were also a number of private baches, and we quickly made our way around to Leck's Beach on the opposite side of the island.

Since we were relying on catching fish for our survival we had brought along a hand-spear, mask, flippers and snorkel. My first encounter was with a sea snake, as I made my way around from the beach and creek mouth towards the rocky headland. This fascinating creature was grazing sedately, head down, tail up, on some mossy rocks. I was a little worried by its banded body so I swam through the light surf to the rocky water's edge, but then thought better of it. If we wanted to survive then we had to spear fish. So after moving further around the headland I re-entered the sea and managed to spear a medium-sized bream, enough for a meal.

As the days wore on we kept the often chilly winter air at bay by piling driftwood on our campfire, and cooked up fish over the hot embers along with our boiled rice. We weren't exactly starving but we had to keep at it, taking turns to spear more fish. We also found shellfish, being careful around the creek mouth where the dangerous stonefish were known to lurk in the murky shadows, and gathered Neptune's necklace from around the estuary. We also managed to find some large field mushrooms, and there was prickly pear cactus with its red fruit. We made the latter into a jam, and also baked the fruit of the pandanus palm, which were similar to a sweet potato.

On one memorable occasion I was just about to spear a fish near the sandy seafloor when the whole bed of sand came alive in the form of a five-metre stingray, which flapped its wing-like body and swam away. We often saw large green sea turtles, and we discovered places up the beach where they had laid eggs, but we left them alone, not wishing to harm them.

After a couple of weeks of subsistence living, by which time we felt considerably toughened up but happy with our lot, our friend Moby arrived to join us. After one day he had endured enough of our fish and rice, prickly pear and Neptune's necklace, so he headed back to the resort to find himself a hamburger. We also went over, in the hope of picking some coconuts which grew in profusion near the resort. We spied a nice bunch up a six-metre-high tree on the beach in front of a small cottage. I shimmied up the trunk slowly but surely, until I amazed even myself by reaching the crown with its bounty of coconuts. Clinging on tightly, I twisted one nut round and round until it gave way and dropped to the ground below, then I twisted off another and another. Meanwhile the owner of the bach had come out and was standing at the base of the tree. By the time I had descended he had retrieved all the coconuts, claiming they belonged to him. So it was time for Plan B. Duncan and I sauntered over to the resort while Moby, much to our disgust, bought himself another hamburger, and we managed to twist off a couple of nice fat coconuts that were hanging quite low down.

One day there was a competition on the island, with a first prize of a meat pie and a can of beer. It was a race that involved swimming from a boat to the shore, then a sprint to the top of a steep sandhill, back down and a swim back to the boat. I was determined to win, and so I did. I managed to swap my can of beer for another meat pie, one for me and one for Duncan, after which we said our farewells and swam back to our camp.

Over the next 12 months we made four subsequent trips to Great Keppel Island, enjoying the solitude, sun, sand, camaraderie and the wonders that nature provided. Most of our Brookie mates paid a visit to our paradise, and the salt air freshened our sinuses and cleared out the toxins we'd gathered from our urban lives.

During this time my restlessness was growing, and insights into the way I really wanted to live were beginning to ferment. Other means of survival stimulated my imagination. My subconscious was storing all this away, deep within myself, until a threshold was reached and my eyes could see consciously, all the way to the horizon.

Towards the end of my second year of study, as the vacation loomed, I felt as if a lid was being lifted off my existence. Perhaps it was a premonition. This particular vacation felt like it was going to be forever. To me, this was like a revelation. Before this I had never seriously contemplated leaving my medical studies. It was completely out of the question.

Every event of my life up to this point had brought me to a threshold which I passed through as the vision of a new world and a way ahead became clear. This occurred as I was reading a book about a New Age community in Scotland. The story was the catalyst that enabled the empathy and concern I felt for mankind and the planet to finally find a way forward.

Universal love and respect are the main movers and sources of our energy. They have the potential to support our standard of living to a much higher level. Man was quickly evolving, so there was hope for us yet. I was touched by the divine natural wilderness to be an agent of change. The time was now. My conviction was total and I never seriously looked back.

I have never doubted the personal conviction I felt at that time. I have continued to focus on the lessons of the past and the importance of the present, and look to the future with confidence and optimism. I realised that the only way I could have an impact was to change my own ways and get on with it. I took strength from my faith that if I did what appeared to be the right thing, then my needs would be met and I would be looked after.

My decision to give up medicine was also about the way the medical system only treated symptoms and not causes. I could see there was a need for more preventative measures, but in the 1970s these were practically non-existent. Instead of the unbridled use of pharmaceuticals, many conditions could be alleviated or improved by changes in lifestyle, attitude and diet, along with more attention to safety issues and less use of alcohol and recreational drugs. We also needed to make this planet whole again.

Despite my doubts I returned to university the following year. In this third year we were being trained in the use of drugs — using drug A to treat a condition, then drug B to counteract the side effects of drug A, then drug C to counter the effects of B, and so forth down to drug D. Psychological conditions were also being treated with drugs rather than counselling patients to help them deal with stress, relationship crises or economic problems. People had become reliant on, and in some cases addicted to, medication.

Having said all that, I must acknowledge the vital contribution the medical system makes to the viability of our lives in the 21st century. I would love to have been able to make people whole again, and to have developed the skills to put people back together again as my Uncle Laurie did. I admired his surgical skills immensely, and have visited him on occasions after he has been up all night sewing people together again after they have been involved in traumatic accidents. His concern is solely for the welfare of his patients.

But logic and my resolve led me to other places. I felt that we needed to evolve a more complementary approach to our health, acknowledge other forms of healing and take more responsibility for ourselves. We needed to adopt lifestyles that would allow our bodies, minds and spirits to heal more naturally, rather than always expecting a quick fix. Of course modern medicine with all its advances still plays an integral part in providing health and well-being, but our modern world also tends to overload us with toxins and harmful habits which could easily be alleviated with better management.

One month into my third year I left university. I felt that the previous 20 years had been like a chrysalis that had folded its wings about me while I contemplated the meaning of life here on Earth in the 20th century. Now it was time to shed the cocoon and spread my wings. All I needed was a place to settle, where I could mix my hands with the earth and watch the fruits of my toil grow. Little did I realise that my wings wouldn't come to rest until I had settled back in New Zealand, my country of birth.

My first priority was to look after my immediate family. My belief that the system was unsustainable and that we were actually poisoning the planet led me to take practical action. In the event of a structural breakdown of society and its supply lines, the most important things would be to have shelter and an adequate food supply. So I set about digging up Dad's overgrown vegetable plot and planting a variety of seeds, such as lettuces, corn, tomatoes, carrots, peas and runner beans, which with frequent watering quickly sprouted away towards profusion.

I also collected macadamia, pecan and almond seeds from wild trees nearby and laid them between hessian sacks to sprout. To my amazement this happened within two weeks. These were planted in nursery pots along with other seeds, so I began the makings of an orchard. We owned about 1.5 hectares of land so I saw much potential there. Dad took me to a council forestry nursery where the trees were small and inexpensive, and I bought many trees and planted them.

Of course my family were very upset and disappointed about my decision to leave university. They had held great hopes for me, and much of their mana was held within my potential. It was my father who was the most upset. My decision was not so much a surprise to Mum, who in the past had occasionally commented that she couldn't see how I would fit into the mould of being a doctor. This I would dismiss as nonsense. In a way I was as surprised as anybody since I had never really seen it coming. To me it was a revelation.

When I began gardening full time and expressing my concerns about my family's welfare there was a mixed reaction. Although my parents could see some sense in my newly expressed philosophy, they were not happy that it was coming from their own son. My father said at one stage that he would 'weep tears of blood'. On the one hand there was appreciation that I actually cared about them, but on the other hand was a disbelief that the system providing all their needs would ever fail them. But my enthusiasm and idealism were unshakeable, and eventually my father announced that they had held a vote. I had been voted out and was to leave and fend for myself. I was given two days to leave.

My sisters were upset, and of course had never voted, nor had my mother for that matter. To be fair, Dad was really just trying to make me face up to the harsh realities of supporting myself in the big wide world, which was not a problem for me and never has been. At this time and ever since I've had total faith in the divine nature of existence to support me as long as I do the right thing.

While I was living at home I'd received an allowance of $10 a week from Dad, and I was doing a lot of work around the property. When Dad asked me to leave I already had a job across the other side of town that my girlfriend Annette had lined up for me, doing some gib-stopping and painting. I already knew that it was time to move on and make my own way.

Fortunately, the weekend before my father's announcement I had found three $2 notes washed up on a beach, which was enough to see me through the first week until my wages came through. Some old schoolmates let me sleep on their lounge room couch for a week, paying board of $1 a day, until I was paid $20 for my week's work. After that I moved in with two of my Brookfield mates, Tim and Nick, who were renting a house, and took on a job as a carpenter's labourer. I had decided that I really wanted to move out of town, and I was preparing for this.

Even though my parents had temporarily abandoned me, over the years they had instilled in me enough confidence to work towards the new beginning I wanted. Nothing was going to stop me from realising my goals. Though it seemed that in a way the whole world was working against me, I put that aside as totally irrelevant. My idealistic vision, fuelled by my inherent confidence and determination, kept me going whatever the odds, hardships or circumstances.

One day, after I'd been staying with Tim and Nick for two or three months, Tim's brother Simon announced that he knew of the perfect place for me to live. Simon was studying at Gatton Agricultural College, which was in the middle of the Lockyer Valley, the food basket for Brisbane. He knew of a place in the hills about 100 kilometres west of Brisbane, above where he was renting an old farmhouse. He was just heading back there and invited me along.

Once we reached his house I jumped on the back of his Yamaha 175 trail bike and off we went, bouncing our way up into the hills along an old disused dirt road. After we had ascended to about 500 metres above the Lockyer Valley we were greeted with panoramic views almost all the way back to Brisbane in the hazy, blue-purple distance. When we finally arrived at the end of the road we found an ancient wooden-slab building with a rusty corrugated-iron roof. The bearers and walls had all been hewn out of eucalyptus timber with metal axes and adzes.

Simon announced that the place was called Egypt, which seemed an apt title considering its far-away nature. The old house was surrounded by cultivated paddocks which quickly blended into the surrounding eucalyptus forest. The view was stunning, and I immediately fell in love with the place. Simon suggested we visit the owner, who lived back down in the valley.

The old dairy farmer was happy for me to live up at Egypt and didn't expect any rent, as long as I helped keep the kangaroos and wallabies away from the crops of barley and oats he was growing up there. Apparently the area had been settled 100 years before by dairy farmers, who would bring their cream down by horse and dray. There had once been a thriving community up there, but no one had lived there for over 30 years, so the area was pretty much abandoned. I moved in straight away and later hired a truck for a day to bring up some old timber and windows that I had been collecting from a renovation building site I had been labouring on.

This was my first taste of complete isolation, though my

nearest neighbour was only five kilometres away down an old dray road that dropped steeply off the plateau. The remoteness of the place carried with it a sense of vastness and connection to the entire surrounding landscape.

The vast blue sky opened above me, and the view extended beyond like the sea. An old water tank collected rainfall off the roof and provided shade during the intense heat of the days. About a third of the slab walls had been dismantled, probably for fence posts and pallets, which made the views even better. There were large hessian sacks of barley and oat seed stacked in the middle of the house, and these provided me with a comfortable raised bed. In an area where part of the floor had been neatly taken away, I built a stone fireplace and paved the ground with flat slabs of sandstone.

Each morning and evening the fire warmed me and cooked my food. Midwinter was soon upon me, and I toiled each day digging and planting the fertile black soil, putting in windows and rebuilding the walls. During the winter months the cold westerlies blew in off the dry inland plains, and at night I buried myself under a pile of blankets to seal out the gale-force wind until the new walls provided a wind-break. Each day I watched the blue skies, hoping for clouds and rain to water my garden. Otherwise I'd carry bucketfuls of water from a dam about 200 metres away to nourish my thriving young vegetable plants. Each evening I washed in the dam as the sun set, then warmed up by the glow of the open fire as I prepared tea.

My friend Moby had lent me an old wind-up gramophone, and one afternoon when I was playing it the old dairy farmer walked in, drawn by the music emanating from the house. He couldn't believe his ears, and he told me that the same music had been played there 30 or 40 years earlier when dances had been held at Egypt. He told me how he had waltzed there with his wife in the old days, and even won dancing competitions.

From time to time friends from Brisbane would visit, but for the first six months I was pretty much alone. Every couple of weeks I would head down to Simon's place, where I kept my 10-speed road bike, and cycle the 100 kilometres down to Brisbane to stay with Tim and Nick for a few days. I would visit my family then cycle back up again. Some days the ride would be especially arduous as I faced the gale-force westerlies all the way up to Gatton. Later, during the summer months, I would ride overnight to escape the sun and heat of the scorching days.

It wasn't long before my very loving father was encouraging me to move back home from Egypt, since he missed me. But I knew that our superficial differences would cause us to grate against each other and I needed my independence to achieve my goals. He and Mum drove me back up to Eygpt on one occasion in order to pay a visit, and they gradually began to realise that the best way to cope with the change was to stop criticising me since this only encouraged me to move further away. But this was a slow process, and it wasn't until about 20 years later that things really improved.

After a while an old school friend, Alan Rogers, began living at Egypt. He was a brilliant scholar and had topped the class in economics and French at school, but like me he had left university and chosen to live on the land.

One day we were astounded when a two-metre-long brown snake appeared from under the house. It stopped, turned around and gazed at us, then went on its merry way.

We also shared the space with a large black snake that hung out near the water tank, a python that lived in the rafters, and a long, thin, green tree snake that occasionally adorned a nearby shrub.

As time went by more visitors came and stayed, and though they loved the area most found the isolation a bit daunting. After about a year Alan and I were well settled there, but the political climate of Queensland during the 1960s and '70s was dominated by a hard-core right-wing government headed by the dictatorial, Joh Bjelke-Petersen, who was Premier for 19 years. The authorities were intolerant of anyone with an alternative lifestyle, and actively pursued them. They believed we were a threat to the community, and demanded that we move on. The irony of this situation was that both the Minister of Police and the Commissioner of Police at that time were later jailed for three years, after being convicted on charges of corruption and vice.

We left Egypt and went back to Brisbane. Mum and Dad were overseas at this time, and I based myself with Tim, Nick and another friend, Chris Kelly, for about a month. By this time they were renting an old farmhouse out at Brookfield. Tim was working as a carpenter, Nick as a labourer, and Chris as an electrician.

During this time I watched some of our old home movies of the family farm at Kawhia, and I decided to return to my homeland, New Zealand. Alan decided to come too. I had had the idea that we might be able to live at the farm, so soon after arriving in Auckland we went to visit my Uncle Lawrence, who owned it by then. But he, bless his dear soul, being a surgeon, and me being a medical-school dropout, would not let us stay there. In later years Laurie encouraged me to live at the farm, but by then I was well entrenched in South Westland.

I was deeply disappointed but there was nothing we could do, so we decided to take a trip up north. From Auckland we cycled up through Waitakere and on to Rewiti. After spending our first night in a tent and becoming drenched, we packed up and made our way toward a farmhouse near what looked like an old barn. A middle-aged Maori man appeared at the door and we asked him if we could stay the night in his barn to dry out. He was obviously taken aback, and replied, 'That's not a barn. That is our marae. If you asked that up north they would have you for dinner.'

It looked as if we had put our foot in it, until his belly began jostling up and down as he burst into laughter. He then said we were welcome to stay there for the night, and once we had settled in he invited us back to the house, where we were fed like long-lost sons or cousins. Not only that, but our new friend recommended that we stop the next night at Glorit, where he knew a fisherman and boat-builder by the name of Frank who lived on the Kaipara Harbour.

As we were packing up the next morning people began arriving to attend a tangi at the marae. The minister, hearing that we were heading north, suggested that when we reached Dargaville we should call in on Sam Toia, who was a youth affairs coordinator with the church there.

For most of that day we rode along hilly, winding roads. We were eventually rewarded with panoramic views of the Kaipara Harbour, New Zealand's largest by area, and at day's end we were welcomed into Frank's humble cottage. Not long after this one of his fishing mates entered and handed us a fresh flounder each for supper. That night we lodged in the hull of a 12-metre sailing boat that Frank was constructing nearby.

The next day we cycled up through Wellsford, and before long headed west onto the road that led to Maungaturoto and Dargaville. Along the way we met a friendly family who invited us to stay with them at their farmhouse near Maungaturoto, so we warmed up in front of their fireplace for a couple of days before riding off again into a westerly gale, complete with hailstones and rain. We dosed up on walnuts dipped in manuka honey, and luckily our final leg from Ruawai to Dargaville was aided by a strong, gusty tail-wind, but we arrived cold and wet on Sam Toia's doorstep.

Sam and his wife Auntie Bonnie greeted us as if we were long-lost family, once again feeding us up generously, and welcoming us onto their marae. We stayed there a week, enjoying their warm hospitality, then we hit the road again, heading up into the Waipoua Forest. This was surely the most amazing forest kingdom I had ever seen, here amongst the ancient kauri giants. After sweating our way up a steep gravel road we pushed our bicycles on up to the top of the forested ridge. From the crest overlooking New Zealand's largest remnant of pristine kauri forest we coasted down into the heart of the kingdom, observing the massive trunks and canopies along the way.

On reaching the bottom of the valley we set up camp on the south bank of the Waipoua River, then ventured along the walkways to pay our respects to Tane Mahuta, the god of the forest, and Te Matua Ngahere, the father of the forest. We were totally in awe of these monarchs, and so glad that this small portion of the originally extensive forest had been saved.

Next morning, as we were once again wheeling our bikes up the winding gravel road, a forestry vehicle pulled up alongside us. The driver offered us a ride to Waimamaku, the next town, just south of the Hokianga Harbour. Much of this valley was inhabited and owned by people living on small organic farms and communes. Before long we were sharing experiences with a 17-year-old lad by the name of Richard who invited us to stay with his mother and sister. Since we were still wet through from a downpour the night before we accepted readily.

Richard's mother, Jane, was a herbalist, and every vegetable and herb imaginable was growing in profusion in their garden. Both mother and sister wore straight, waist-length hair (even Richard's was shoulder-length), and they reminded us of Lady Guinevere from the King Arthur legend. They milked their own cows and goats to produce their own butter and cheese, and they served the best cup of tea I have ever drunk, poured majestically into a fine china tea service.

Alan and I helped collect and chop firewood and worked in the gardens, then after a thoroughly enjoyable stay we cycled a short distance to the head of the valley to a forest commune called Long Louise, nestled amongst the towering kauri stands. Here we were lodged in a large Indian teepee occupied by an English girl named Sue. We also met a kauri wood carver who directed us towards a massive twin kauri complete with a rope ladder ascending high into the tree's crowns. We climbed carefully up between the tree trunks for 20 metres until we reached the forest canopy. There, tied among the massive limbs that branched out to form the twin crowns, was an extensive rope cargo net like a bower. This provided a safe and secure platform from which to view the surrounding giant trees.

From this vantage point I could imagine a world where instead of chopping these great giants down, then turning them into lumber and houses, we could instead actually utilise their tree trunks as foundations for houses constructed within the canopies of the forest with walkways in between. Hanging gardens could be established to harness the sun's energy.

At this point my journey north came to an end for the time being. Alan eventually reached Cape Reinga, but I returned to Auckland as my sisters, Annette and Vivienne, Annette's future husband, Ralph Westera, and my girlfriend, Jackie Oakhill, were about to fly in. We all travelled together for about three weeks, visiting Kawau Island and Rotorua before driving over to the west coast to spend a few days exploring the old family homestead and farm at Kawhia.

Jackie stayed on after the others had flown home to Australia, and we cycled down the Hauraki Gulf and over to Coromandel and Whitianga, then back to Auckland before Jackie, who had become homesick by then, flew back to Brisbane.

After she left I went and stayed at Panmure with my octogenarian godparents, the Malones, and caught up with old family history. In October 1977 I stood at the grave of my great-great-grandfather, Robert Long, on the hundredth anniversary of his death, alongside the grave of my grandfather, Robert Baskerville Long.

These marvellous old people, the Malones, passed on to me a sense of family and commitment to the land which has held me in great stead to this day. At this point in my life I was considering walking south to find somewhere totally isolated and just fade away into the ether, to leave the Earth that I was so disillusioned with. I seriously contemplated fasting and meditating until I passed on away, but eventually felt there was more to be done here in this world.

So I walked most of the way down the coastline around

the Hauraki Gulf, and over to Coromandel to visit my friend Alan at Sandy Bay, where he had settled into the Moehau Community with his partner, Ellen Appleby. I enjoyed working in the gardens and catching up with the various people who were living in or visiting this community. I slept in a large geodesic dome, and each morning I milked one of their cows and enjoyed the frothy, fresh, creamy milk.

But I was missing Jackie, so I hitched back to Auckland and a few days later had sold my 10-speed bicycle and booked a flight for Sydney. In November 1977 I arrived back in the Land of Oz, and hitchhiked through the night up to Brisbane.

chapter 6 a timeless land

Once back in Australia, it wasn't long before I decided to hit the road again. Jackie had moved on from me, and I had had enough of Western culture. Something was telling me to leave it all behind, to learn to live without money or gear. One day, I thought, all this material world may just melt away, leaving only the humble and hardened — those who had been hardened by the elements, but were still compassionate toward others.

I decided to head across to Western Australia via the Nullarbor then up to Darwin, and see if I could get a boat across to Asia. I would see if there was more to offer further afield.

So, dressed in shorts and a shirt, with $20 in my pocket, no shoes or jandals, no tent, groundsheet or raincoat, I headed off. I carried an old navy duffel bag, in which I had one blanket, a woollen jumper, and a pair of woollen socks to wear at night. Each day I walked until some kind person stopped to pick me up. With my light pack I chewed up many miles each day between rides. My bare feet quickly became pretty tough after travelling over concrete and gravel, and even broken glass at times. The soles of my feet felt more like leather than anything else.

As I walked the highway I kept a lookout for fruit trees growing around deserted farmhouses or leaning over garden fences. They were fair game, and as the days went by I built up a store of apples, apricots, peaches, lemons or grapes. During this period of my life I was mainly living on fruit, nuts and vegetables, so I lived on what I could collect along the way and the meals of vegetable and grain that people gave me. It was now about March, so harvest time was near, a good time for living off the land.

Water was a necessity, of course, and I carried a leather water bottle that I had bought in Barcelona, and later also an old beer bottle with a cork. At night I bedded down in the trees or grass near the side of the road, or in old barns away from people's houses. I was treated with kindness and generosity by the people I met, many of them offering me a place to stay for a few days, or a piece of extra clothing when the weather turned cold. About 150 kilometres out of Adelaide, on the Whyalla turn-off, an old 1960s Holden stopped to pick me up. This was to be my ride for the next 1800 kilometres. The drive across the Nullarbor lasted for two days and nights. We would pull up after dark and I would sleep beside the car, under the stars. After the seemingly endless straight road the gumtrees of South Australia had gradually given way to saltbush, and the red earth and dust penetrated everything.

I was becoming aware of how timeless a place Australia is. I was also beginning to enjoy the journey. I was a nobody, set free of pretence, living for the days that unravelled ahead of me. At the same time my strength and determination seemed to be building. The less I owned, the more my spirit and resolve grew. And my faith in human nature and the charity of mankind increased each day.

I didn't travel without money just so I could rely on charity, but so that I could connect with that side of people's nature, to see the worthiness in people. Their hearts opened. I was no threat to anyone, so I could drift along with the winds that blew me; I had faith that the universe would look after me. The vast open land and sky began to own me and nurture me, its hardiness just a natural character like any other.

Before I reached Perth I spent time with a couple of groups of people who were living on cooperative land. They were growing their own vegetables and had livestock such as dairy cows, sheep, beef and chickens, but they used a subsistence permacultural style of growing things, using natural processes and resources. I fitted in well enough there and they would have made me welcome if I had stayed on, but my restlessness urged me on. These people seemed too domesticated.

As I headed north from Perth I left the green tree-clad southwest corner of Australia for the barren red reaches once again. The coast of Western Australia stretches up through Geraldton, Carnarvon, Port Hedland and up to Broome, with little else in the way of settlement in between. Some days I must have walked 40–50 kilometres or more along the stony roadside, the hot, barren ground becoming one with the soles of my feet, the open blue skies blazing overhead, the stunted trees surviving on the edges of some of the world's driest deserts.

From Broome I headed northeast, along a road that is basically gravel, clay and sand interspersed with potholes all the way across to the Northern Territory. There are few bridges, and during the midsummer monsoon season floods make the road impassable. The country is flat and low-lying, and borders the Great Sandy Desert to the south.

My first ride left me 150 kilometres along the road in the middle of nowhere. As the shadows lengthened I kept trudging along the sandy road between low shrubland with views to the horizon. It was an expansive feeling to be wandering along this byway miles from anywhere, no towns for hundreds of kilometres in any direction. The traffic was almost non-existent — it was just me and the natural world about me. The broad horizon and endless sky began to unravel any of my remaining attachment to objects, material things or money. There came a point where they became almost irrelevant to my day-to-day existence. Wasn't there some other virtue greater than all the riches of the world? Some greater form of contentment? I felt it glowing within me.

As the sun set and the red-golden glow slowly died, the stars broke through the deep dark blue of the night. My journey kept on, the road ahead dragging me on through twilight and darkness until I was too weary to carry on. Laying my blanket out on the hard earth I slept soundly until, in the early hours of the morning, a light began to create shadows, flickering among the grasses and shrubs. I quickly packed up my swag and began walking, and for half an hour the light gradually strengthened as a vehicle came closer.

Eventually the blinding lights surged past me then hauled to a stop. I thanked the friendly soul for stopping and we headed on through the remaining night until we reached Fitzroy Crossing around daybreak. Here we parted ways. We were now in the beginning of the Kimberley Ranges, rolling hills sparsely populated by eucalyptus trees and green grass. I continued my journey, eventually arriving at the Victoria River, which had a proper signpost and an actual bridge over it — the first I had seen for about 600 kilometres. I was now in the Northern Territory. As I neared Katherine the road began to improve. The gravel was replaced by a strip of bitumen just wide enough for one car, so when another vehicle came the other way, every hour or two, one side of the car would be on the tarseal and the other would be in the gravel.

From Katherine it was only a few hours to Darwin, and from there I headed out into Arnhem Land, to the South Alligator River. My friend Alan Rogers had told me about a small settlement of people there, and had recommended I visit them. It was a sparse settlement comprised of about three huts 500 metres apart, around a small lake or billabong. The people here had staged an anti-nuclear protest and had blockaded the road to stop trucks carrying uranium ore. They were interesting people, and I spent a week there, but once again it was time to move on. I hitchhiked back to Darwin, then decided to head back to Brisbane.

My parents had been travelling for the last year and a half in Europe, India and the East, and they were due home soon. I longed for their company and a rest from this long journey. I had been on the road for nearly three months.

As I left Darwin I found an apple on the roadside. What a gift. I was being looked after still; breakfast had been provided.

The road south across the plains to Tenant Creek and then east towards Mt Isa brought me back into the dry grasslands of northwest Queensland. I travelled onwards through Cloncurry and another 1000 kilometres to Charters Towers, where I teamed up with a truckie, becoming his 'offsider'. He drove a road train, a truck and two trailers with sheep on board, and we headed south down the inland gravel road.

After two days we parted company at Kingaroy, and I finally arrived back at Brookfield to be greeted by the open arms of my parents.

I had circled a timeless continent, where one landmark merged into the next, where one gumtree among millions stood out along the track. The land and the generosity of her people had sustained me.

chapter 7 journey to the east

I stayed for a few months in Brisbane, and it was good to catch up with my parents and sisters again. During this time both Sue and Annette got married; Sue and her husband John then moved to Darwin, and Annette and Ralph to Cairns.

After a while I decided it was time to put down roots for a spell. My friend Johnny Rogers lent me a 10-speed Raleigh pushbike, and together we rode south into northern New South Wales to look for somewhere to settle. We were searching for a basic house, or even just a shed or shelter. After riding through rainforest we dropped into the head of the Uki Valley, not far across the border, where we found a suitable dwelling. It was a humble shelter, owned by a farmer who let us rent it for $2 a week.

Murwillumbah was the nearest large town, far down the valley. Nimbin was a smaller town nearby. It was run by hippies, and most of the surrounding countryside had been bought up by cooperatives and communes. Our next-door neighbour, who lived about a kilometre away, was Zarco, a tall Yugoslavian man with black waist-length hair. We also had friends who belonged to a land cooperative up through the nearby forest, and they became regular visitors. Sometimes a couple of other people would live with us at Uki for a while too.

The farmland ran into untouched rainforest where there were large native fig trees with their characteristic massive buttress roots. There was one inspiring tree in particular that was a mesh of large vines coming up off the roots. It had grown around and up a large, tall host tree that had since died, leaving a tree that I could climb for about 15 metres, holding onto the mesh of vines. At this height there was a hole large enough to enable me to squeeze inside the tree then climb back down inside the hollow core, with the sunlight dappling in through the gaps in the mesh. The tree extended about 30 metres to a large canopy that dominated this area of the rainforest. It made me think of the treehouse in *Swiss Family Robinson*.

Every so often I would hitch a ride back to Brisbane to work as a landscape gardener for some of our Brookfield neighbours, helping to create and maintain their dream gardens. They always made a point of giving me a nourishing lunch, and nearer to home I would sometimes stock up on bananas at a nearby plantation. Near Murwillumbah there were sugar plantations where I could collect a few metres of sugarcane to eat. There were wild macadamia nuts to harvest, along with wild passionfruit vines and avocado trees hanging over fences along the roadside. I also planted a vegetable garden and had a peach tree growing out beside the water tank.

I was basically a so-called hippy myself, a flower child, pacifist, anti-materialist. I visited many places around the valley and made many friends, but nowhere held me. My ideals were taking me further and further away from places where people had settled, away from farmland, away from roads. I loved these people; we shared many great and thought-provoking discussions on the meaning of life and the universe, as we all do, but the road still held me. My new home was still somewhere along the narrow twisting highway, somewhere beyond the hills and ranges, far beyond the misty blue mountains.

My soul began to search for new meanings and beginnings, and my heart sought to find direction and hope away from Western civilisation, of which I had had enough. I made my way north to Cairns to stay with my lovely sister Annette and her husband Ralph. I decided to get work on the trawlers and wharves there so I could earn enough money to head towards India, that golden jewel.

I worked for three months on an old survey vessel that was being refitted with freezer space to service the prawn trawlers that work up in the Gulf of Carpentaria. This was a job I loved and hated. I worked long hours, 10 hours a day, six days a week, and saved whatever I could. It was great to be working on the water. I had always dreamt of working on a fishing boat; that was yet to come, but here I worked alongside mariners of all flavours — yachties, fishermen and hard-case crewmen. The boat was a madhouse of activity since the work had to be completed in time to take advantage of the coming prawn season. My bedraggled appearance earned me the nickname 'Shag', which the skipper always called me. Later I also worked loading and unloading boxes of prawns from containers into port freezers, working with a team of labourers day after day.

Eventually I had enough money in my bank account to see me off from the shores of Australia, so I hit the road to Darwin, where I planned to fly or take some sort of boat to India. My eldest sister Susan and her husband John Chambers owned a veterinary hospital in Casuarina, in Darwin, and after a long, dusty hitchhike to Cloncurry I took a bus to their tropical hideaway in the suburbs. John took me on as a carpenter and gardener around his veterinary business, and kept me busy building planter boxes to service his passion for growing palm trees, which grew in profusion about his property.

On 18 July 1979, after a busy month and with a few more dollars in my pocket, I bade Sue and John farewell and flew to Singapore and then on to Sri Lanka, arriving in Colombo in the early hours of the morning. A new adventure had begun. I had finally broken away from the chains that bound me. It wasn't that I didn't love the people. I did and always had loved everyone. But it was the system, the establishment, whatever you wish to call it. There seemed something misguided about it. The powers-that-be were alien to the basic happiness and wellbeing of the common people. It was time to shake off the shackles and find my own way.

The vast continent of India and Asia lay ahead of me — new customs and cultures unknown to those left behind. My search was about to begin. If you search hard enough, the solution will be found.

I stayed for several weeks in Sri Lanka, first in Colombo, where I was made welcome by friends of my parents and introduced to their Buddhist culture. Later I travelled south with their nephew, through what seemed like a Garden of Eden — there were coconut trees everywhere, and in the rainforests tropical fruits such as banana, avocado, cashew nuts, jackfruit and oranges. But it was in the highlands of Sri Lanka that I spent the most momentous day, since this was where I conceived the intention to live in South Westland.

As we gained altitude the terrain became steeper and

more clothed in rainforest. We began to leave behind the steaming humidity and heat of the lowlands. After a while we began to see rice being dried out on the middle of the bitumen road between the wheel tracks. Someone would be squatting nearby, ready to sweep any stray grains back into place after the passing of each vehicle.

This place of misty fog and cool breezes reminded me of where we used to travel as kids in the back of the old Vauxhall, up past Taupo, towards Mt Tongariro and Ruapehu, up through the ponga ferns and rainforest of New Zealand. I realised that was where I longed to live — but not in the North Island; in the South Island, on the West Coast near the southern end where I had heard there were no roads between the ocean and the mountaintops. That was where I must go.

I had never been to South Westland at that stage of my life, but friends who had visited and tramped there had told me about it. In 1977 Philip Wilkie, a friend of one of my cousins, had given me an extensive geography lesson on a map of the South Island which went from the ceiling to the floor of his bedroom in Mt Eden, Auckland. Philip understood what I wanted to do, and indicated then that South Westland to Fiordland was the place for me to go.

First, though, I still wanted to see Mt Everest, so after a few weeks travelling round Sri Lanka I headed off for mainland India. I caught the bus up to Anuradhapura and visited the bodhi tree where Prince Siddhartha, better known as Buddha, gained his enlightenment. This was a thought-provoking place. From there I continued on to Talaimannar, where a ferry departed for Rameswaram in the southern Indian state of Tamil Nadu. I was now surrounded by throngs of people of a completely different culture, simply one nameless and faceless person in the mass of humanity.

After exploring the area, and learning to deal with the endless hustle and bustle, the never-ending music and the attention I attracted as a Westerner, I set off to walk south, following the beach. After following the coastline for about 150 kilometres I headed inland to a nearby village and caught a bus for Tuticorin, then on to the west coast state of Kerala. From there I travelled up the coast before heading inland by train for about 1600 kilometres, right up the central plateau-country of India as far as Varanasi. My health was poor during this journey, and I often spent days bed-ridden between train journeys, suffering from the flu and diarrhoea, abscesses and intense toothache. I lost so much weight I was skinnier than most Indians I had seen — one of the reasons I couldn't remain in this continent.

From Varanasi I travelled up to Kathmandu, staying in a Buddhist monastery where the monks ran an orphanage for homeless children. Later that week I experienced the most amazing and spectacular scenery of my life, as I watched the sun rise from above the town of Dhulikhel, about 80 kilometres from Kathmandu. You can see the highest mountains in the world stretching from one end of the horizon to the other, with Everest among them. As the sun rose, every colour of the rainbow glittered and glistened off the array of permanent glaciers, just like jewels. The clarity of the air allowed the sunlight to travel unhindered, hundreds of miles across the massive mountain ranges.

After a week walking around the foothills below Mt Annapurna, crossing footbridges above tumultuous rivers emerging from the Himalayas, I returned to Kathmandu to begin the journey home. Throughout my travels through the heartland of India the decision I had made in the highlands of Sri Lanka remained unchanged — my goal was still to head home to the West Coast of the South Island.

I headed to Christchurch via Calcutta, Bangkok and Brisbane. The culture shock was immense, but it was a relief to be in the South Island. I arrived on 17 January 1980, ready for the sea, the forest and some wide open spaces.

chapter 8 home at last

After arriving in Christchurch I headed over Arthur's Pass to Greymouth. From there I continued hitchhiking north to Westport, then Karamea to walk over the Heaphy Track to reach the Nelson area where I planned to pick apples. My money reserves ran out about the time I secured a job at the second orchard I enquired at, just east of Motueka. After the last apple was picked about three months later, the orchardist dropped me off at the start of the Abel Tasman Track. I walked through to Collingwood, then back over the Heaphy Track, stayed with a like-minded friend, Jonathon Lodge, up the Karamea River, and eventually explored the coastline and valleys as far south as Franz Josef. After that I headed up to Auckland to see Uncle Jack and Aunty Doreen, then I hitchhiked down the east coast of both the North and the South Islands.

By September 1980 I was hitchhiking down to Bluff on my way to Stewart Island. As I was walking out of Invercargill, Buntie McCrystal and his wife Ivy stopped to pick me up. Buntie, with his gravel voice and twinkle in the eye, struck me immediately as one of life's treasures. By the time we reached Bluff my plans had changed and I was on my way to Puysegur Point and Preservation Inlet, the entrance to Long Sound, the southernmost haven of Fiordland.

A few days later I was on my watch skippering the *Komuri* as we journeyed west from Centre Island towards the wild oceans off Puysegur Point. I was navigating by the stars in the west as they slowly fell into the sea.

'Just pick a bright western star and follow it,' advised Buntie. There was a compass bobbing about in its case to provide the westerly bearing, and another fishing boat about a kilometre ahead of us that was heading in the same direction.

This was my first experience of driving a fishing boat, or any large boat for that matter. Buntie and Dean West, the 18-year-old crewman and owner of the boat, had watched me for half an hour to make sure the boat was in safe hands under my watch. Then about midnight they had both gone forward to the sleeping quarters to retire for the night. So here I was travelling across the Southern Ocean off the south coast of Southland.

It was magic. The sole light of the boat ahead of us appeared and disappeared as we negotiated the ocean swells that incessantly roll across this stretch of sea. The moon was full, and as we neared Fiordland across and out from Te Wae Wae Bay the snow on the mountains sparkled with brilliant white light. I was seeing for the first time the crystalline, pristine nature of Fiordland, which was to be my home territory for a greater part of my life.

As the brilliance of the stars led us west my concentration never wavered, held by the responsibility Buntie and Dean had laid in my hands. There was also the amazing fascination of watching the brilliant star I had selected gradually sinking into the ocean, to be replaced by another chosen bright star before the previous one had sunk. Bearing west was a basically simple process. It was surprising how quickly the selected stars disappeared. I suppose the time was drifting away quicker than I realised as I maintained my unwavering grip on the large wooden steering wheel.

The wheelhouse was not much larger than two telephone boxes, and perched just forward of the rounded stern section of the *Komuri*. She had negotiated these waters for nearly a hundred years, and found her way from peak to trough then peak again like a large dolphin playing in the waves. Between the wheelhouse and the forward cabin lay the work deck, laden with a selection of rusty steel-framed craypots, week-old bait, ropes and buoys. Occasionally the larger swells would surge up and through the scuppers, leaving the deck glistening in the moonlight.

As the night wore on the adrenalin in my veins kept me alert, and even as the first dawning light began to glow upon the distant snow-capped mountains, I continued to keep adjusting the wheel, now almost by instinct, as if I had spent years of my life at sea. The compass had become a friend, leading us safely on our way across the vast inky-blue waters.

Ever since my boyhood days I had dreamed of this, to be the master of my own fate, out in the arms of the mother sea, journeying off to adventures that only those who have known them can relate to. I could feel there would be no turning back; the thrall would be too great to escape. I was captured by the wild hands of the deep that held me safely aloft and in the arms of a watery queen, a child to explore the stars and the Milky Way. The roll and the heave were lulling me into a new realisation and a space I would never leave.

'Time for a PG Tips,' Buntie croaked as the sun finally broke the horizon and highlighted the deep-green walls of seawater with silver and gold. 'Here's a cup of tea. You've done well. We're still on course.

'Our first pots are still a couple of hours away, so take a wee nap if you please.'

Heeding his advice I headed forward, blinking in the bright morning light. Then I descended below deck level and collapsed into my welcome bunk like a babe in a cradle.

Some time later I awoke to the smell of sizzling bacon cooking on the galley stove nearby. The old range was being kept alive with liberal shovelfuls of Southland coal, keeping the cabin cosy and warm. As I came on deck Buntie and Dean were getting into action. The first pot of the day was looming on the horizon. They began checking the gear and stringing ropes, buoys and bridles on the new pots.

'What are you like at stringing up bait?' Dean asked me.

'Show me how and I'll set to it.'

He grabbed a bait hook, which looked like an oversized safety pin, about 30 centimetres long.

'Thread this through the eyes of the bait fish and you're in business.' Dean motioned me to a stack of large cardboard boxes piled chest-high against the side of the wheelhouse. 'Here's your bait hook, there's your bait, and you're away. You've a choice of cod or Nelson albacore heads.'

I could see this could be a messy task so I donned some yellow PVC overtrousers, but nothing had prepared me for the stench that met me as I opened the first carton on the deck. The *Komuri* had been built before freezers were invented, so they relied on companion boats to store their fish. This particular bait had been out of the freezer for over a week during their R&R back in Bluff. Aware that this important moment was my initiation into the real world of fishing, I picked up one bait hook after another and pierced the eyes of the wretched cod. I threaded four or five onto each bait hook, managing to quell the churning in my stomach and drawing in deep breaths of air as welcome gusts came my way, until finally the job was done — for the moment.

'Ah, we'll make a fisherman out of you yet,' Buntie cried with a broad smile on his face.

Dean was steadying himself against the roll of the boat as he coiled up the rope of the grappling hook. There was a new sparkle in his eye, like a pirate surveying the booty in his treasure chest. He lurched to the side and tossed the hook with a deft 10-metre throw, as Buntie hauled the boat into reverse to halt our momentum. The grapple had hooked over the pot rope and Dean quickly took in the slack, pulling the bright yellow and green buoys towards the gunwale of the boat then flicking a loop over the gantry pulley and one through the winch hauler. The ropes were screeching as they flew between the whirring wheels, sending up a tail of spray. Buntie's face was framed by the wheelhouse window as he stared intently as the rope coiled and piled up on the deck. After three or four minutes of hauling, out of the depths of the deep blue-green water a rectangular steel cage appeared in a red-orange glow, bursting the surface of the ocean.

Dean steadied the wildly rocking trap and I went to his aid as the craypot crashed down on the landing bay. The chattering, leaping crayfish were two layers deep. Dean and Buntie's smiles burst into cries of elation. We released the rubber-tethered hooks that held the door, then tipped the pot so the fish could fall to the deck. Dean began measuring them, and instructed me to swing a fish-laden bait hook in through the trap and hang it under the wire top of the pot. We then retethered the door hooks.

Buntie had run out of the wheelhouse for a closer look,

then rushed back to the wheel and studied his depth sounder before shouting, 'OK.' Dean and I pushed the freshly baited pot over the side and watched the coils quickly disappear. With a toss of the buoys, the first pot was done.

Before long the fish were all sorted. The shorties and eggy females went back to the ocean, while the 'takeables' were gently tossed into a wooden holding bay on the deck.

As we steamed from pot to pot, I rebaited the hooks and watched the ocean in all its morning glory. Albatrosses and mollymawks soared away above the waters, often gliding between the masts of the *Komuri*, the sooty shearwaters and black-backed gulls joining the fray along with myriad terns and other gulls. The sea was alive and overhead the sky never stopped moving.

The southerly breeze gradually freshened as the day wore on, occasionally wiping the top off the waves and sending a crisp shower of spray over Dean and me as we leant and swayed throughout the day. Sometimes the scuppers would come to life as the cleansing sea rushed across the deck and drained again between swells. The bow of the *Komuri* was untroubled by the heaving waves beneath us, but the rhythm of the ocean occasionally led me to dry retching. 'Get it in the pot!' Dean and Buntie would say. 'The fish will love it.'

After about 50 pots we began to draw level with Puysegur Point, which loomed above us. Once we reached the mouth of the inlet, Buntie skippered us into Preservation. Here calm water welcomed us and we entered what seemed like a paradise. Further up Long Sound, which pierces the land for 35 kilometres, cloud lay over the distant mountains, with rays of sunlight finding their way into green and golden valleys. Distant showers of rain mingled with the sunlight. It was obviously a moody place, full of surprises.

Our sister ships, the *Neroli* and the *Hakawai*, already lay at anchor. We hauled up alongside, their crews catching our bow and stern lines and fastening them to their bollards. We'd return here at the end of each day, tying up alongside like a small, watery village in the vast untouched wilderness, watching over one another. One anchor held all three boats, so as the wind changed direction we all drifted around together. We'd transfer the bags of crayfish tails to the freezer of either the *Hakawai* or the *Neroli*, and in the evening we'd move from boat to boat and catch up on the local gossip.

This was a unique place, the southwesternmost region of New Zealand. The colours and wildlife were in a world of their own. As we looked north from out in the ocean the sea emitted aquamarine colours I had never seen before. The brilliant golden morning sunlight pierced the crystal-clear blue-green depths at a unique angle as we gazed landwards, and the distant mountains disappeared into the mauve mists.

The 'village' was our base, and each morning we ventured from the safety of the sound back out onto the heaving Southern Ocean. Some days we fished among waves that were up to 10 metres high. Even Buntie was awed by these very intense days. Sometimes as we were working a pot on the landing bay — Buntie intent, studying the advancing sea, keeping the bow in to the waves; Dean and I clearing the fish and rebaiting the pot — a wall of water would surge over the bow, lurch across the deck and bodily lift us and the pot up and over. A number of times I ended up on the deck pinned under a craypot. Dean and Buntie would come to my aid as I struggled to get out from under the heavy pot.

After a couple of weeks Buntie cried, 'We can't take much more of this. The sea is too big!'

So he turned our bow eastwards and we steamed for Bluff with the sea up our chuff. Ten hours later *Komuri* chugged her way back into Bluff Harbour, and our exhaustion quickly evaporated in the excitement at the dock as friends and family welcomed us back. After our gear was unloaded and stowed away I headed back with Buntie and Ivy to the comfort of their warm home perched on the hillside. I was now a different person to the hitchhiker they had picked up all those weeks ago. I had become family, and the Bluff people accepted me as part of their community. We stayed in port for two weeks, partying at the local pubs, the Age and the Exchange, or in Buntie and Ivy's home. Then, after two weeks of drinking and gambling, Buntie stated, 'I'm broke. It's time we went fishing.'

I did several more trips with Buntie and Dean, enjoying the hard work and the camaraderie of the fishermen, and getting my first taste of the magic of Fiordland. But finally it was time to resume my journey, so I farewelled Buntie and Ivy, and crossed Foveaux Strait to Oban.

After spending several weeks tramping on Stewart Island I returned to Bluff, caught up with Buntie and Ivy, then headed across Lake Manapouri to walk in to Dusky Sound. This was a profound and life-changing experience. My 10-day journey into this isolated region of Fiordland captured my heart, soul and spirit. The lush green elfin forest and cascading streams became part of my fabric. Dusky emanated a musicality that I had never heard before, and I felt a sense of loss once I had returned again to the eastern shores of Manapouri. From there I decided to head back up the west coast, but rather than travelling by road through Queenstown, I opted to hitch up to the Hollyford Valley, walk out to the west coast and head north from there.

I made it as far as Big Bay, where I sheltered overnight in a forestry hut as the rain set in to a steady stream. It continued into the morning, so rather than continuing my tramp I decided to explore the area and meet some of the whitebaiters whose huts were dotted around the mouth of the nearby Awarua River. I knocked quietly on the door of the first hut that had smoke rising from its chimney, and before long it was opened by a jovial, well-fed Maori man who introduced himself as George.

'Welcome to Smokey Range,' he greeted me.

Before long I was sipping on a cup of hot tea and chewing on a slice of homemade Maori bread, fresh from George's camp oven and cooked in the hot coals of the large open fire that was the main feature of his living room.

George was an elderly man of mana and pride, one of those people who you feel privileged to be in the company of. It turned out that he was of Tainui origin and hailed from the Aotea Harbour, north of Kawhia. He had been a neighbour of my grandfather, Harry Smith, and had known him well.

After a couple of brews George decided we should go and visit the whitebaiters. We trudged along a sodden, muddy track through long grass and a glade of bush, then entered another hut that was full of people. They were obviously wasting no time on their day off, drinking beer and rum like it was going out of fashion. There were a couple of local whitebaiters, as well as two helicopter crews, a shooter, and another pilot. They got more and more worked up as the storm raged outside, buffeting the walls and roof with gale-force intensity, until in the end we were all rolling around with laughter.

By the next day the rains had abated, giving birth to a clear, bright morning. The helicopters had all left at first light, off hunting for red deer. George had offered to row me across the Awarua River, and as the shadows shortened the heat of the late November sun began to beat down on the land, raising pockets of steam and mist off the surrounding foothills and mountains. When we reached the northern river bank we were met by two of the whitebaiters, Mitch and Dobbie, who reassured me that the next few days would bring fine weather. They warned me not to take the Hacket River too lightly, since the floodwater there would still be abating, but said it would probably be manageable by the time I reached it.

I bade them farewell and set off, letting my pack settle upon my back, quickly finding my stride and letting the day's walking begin. I whistled across the sandy Awarua mouth and set upon the stretch of boulders that stretched as far as the eye could see towards what must be Crayfish Rock away in the distance. This stretch along the north side of the bay was a change from the five kilometres of sand and cobblestones along Big Bay beach, and I greeted it with enthusiasm.

I made my way past Big Bay Landing, out towards Crayfish Rock and on to Awarua Point. The view back towards the Main Divide was one of pristine snow-capped mountains on a scale as grand as you can get. Mt Tutoko rose above all else, then the view of coastal Fiordland extended way down from Martins Bay, Kaipo, Milford Sound to Bligh and Sutherland Sounds, finally diminishing in the distance into the watery horizon. The constant feature of this landscape is the sea, with perfectly formed waves peeling off the north reef of Awarua Point for miles out to sea then rolling into Big Bay. Little did I know that this was to become my workplace for years to come, surfing these enormous sets to bait pots for crayfish.

As I rounded Awarua Point I passed a greenstone boulder about a metre across, sparkling green and glistening in the late morning light, one of the millions upon millions of boulders that bedeck the coast from Awarua to the Hacket. Some were the size of houses, others one or two metres across. Then, as the boulders began to thin, becoming sparser and more like cobblestones and shingle, a river appeared — just shingly, sandy riverbed and banks adorned with flaxes and forest, a medium-sized flow of water descending straight from the mountains. No huts, no sign of man. This must be the Hacket.

'I could live here,' I exclaimed as I took this all in. I let out a sigh of relief. My searching was over. This was the first time for many long years that I had said this to myself. I knew that this place was to be my home.

So I carefully forded the river, put my hands together, nodded, paid reverence and respect to the waters rushing out to sea from the previous day's flood, and continued on my way, knowing that I had made the greatest discovery of my life.

After walking further north, across Ryan's Creek and beyond, I reached Gorge River as the shadows were lengthening. Dobbie and Mitch had said there was a hut here, on the south bank of the river mouth near an old airstrip. So I made my way to the shelter where I intended staying the night, set down my pack and began to sweep out the hut and settle in, content to know that I was in home territory.

A bit later I went for a walk and was surprised to see another place just around the corner of the flax thickets, a little upstream but still near the airstrip. There was a sign near the front door, with 'New Zealand Forest Service Gorge River' boldly etched and painted on it. This cottage certainly had character. I grabbed the broom and began to sweep it out. And this was where I slept the night of 26 November 1980. It was the first of what turned out to be many nights I slept there.

chapter 9 living off the land

The following day I continued on north, since I was expected in Karamea to collect my mail and spend Christmas with Jonathon Lodge and other friends up there. But I knew now that I would be coming straight back to settle in the Deep South.

I tramped up the coastline to Barn Bay, where I met fisherman Lou Brown, his partner Jude Batson and her children, Kate and Quinn, then I headed out and forded the crystal-clear Cascade River. Overnight I slept in a small musterers' hut, then I walked out along the Jackson River road to the Arawhata Bridge. From there I hitchhiked up to Karamea.

Several weeks later I returned to South Westland. I spent a night sleeping out under a beech tree beside the beautiful Jackson River, not far up from the Arawhata Bridge. Early the next morning I set about walking up Jacksons Road and back towards the Cascade Valley.

After I had been walking for a couple of hours a Forest Service vehicle pulled up and the driver offered me a ride. Aboard the 4WD were Dave Hilliard, the head forestry ranger for South Westland, based in Harihari; ranger Shane Hall; and the local Haast ranger, a blond-haired outdoorsman by the name of Clint McGee. I was in good company as I headed back in to my new home. They left me near the road end, and I thanked them, bid them good-day and headed on to Barn Bay.

The day — 17 January 1981 — was electric. I could feel it in the air as I forded the awesome Cascade River, her muted blues melding into the shingle and boulders that lined the riverbed. The blue skies and gentle breeze highlighted the cool, crystal-clear, rushing waters, watched over by the bush-clad hills and mountains of this beautiful valley. The tawny, grassy river flats were a perfect place to put many miles underfoot, the river silt providing comfort for my bare feet. This was the first anniversary of my arrival in the South Island, a day to celebrate. To me this was a milestone, though most would have taken it for granted.

It was with energy and excitement that I frittered away the miles of mossy, muddy track through glades of forest filtering the brilliant sunlight coming through the canopy. Mossy, lichen-covered podocarp trunks were dappled in golden, tawny and raw umber shades, the sap-green understorey of coprosma and fuchsia adding to the mystery of the forest gloom.

Before too long, as the afternoon was beginning to lengthen, I broke through the layers of forest and out onto the Hope riverbed. I followed its meanderings down to Barn Bay and Lou Brown's tin hut, in behind the flaxes. Welcome faces greeted me: Lou and Jude, Kate and Quinn, also Chris and Mary, crew for Dale Hunter, who would become an important part of my life, and Lou's new crew, Leslie Hadley. They kindly offered me a beer; it was time for a catch-up, since a month or two had passed since our first meeting.

The hut was two-storeyed, and as I walked in the door from the back landing at the top of the stairs I was once again struck by the awe-inspiring view of the Barn Islets out in the bay. The hut was actually an old aircraft hangar, and there was a large window facing the sea. The sea was dead calm, but the small living room was full of faces. Geoff Robson, a Jackson Bay fisherman, had come ashore off the *Coruba*, and there was George McInroe, a Greymouth fisherman, and his crewman-skipper, Kelvin, off the *Erynne Kay*. As we shared some homebrew I also met Jimmy Shepherd and John Kelman, skipper and crew of the *Sea Shag*. They had all moored out at the northern end of the bay in behind the Sugarloaf Needle. The fishing had gone quiet so they had come ashore to stir up some fun and mix with the locals.

Just as we were settling down for some friendly banter an aeroplane zoomed overhead, nearly taking the roof off. It then circled round and landed, and out hopped a nimble, smiling Don Mahon, his wife Jude and her daughter Xavier. Now this really looked like we had the makings of a party.

And party we did. The floor of the living room, whose supporting beam was an old ship's mast, was gyrating and bending up and down by about 45 centimetres as everyone began dancing and bouncing around. George and Kelvin were below, taking bets on how long the ship's mast would last before the floor came crashing down.

This was my welcome home party, with these people who were to become part of the fabric of my life. From the moment I walked in the door I felt as if I had always lived on this coast-line. It felt as if I was arriving home to visit a long-lost friend, and I felt just as much part of the place then as I do now.

The South Westland and Fiordland fishing community welcomed me as one of them, and told me that if anyone wondered what I was doing, I was crewing for them. They encouraged me to settle at Gorge River to bring it back to life and be a bastion of hope for when times were tough, as all fishermen know they can be.

There are four shipwrecks within six kilometres of the Gorge River mouth. Just the year before, the body of crewman Russell Horne had been washed up after the *Empress* had overturned and sunk. A rogue wave had struck her at the Steeples, one kilometre north of the Gorge. Russell's spirit still lingered in the minds of these folk, and in the foam and boulders of this unforgiving coastline.

I stayed a couple more days at Barn Bay, catching up with the locals, then I strolled down the beach to Gorge River, my plans strengthened by their encouragement. My sense of place has become more complete as the years have gone by, but my sense of belonging has always been much the same.

I settled into the hut at Gorge River, sharing it at various times with trampers, hunters or fishermen. For the first three years my isolation could be broken at any time, since the sign on the front of the hut indicated that it was the Gorge River Forest Service hut. I kept the hut as clean and tidy as possible, and people were free to come and stay as they pleased, as in any public hut. Occasionally they would stay in the hut next door, but usually they preferred the character of my hut, which had more room and a better view.

Sometimes a plane would land and for the next week or so a party of hunters would base themselves at the hut and scour the hillsides for the elusive red deer. All sorts of characters from around New Zealand and the world would appear. My sense of isolation would soon return when they left but I always appreciated their companionship. At times I felt a bit invaded, but it was their hut as much as mine so who was I to complain?

I left on my first tramp out to Haast on the shortest day of the year, 21 June 1981. I walked out from Gorge River to the Cascade Martyr Homestead, a distance of about 50 kilometres, in one day.

About 200 metres upstream from the hut and the river mouth high limestone bluffs rise up out of the deep river water. These bluffs extend for a further 300 metres upstream. When the tide is out there is a ford just downstream from the start of the bluffs, but when the tide is in there is no ford to cross unless you climb about 200 metres in altitude and head inland for 400 metres past the bluffs. It could take you up to an hour to complete this diversion. Nowadays we have a dinghy, a small inflatable boat and a canoe to cross the river at high tide, but in the early days I had none of those.

On this day, because the tide was high, I started my journey by paddling a mohiki or flax-stalk raft across the river. It took 156 stalks to support my weight. I then travelled up the beach to Barn Bay, and out to the Cascade River. When I came out near Robbie Nolan's hut all the musterers there started howling at me, since they had heard there was a wild man living at Gorge River, and their dogs joined in.

By the time I arrived in South Westland, Robbie Nolan had already passed away, leaving his farm on the south side of the Cascade to his son Maurice, but he was such a legend that this hut was known for many years as 'Robbie Nolan's hut'. Robbie's brother Des owned the farm on the north side of the river where the homestead was, beside the Martyr River, a tributary of the Cascade. It was originally built by the Macfarlane family over 100 years ago, and stood there until the late 1990s when it burnt down.

A few days after I passed through here Maurice Nolan

came up to me in the Haast pub and wanted to see my feet. He had ridden his horse back along the track looking at my footprints, which seemed very long since I was travelling quickly. I said to him, 'You can take my gumboots off if you want to.' He smiled and grimaced at me and walked away.

That first night I camped in a cosy little hut across the paddock from the homestead, then I headed off up the hill, along the road through Monkey Puzzle Gorge, up over the Martyr Saddle and along the road that wanders beside the Jackson River. The scenic walk was a blessing, since there was time to study the trees and terrain as I walked along the gravel road. After about 15 kilometres a vehicle pulled up beside me. The door of the white ute opened to reveal the smiling face of Clint McGee, the Haast forestry ranger. I climbed aboard, thanked him, and breathed a sigh of relief that my body would have a chance to rest for a while.

As we travelled Clint and I chatted, and he quizzed me on travelling times and the state of the Gorge River hut. He asked me if I was keeping it tidy, to which I answered in the affirmative. Each year he usually flew or walked into the Gorge for a hut check and a tidy-up of the airstrip. I let him know that I had been trimming the flaxes along the sides of the strip.

I was heading to Jackson Bay to stay with Jim and Carol Sheppard so I asked Clint to let me off when we reached the Arawhata Bridge. Before he drove off he said, 'I'll drop you off some paint and a taste of tucker and you can paint the hut.'

'Good as gold,' I replied.

It was another two years before Clint reappeared. On a memorable day in the spring of 1983 a Hughes 300 helicopter landed, flown by Dave Saxton. I saw Clint jump out, and as he walked up to me he said, 'We haven't come to kick you out.

You can be the caretaker forever if you want. Just look after the huts and maintain the airstrip and the tracks.'

'Good as gold,' I agreed, and we shook hands to settle our gentlemen's agreement.

When I consider my life on the Coast, it is a story of contrasts: my life at Gorge River compared to those in other places, and my life during the 1980s compared with the present day.

In the early days I was always amazed by the meals that would appear on the table at people's homes, either at Big Bay or beyond at Haast, Te Anau or wherever. They would always be so different from those at my place. No way could I serve up a meal that resembled theirs. After my first long, cold winter at the river, the Southland swedes, pumpkins and potatoes served up by Terry Fischer at his Big Bay whitebaiter's hut were truly something out of a dream. My homegrown potatoes would be small or wireworm-eaten, my swedes would be tough and chewy, and the salads were comprised more of weeds than succulent lettuces. Tomatoes wouldn't grow. The soil was so acidic that even silver beet was difficult to grow, and the ground so hard and rocky that the carrots would be stunted and bent. My one success was with cabbages, which flourished in the early '80s and helped keep Dobbie and Mike alive when they ran out of food while crayfishing the Gorge.

Right from my earliest days I would collect the seed heads of the club sedge grasses that abound along the margins of the airstrip. Long before I arrived at the Gorge I had realised that wheat and rice are just domesticated grass-seed heads, and that any or most grasses produce an edible seed head, providing protein, oils and starch. Our native seed heads are easy to harvest. In the late autumn they are dried out on the tops of their stalks, ready for picking. I would gather the seeds into an old leather school pouch and bring them back to the hut to dry out more. Once they were dry enough to crumble between my fingers I would grind them up on a large flat stone, pounding them with a wooden mallet or a stone.

Once I had sifted out the flour from the husk I would mix this into a dough with bought wholemeal flour. After the dough had thickened I would roll spoonfuls in the flour, coating the outside, and press them into flat cakes. I would usually cook these on the steel plate on the top of the stove, turning them over from time to time until they were baked. This bread, made from half sedge grass seed and half shop-bought flour, was my staple food for many years.

Similarly, the bull kelp that was thrown up on the beaches during large storms was a staple food for my first 15 years. Collected fresh and then hung high above the stove to dry, the thinner ends could be eaten like crisps. But most of the dried fronds would be ground up into a powder, to be added to soups or bread.

One of my initial purchases, within the first couple of years, was a grain grinder from a shop called Sprouts in Christchurch. I used this to grind the kelp and sedge grass seeds to a finer powder. The bull kelp could also be cooked for two or three hours to soften it into a jelly, which I enjoyed mixing with dough or stews. I would also eat it as a dessert with milk and sugar when I had some.

During my early days at Gorge River, when I was living on my own, my food was very basic. I didn't bring in butter, milk, sugar, cooking oil, eggs or cheese. A typical shopping list would include brown rice, peanuts, honey, rolled oats, raisins, wholemeal flour, mung beans and brown lentils. In 1981 I could head to Haast, spend $20, load my pack up and head home. I could pack in 20–25 kilograms of gear. I could buy 10 kilograms of chicken wheat for $5, which would go a long way. I loved reading novels, so they would be in the mix too. (In comparison, nowadays our monthly aerial supply drop will cost us around $300, and include sausages, eggs, bacon, mutton, flour, cheese, butter, oranges, apples, bananas, sugar, cooking oil and sultanas.) In my first year at the Gorge I spent about $500 on food and living expenses. I was still living on money I had earned from apple picking in Motueka.

Every few days I would browse through the forest, picking fresh and tender supplejack shoots which grow on the ends of the tough vines blocking your way in the understorey. These shot up in the spring, and if the deer hadn't eaten them they would climb up towards the canopy. If you noticed a young green vine you could pull it down and often the end shoot would still be tender. The young inner fern fronds were also a nourishing source of vegetable greens, and when I had collected these I would add them to most of my meals, such as porridge or vegetable stews. As my garden produced more food my reliance on the ferns decreased, except when I was away tramping or staying at Big Bay or Barn Bay.

Occasionally visitors who had flown or boated in would leave me some supplies, which would provide a welcome change of diet for a few days. But I was used to my simple fare, and I didn't have the money or energy to carry in a greater variety of food. I lived off the land and garden as much as possible, eating the seed heads of plants such as turnips, parsley, swedes and cabbages, which all provided nourishing food.

As time went on I began hunting for fish. At low tide I could spear fish that had been stranded in rock pools, collect mussels and paua, and go for the odd dive. The crayfish were harder to find in the 1980s than they are now.

When Clint visited in 1983 he told me of plans to renovate the hut. He and Barry Perrin, a Forestry Service carpenter from Harihari, undertook an inspection, crawling around beside the hut and the old shelter next door for about half an hour. They then decided it would be easier to do up the other hut, since the piles of the one I was living in were shot. I cranked up the old Shacklock and over a brew of hot tea they hatched a plan.

November came and with it two loads of timber, plywood, nails, paint, food and other gear flown in by Jeff McMillan, whose father Alister owned Aspiring Air based out of Wanaka. Then, around 20 November, Clint, Barry and a Forestry labourer by the name of Peter flew in with their carpentry tools and shovels, ready for action. Since they were working next door they settled into what was evolving into the 'Caretaker's Hut'.

In those days the Forestry Service workers were down to earth and cool. They always boiled their billies using firewood rather than gas, and they lived closer to the elements than the DoC workers of today. As we began to chew the fat that first evening, sitting by the warmth of the old wood stove, I announced that it was a couple of days after my birthday.

'Oh, great!' cried Barry.

He grabbed the bottle of whisky he had plonked in the middle of the table, quickly took the top off, threw it onto the floor, stomped on it and exclaimed, 'Well, that's taken care of that.'

So along with their crate of a dozen bottles of beer, the whisky and homebrew kept us entertained until the early hours of the morning. Clint and Barry were a source of delight with their stories and yarns, taunting each other in playful jest. It was one of the best birthday celebrations I had had.

The next morning dawned fine and clear, and after taking a few healthy lungfuls of fresh air Clint exclaimed, 'Too good a day to work. We'd better go hunting.'

So off they went across the river. Around midday I heard shots away in the distance, and later I heard them crashing and shouting their way down off the top of the high knoll across the river. Every now and again I could hear a crashing of branches and a thud as they struggled with their quarry. Eventually they appeared on the opposite river bank, so I launched my dinghy and rowed over to bring them back. Two red deer lay at their feet. The hunters' white teeth gleamed with pride as they tossed them into the bottom of the boat.

'Damn those bluffs!' they cried as we laughed our way back to the hut.

The following day was another 'cracker'. The ocean was beginning to settle down to a lazy, oily appearance, with little breeze and minimal roll. As I was standing down the beach studying the river mouth, Clint and Barry appeared and stood beside me.

'We've got a problem. We've got 10 gallons of paint but no paint brushes.'

'Oh,' I replied, seeing a pleading look in Clint's clear blue eyes.

'You couldn't row out and find some paint brushes, could you? There's bound to be some among the fishing fleet.'

I pondered this point. The boats usually go up on the slip each year for a coat of anti-foul paint, so there would have to be a paint brush aboard one of the fleet of about seven fishing vessels that were currently working their way up and down the coast each day.

'Yes, I'll go,' I volunteered. 'Looks like a good day for it.'

I stood there for a while longer studying the river bar and the lay of the break, the deeper channel, along with the magnitude of the larger sets coming off the ocean and passing though the river mouth region. Many a time I had rowed out to sea, a task not to be taken lightly since the mighty Tasman takes no prisoners. Many a day had been spent searching for an opening, a way beyond the breakers that roll in continuously, caressing the beaches and boulders of this rugged and exposed coastline, so that I could rendezvous with fishermen, my partners in this quest but on the other side of the watery fence we call the breaker line.

This barrier holds us to ransom, so close but so far. They were out there earning their living from the briny deep, and we here only hundreds of metres away going about our daily chores, ever conscious of our neighbours wallowing about outside the waves, heading our way. Sometimes the danger of crossing the barrier was not enough to stifle the pangs of isolation.

It's all in the timing. Sometimes it takes days of watching the waves, searching the horizon for signs of a change in the weather, for mares' tails, looking for dark bands where the sea meets the sky. As the weather abates following a storm, the seas gradually settle. The southwesterly gales finally blow out to a calm just before the next northerly blow. The five- to 10-metre waves die down to a more manageable one to two metres but never quite settle away to nothing, except on very rare occasions. There is little room for error, and the timing of the waves becomes etched in my brain. I gauge the size of the bigger ones during each set of seven or eight waves, then watch for extended periods to see the largest ones every five to 10 sets. Hoping for a rendezvous to pick up stores has often taken many days spent observing, until I almost feel like I have become the waves. At times it might have been easier to walk out to Haast and back to obtain them.

Meanwhile, the tide was coming up to high, the optimum time to row straight down the river bar channel and out to sea.

'You look a bit reluctant,' Clint hinted as I studied the situation and took it all in.

'It's better to look before you leap,' I replied. 'It's looking pretty good. I'll grab some gear and I'll be away.'

'Ah, beauty,' he sighed. 'That's the spirit.'

The previous day the fishing fleet had worked its way north. So on this day the boats would begin to appear from the north. Already the first of the fleet was away in the distance, off Sandrock Bluff, gradually working its way on the glassy sea towards us. I picked some parsley and watercress from the garden and placed them in a glass jar full of water, along with some violet flowers to brighten up their wheelhouses. The fishermen love some fresh greens to ward off the scurvy. Along with my faithful Swanndri, I collected my carved-out totara oars, which were leaning on the wooden weatherboards at the front of the hut, and quickly headed up towards the dinghy, tied to rata trees up at the bluff. Clint and Barry helped me launch the dinghy — a three-metre aluminium Parkercraft — into the cool, emerald waters of the river. After fitting the oars into the rowlocks and tying them in, I tied in my backpack with Swannie and carefully placed the glass jar upright against the seat.

I leaned on the oars and set my loyal dinghy into action, quickly leaving behind the overhanging rata reaching out above me, urging me on as I settled into a sustainable rhythm and pace. I negotiated my way through the vibrant emerald-blue waters glistening about the river bar. Gentle waves were lifting and crashing either side of me onto the bar as I rowed down the deeper channel, the flow of the river speeding me up. A few larger swells flowed beneath me. Up and over I went, but luckily not breaking in the depths of the channel. Before I knew it, the rocky bottom eased away, replaced by the deep blue-green of the Tasman Sea, overlaid by the sap-green and umber bush-clad hills and mountains. They grew in stature as I drew further out onto the ocean, out past the Gorge Islets, heading north.

The first boat coming my way was the *Bonita*, a large blue wooden vessel. She was slowly working her way down from Cutter Rocks off Brown's Refuge. Each boat had set a line of about 100 craypots from Cascade Point to the north reef of Big Bay, so the process gradually brought each one along this line, which averaged about one to two kilometres offshore in eight to 12 fathoms of water. By the time I had left the craggy Gorge Islets in my wake two kilometres behind me, the *Bonita* had begun to loom large above me.

The boat hauled into reverse and eased to a standstill beside me. The smiling face of David Buchanan, better known as Crockett, appeared through the wheelhouse door. 'Radar', his crew, had come forward and was standing beside him.

'What're you up to, Beansprout?' they enquired.

I rowed over towards them until my dinghy was nearly touching the wooden planks lining the *Bonita*'s bow. I eased off the oars, stretched my fingers, looked up and answered, 'You haven't got any paint brushes, have you? You wouldn't read about it. The Forestry guys are in, working on the hut. They've got 10 gallons of paint but no paint brushes.'

'Blow me down,' they replied, shaking their heads. 'We'll have a look below.'

They disappeared for five minutes as the boat drifted around on the tide. I could see other boats slowly appearing from the north, some up as far as the Barn Islets about 15 kilometres away. Surely there would be a paint brush or two on one of these boats.

The sea was beautiful, not a breath of wind, so glassy, yet there is an awesome feeling of vulnerability when out on the ocean in a dinghy. The depth of the sea is immeasurable. It is a feeling I love. The adrenalin flows and your body is working on hyperdrive, almost like on borrowed time. You look back at the mountains and know that even on a good day a landfall would be quite hazardous except in selected places.

Before too long Crockett and Radar reappeared. 'Sorry, Beansprout, can't find any brushes aboard this boat. I'll give Jack and Stewie a call on the blower.'

Crockett picked up the mike of his radio transmitter, which was mounted close by above his large wooden steering wheel, and began making enquiries around the fleet. I thought to myself, 'If all else fails, Lou Brown would definitely have some paint brushes up at Barn Bay.'

'Oh gee, Beansprout,' Crockett came back to me. 'I asked around and nobody can find a paint brush.'

'Oh well, it's a beautiful day. I'll just keep heading north to Barn Bay. Lou should have some paint brushes.'

'OK, Beansprout. Good luck. The boys will look after you if you need any help. We'll see you later. Here, do you want a feed of fish? Here's some flounders we trawled up this morning.'

After they had tossed a couple or three big fat fish into the boat they steamed off south. I took up my oars with renewed vigour and headed further north. The steady rhythm of my rowing eased me further and further on, my body enjoying the moderate pace and my senses relishing the challenge as the Cutter Rocks gradually eased past me and I began heading out toward the Barn Islets.

Next Jack Hammond, skippering the 15-metre *Jeanette*, eased up beside me for a chat, his crewman, Craig, watching with grappling hook in hand.

'Great day, Beanie. Sorry we've got no brushes.'

'Ah, that's OK. A couple more hours will see me to Barn Bay.'

After we had chewed the fat for five minutes we went our separate ways. By now I was beginning to get quite thirsty. I hadn't brought any water bottle, so I thankfully began drinking from the glass jar with the parsley, watercress and violets in it. I made a mental note: always bring a water bottle when rowing out to sea since you never know where you might end up. So far I was about six kilometres north of the Gorge and two kilometres out to sea, an expansive place. You get a great perspective of the landscape looking east across the blue-green sea towards the snow-capped mountains which are usually hidden by the lower foothills.

After rowing another couple of kilometres the *Erynne Kay* appeared alongside as George McInroe senior eased up on the throttle. The low-slung black steel hull, about 12 metres long, had a prominent trawling gantry mounted on its stern deck.

'How are you going, Beansprout?' asked George. His crewman, Johnny Monachan, who was leaning on a rusty steel craypot, had little to say. He was probably wondering what the heck I was doing out here.

'Pretty good, George. I'm on a mission. I suppose you've got no paint brushes?'

'No, sorry, Beansprout.'

'Ah well, I'll just keep heading to Barn Bay. I'm nearly halfway anyway.'

'At least you picked a good day for it,' George added as he headed off south.

Away in the north I could see the *Compass Rose*. At least I wasn't short of company out here on the Tasman. I hauled on the oars and returned to the rhythm of blades catching the water, pulling through, releasing and back to the water again. My hands were toughening up but I could feel the odd tender spot developing. I quickly closed my mind to any physical inconveniences and concentrated on my wake disappearing out behind the stern of my faithful dinghy. I normally called her *Ding Billy* or the *Good Ship Lollipop*. She was enjoying her day out and so was I. There is a magical feeling when one is defying all the odds while the awesome ocean passes beneath us. *Ding Billy* was the perfect-sized vessel for me. I could carry her upturned on my shoulders and back, and she could handle the odd wave over her bow when pushing through the surf. She was no stranger to these waters since she had been used as Eion Wylie and Noel Boyd's crayfishing boat during their first season. Eion and his wife Janine had lived at Gorge River in the mid-1970s, making a living by crayfishing out of the river mouth.

Out off Sandrock Bluff, the largest promontory between Barn Bay and Gorge River, I finally met the *Compass Rose*. The Barn Islets were looming larger on the watery horizon towards Cascade Point. I was now 10 kilometres from home, over halfway to Barn Bay. I was resigned to the fact that I would have to row the rest of the way to achieve my mission.

The enormous white and blue wooden hull of the 16-metre *Compass Rose* loomed above me. The smiling face of her skipper, Stewie, appeared as he leaned out of the wheelhouse and peered over the gunwale. Alan Burns, better known as Burnsie, beamed from midships, holding something up in his hand.

'We've found you a paint brush.'

'Is that right?'

'Yes, we found her down in the bilge.'

'Ahhh!' I breathed a sigh of relief.

'Toss us your bow line and we'll haul you aboard.'

After a couple of swift paddles I drew alongside, coiled up my bow rope and tossed it towards Burnsie. Once in hand, he hauled us up close and I climbed aboard with footholds in the scuppers and launched myself up over the gunwale and onto the smooth wooden deck. We then hauled *Ding Billy* up and perched her on the back deck, dwarfed by the trawl gantry. At some point I handed them the jar of watercress, parsley and violets.

'Sorry I drank all the water but it was thirsty work getting here.'

'Good as gold, Beanie. Come and have a brew and we'll take you home.'

The smooth purr of the Gardiner engine felt reassuring as Stewie negotiated the *Rose* through the minefield of pots lining the coast. Burnsie's skilful use of the grapple ensured they wasted no time in hauling up their pots. Luckily the ropes and buoys of all the different boats lined up with the run of the tide, allowing the vessels to work between them without taking the ropes around their propellers.

We jived away to Scenic Radio's classic hits, leaning into the rhythm of the waves along with the music. I loved being aboard the *Compass Rose*. I thought of her as my home boat, and had often rowed out to sea and ended up walking her smooth wooden decks in my bare feet. Burnsie's birthday was on 15 November, two days before mine, and Jack Hammond, skipper of the *Jeanette*, was born on the 20th, so we often celebrated our birthdays together during the crayfishing season. When the weather came away the *Compass Rose* and *Jeanette* would head to Milford Sound for shelter rather than have to sit on the pick at Jackson's Bay. The crew were from Greymouth and would sometimes travel by road or air to their homes and leave the boats safely in Milford Haven.

Occasionally a journey out in my dinghy to visit a passing fishing boat resulted in two or three weeks at sea — down to Milford Sound, then taken on as replacement crew and up to Jackson's Bay and down to Milford a number of times until the crewman returned and the weather settled enough to row safely back ashore at Gorge River.

I could often pay my way by diving on ships' propellers to clear them of rope coiled around them. One rope in particular had melted itself like a plastic casing around the stainless steel shaft, and it took half an hour of hacksawing before I managed to clear the rope away. Luckily they had a diving tank with air to help me complete the job. Most times I went to Milford two or three skippers would ask for attention, and this would provide pub money. Stewie or Burnsie would deck me out in better gear so we could enter the private bar at the Tourist Hotel Corporation establishment in Milford Sound.

Milford Sound is actually my closest town as the crow flies, being 65 kilometres away, and I love going there. There is a vibrant spirit amongst all the people who work and visit there, as a result of the isolation. They know how to make their own fun.

Some of the best dances that I have ever attended have been in Milford, especially when there was a live band. The old fishermen would say, 'This is the best night we've ever had.' Inhibitions are lost in this smallest, most remote metropolis of New Zealand.

Each year the Milford and Te Anau fishermen would book out all the motel units at Cascade Creek on the Milford road for their annual get-together. This would be followed by a golf match near Te Anau, and some of the fishermen would hire the Milford helicopter to fly over to Queenstown for a few beers before returning to the party.

On one occasion the head chef at the Milford tourist hotel stocked me up with supplies, leading me into the kitchen larder and inviting me to help myself. I later gave him a painting. A few days later when I rowed ashore from the *Compass Rose* there was a large roll going in, plus a cross-wind prevailing. They were in a hurry, and the breeze blew me off my line as I tied in my gear. A lot of energy was spent getting back on my course midway between the Gorge Islets and the lone pinnacle just south of there. It was a beautiful sunny day so it wasn't so bad when a large roller tipped me up just offshore in waist-deep water. The tea bags were hung out to dry but everything else was OK. I was home after 18 days at sea.

As all these memories drifted through my mind, I watched the coastline and the ocean flow by until we were closing in upon the towering, limestone Gorge Islets rising from the briny deep like a whale's fin. Before too long we had slipped the dinghy into the water and Burnsie began tossing live crayfish into the bottom of the boat. I carefully placed the precious paint brush in my pack and climbed back over the side, bidding Stewie and Burnsie a good day and many thanks. After setting the oars in the rowlocks I once again leaned upon the totara blades and quickly headed for shore.

Since the tide was now out I steered towards the landing 150 metres north of the river mouth. The swell was picking up so I waited for a lull and poured on the pace as I worked my way inshore, bringing the rating up to maximum over the last 100 metres to spurt ahead of a looming breaker. Once in shallow water I whipped the bow around into the waves, backed the dinghy in, jumped out into the water to secure it against the surf coming in and zoomed up onto the beach, all in one swift motion. By the time I had carried the dinghy, fish and gear back over to the river, Clint and Barry were on the other side waiting. I rowed across, announcing as I neared the bank, 'Mission accomplished. We've got a paint brush and a feed of fish.'

Over the next two weeks the Forestry boys worked hard lining the hut with plywood, digging rubbish and toilet holes, installing new windows and painting the hut. After a few days of thirsty work they rummaged up their spare cash, presented it to me and asked me if I could scrounge up a few bottles of beer from out at sea. Of course I complied, and once again found myself out at sea aboard the *Compass Rose*. Stewie instructed me, 'Get on the blower, call up "DB Tasman" and see if you get a response.'

I took the radio microphone in hand, pressed the lever and called, 'DB Tasman, DB Tasman, are you about there, Crockett?'

Within a couple of seconds there came a reply, 'Yeah, how you going, Beansprout?'

'You haven't got a spare couple of bottles of beer, have you? The Forestry guys are getting a wee bit thirsty.'

'Oh, good as gold. We'll stage a rendezvous.'

Crockett, on the *Bonita*, had a whole pallet of beer crates, so he was happy to hand over a dozen in exchange for the cash that Clint and Barry had sent with me. By the time I arrived back ashore we had the beer plus crayfish, blue cod and more flounder. The workers were so busy eating fish that they ended up burying the long-thawed-out frozen chicken and steaks that they had brought down with them.

After the two deer had hung for a week Clint and Barry were concerned that they would lose the venison, so I rowed them out to the *Compass Rose* and Stew and Burnsie tossed them in their large freezer. Clint and Barry could pick them up from Jackson Bay wharf after their return to Haast.

To complete their mission, Clint and Barry removed the Forestry sign from my hut and proudly installed it on the front of the newly renovated establishment next door: 'New Zealand Forest Service Gorge River'. Since then I have been responsible for the upkeep of the 'Caretaker's Hut'.

chapter 10 nickel spoon

O ver the years since I moved into the 'Caretaker's Hut' I have virtually rebuilt it from the ground up. The original three-metre-square section of the hut was built by Nickel Spoon Mining, an Auckland-based company that was registered in July 1968. They obtained prospecting warrants for 18,000 hectares of land, and issued an extravagant prospectus. Members of the public were invited to subscribe for 100,000 shares, which were selling for $1 each. The company's aim was to get this nickel, tin and gold field producing $10–25 million a year.

The shares sold well and within a month the Nickel Spoon, or 'Pickle Soon' as they became known locally, had six men at the mouth of the Gorge River clearing land for an airstrip. During February 1969 seven men were prospecting in the Gorge, Jerry and Spoon Rivers. A press release issued by Arthur Fleming, one of the company's founders and prospectors, stated that preliminary results showed an 'almost embarrassing prevalence of gold' and that any risk was 'almost a laughable absurdity'. On the strength of this, the $1 shares rose to $10.

In April 1969 two West Coasters, Warner Adamson and Harold Butler, on contract to Nickel Spoon, drove an HD6 bulldozer from the Arawhata River bridge down to the mouth of Gorge River. This was the first bulldozer to travel on what had previously been a much overgrown walking track. They drove the bulldozer up the Jackson River, then crossed the Martyr Saddle and negotiated what came to be known infamously as the 'Corduroy Straight'. The bridge over the Martyr chasm had been built with logs snigged out of the bush by Nolan horsepower, the Cascade Valley being the exclusive preserve of the Nolan family and their cattle. The chasm was about 10 metres wide at that point, and the bridge stood about 25 metres above the raging Martyr River.

When they saw the bridge Warner and Harold weren't that keen to cross it, so they just lined up the dozer, put the throttle to idle and set her on her way. When she started to go off course one of them had to jump on, shaking bridge or not, and set her right. They had removed the blade to lighten the load for the crossing, and then had a job winching it across, reattaching it and turning around so they could doze their way out the other side. It took them a couple of days to get themselves out of there.

At Barn Bay Ron Auger and Jim Finnie had been attempting to build a strip with a little Farmall Cub tractor that they had stripped down, flown onto the beach with a Cessna 185 and reassembled. Warner and Harold completed this strip after tidying up one on Robbie Nolan's farm for Tony Hawker. He'd gone crook at them when they'd tried to remove a big beech tree that was right in the way at the end of the strip. It was there to make things difficult for unwanted intruders, but not long after this Tony hit it himself. That was just one of the 13 prangs this fearless pilot chalked up before he was killed by a helicopter tail strike in the Roaring Billy, a tributary of the Haast River, in 1971.

After they'd cut a way up Sandrock Bluff they came down by winching themselves off a beech tree. This worked OK until they pulled the tree over on top of themselves, smashing the back end of the dozer and punching it straight down the bluff onto a bench above Bluff Creek.

Here, because they had taken so long, the men ran out of tucker and fuel. After building a chopper pad they walked back to Barn Bay, only to find the Auger/Finnie camp a smouldering ruin. There was smoked crayfish on the menu that night. The next day Harold flew out with a heavily laden Tony Hawker from the Martyr Homestead, while Warner rode double with Des Nolan on his horse. John Sharbrow later flew them back in by chopper with their supplies, and the journey continued.

While they were working their way down the coast towards the mouth of the Gorge River, Hawker landed beside them on the beach to inform Warner of the imminent birth of his first child. They struck ideal conditions on the hazardous bar at the river mouth, with the sea calm, the tide out and the river flow running low, so a celebration seemed in order. Warner had arranged to fly out with Hawker but the airstrip looked short to say the least, so he spent the time doing a quick extension. The seven stags they had shot went into the plane first, and Warner went in on top. The date was 9 May 1969. Harold and Warner had battled over nearly 70 kilometres of extremely demanding country and reached the mouth of the Gorge River within a month. Harold stayed on and made the strip suitable for use by Cessna 180s. During the school holidays he was joined by his wife Margaret and their kids, and they'd all camp in the original hut here.

In May, a geologist's report concluded that there were stream sediment anomalies in copper, zinc, nickel and gold, and sluicing operations were to begin right away. In December, the geologist's second and final report stated that while nickel did occur it was too spasmodic to be of economic significance.

Not much more was heard about Nickel Spoon Mining until it leapt into action in June 1970. The bulldozer that had been lying idle at the river mouth was taken upriver by Ivan Thompson and John Armstrong, travelling about 12 kilometres up the narrow, boulder-strewn riverbed and then zig-zagging its way up Plateau and Gorge Creeks to Junction Hill. Once on the flanks of the hill, they bulldozed an airstrip which today stands out as a red, stark and bare scar on the surrounding green landscape. This rolling plateau comprises ice-age moraine and supports the largest continuous severely leached heath bog on Westland moraine. The slopes of Junction Hill are a gigantic wetland and home to a fantastic mosaic of stunted forest, the most picturesque of which are the silver and pink pines.

John Armstrong built the strip; Ivan Thompson, known as Boom Boom, was the explosives man. They kept working on upgrading it but they didn't achieve a lot with the rock-hard granite. They would shoot a few deer from time to time and Tony Hawker would land his Piper Cub and fly the venison out, paying them in beer and whisky. Finally, on 27 November 1971, they received a message to put a nail in the door and go home. Tony Hawker flew them out. Two days later he was dead, killed by helicopter tail-rotor strike in the Roaring Billy up the Haast Valley.

The airstrip runs noticeably downhill and has several large dips and boulders poking through its rough surface.

Pilots could only land uphill, and had to ensure they had sufficient power to make the turnaround area at the top. At the head of the old airstrip lie the remains of a hut, built with four bunks, a coal stove and a 90-gallon tank. When the men were pulled out the hut was abandoned to the keas and rust, although the strip has occasionally been used in an emergency as recently as 1995.

After this burst of activity Nickel Spoon lost momentum. Unfavourable publicity prompted the company to change its name to South Westland Minerals Ltd, and in May 1972 it was announced that two suction dredges would soon be working in the Gorge River. However, little was heard again. Most of the directors, who were Auckland-based, failed to turn up at the 1973 annual meeting, and having blown close to $200,000 in shareholder funds, the debt-laden company was wound up.

Denis Litchfield, a venison hunter, used to shoot in the area around the Gorge River mouth, and camp in Nickel Spoon's rough shelter. He once said, 'You very seldom saw the prospectors. I don't think they ever did any more than throw a few colours across a pan.'

In the mid-1970s Eion and Janine Wylie had built on to the original Nickel Spoon dwelling, and also built a separate crew's quarters with the help of Lou Brown and his Canadian mate, Quinn. This new hut eventually became the present-day DoC hut that was upgraded by Clint McGee and Barry Perrin. As well as crayfishing, Wylie used to hunt the Upper Gorge flats using strips pioneered by Tony Hawker. He and Noel Boyd built a large freezer and generator shed 50 metres from the northern end of the Gorge River airstrip. During the early '90s I pulled down the remains of the old shed and salvaged any sound timber for use on my hut, but the freezer is still here today and is used for storing firewood and timber.

Wylie increased the area of the old dwelling to about six times that of the original tin-clad Nickel Spoon Hut. When I arrived, the cottage, though in a rather run-down condition, had two bedrooms, a kitchen, living-room area, a roofed concrete verandah and a small bathroom with a shower and a flush toilet, the first south of Jackson Bay.

I always wondered why there was a sag in one end of the roof, until I saw a photograph of the original Nickel Spoon hut. The roof beam running along the apex of the hut extended out into thin air for about 3 metres with no support. The beam must have sagged before Eion Wylie built the next stage of the roof off the same timber.

During the 1980s I undertook some remedial work on the sagging floor, putting in new stumps here and there. I rebuilt the floor of the bathroom, which had rotted away, splitting totara logs and sections with wedges that I had made out of rata. After smoothing up one side with a chisel I laid down a new bathroom floor, hoping the totara would stand up to any water that was splashed onto it.

The old coal range had also seen better days when I arrived at the Gorge in January 1981. It was a Shacklock Orion 501, and being a left-hand oven it was quite rare, but it was in a wee bit of a state with both door hinges broken. I tied them up with stainless steel wire off an old craypot frame, so at least the door wouldn't flop onto the floor when it was opened. The surrounding concrete had caused the stove to bend and warp when heated up, as it couldn't expand sideways. It displayed a noticeable upward arching and so required a university degree in physics to operate it without smoking the hut out. On a regular basis, I would clean out all the obvious cracks and plug them with a slurry of clay from the river bank near the bluff. When it was available, I would add powdered cement to the mix. This would allow the fire to draw better through the stove and up the chimney, and I also had holes drilled in the ceiling to let the smoke out.

chapter 11 fishing big bay

I n early September 1981 I was working at the Awarua River mouth with Graeme Mitchell, his wife Anne, and their children Kelly, Grant and Warrick. We had been busy setting up their whitebait stands, collecting firewood, digging vegetable gardens, and dealing with buckets of whitebait that had been netted as they migrated up to the Waiuna Lagoon.

One day Graeme announced that he had met Dale Hunter on the beach that morning, on his way south to his crayfishing base at the other end of the bay. Dale had wondered if I could come down to see him, as he was short of a crewman for the coming season.

So next day I headed down Big Bay beach to see Dale. I had met him briefly the November before when I had first walked up the coast. Now, after welcoming me in, he threw some fresh kindling onto the embers smouldering in the large open fireplace that dominated the back wall of the hut. He motioned me to one of the large armchairs on either side of a long, linoleum-covered table. Before long the kindling wood had leapt into flames, and Dale rinsed out a billy, filled it with tap water and set it upon one of a row of blackened hooks hanging from an iron bar fixed across the chimney. As the billy came to the boil I gazed around the hut, taking it all in. Camp ovens and other blackened pots lay on flat stones stacked beside the hearth and around the inside of the lower chimney.

Meanwhile Dale rinsed out the teapot, placed it on the table and carefully measured out a couple of spoonfuls of loose black tea. He had an intensity about him that gave him a sense of presence. Nothing was taken too lightly. Perhaps in the rush of things something could be skipped over, but not if it could be avoided.

Once the tea was made, settled and poured Dale sat down in the armchair opposite me. He poured a liberal dose of sweetened condensed milk into his cup, followed by two spoonfuls of sugar, and set about vigorous stirring. Dale was a man of few words. He gradually worked up a flow of interspersed conversation, but spent most of his time gazing out at the nearby sea through the shopfront-sized windows that lined the entire coastal wall of the hut.

It was certainly a great view. From my seat I could see clearly out to Awarua Point, the north heads of the bay. The panorama was beautifully framed by the cabbage trees that perched above the gravelly beach five metres in front of the hut. We would be about one metre above spring high tide on a rough sea.

Little did I realise that this ritual was the beginning of a partnership that was to last for the next 12 years. Somehow our kindred spirits had sought each other out. In many ways we were totally different, seeing and having seen life from widely divergent perspectives. But in other ways we mirrored each other. The silence that imbued most of our working days was as necessary as the ocean that we worked upon. We became a working team where words were irrelevant.

We drank down our hot tea as we sized each other up, until Dale finally came to the point of the brew and asked me if I was available to crew on his fishing boat for the coming season. I pondered the question to prolong the occasion, then agreed to come back down by 1 October.

As I headed back towards the whitebaiters' settlement at the northern end of Big Bay I was confronted by severe whirlwinds that were coming down the gravel and sandy beach about every five minutes. Since I was out in the open all I could do as they approached was curl up on the sand with my oilskin cape wrapped tightly about me and let the 60- to 70-knot winds whirl about me, whipping the sand to a biting, stinging storm for a minute or two before they passed on as quickly as they had come. The beach would then return to normal again before the next onslaught. It was an overall easterly day, and the pattern was created as the easterly wind curved around the Awarua River mouth and then headed south down the open, flat beach.

Despite the occasionally bizarre local weather patterns that come to life here, walking the beach is always a pleasure. The panorama of rocky and snow-capped mountains behind the bay always captivates me, and the place feels almost like the centre of the universe. I always feel privileged to be able to walk this stretch of coast.

By now I was nearing the end of my working spell with Graeme Mitchell, so he organised an order of groceries to come in with Peter Plew from Aspiring Air on their next supply drop. This was an agreeable arrangement since I enjoyed the work and the company at Big Bay. At the end of the month, I would end up with a large box of supplies such as wholemeal flour, rolled oats, honey, peanuts, brown rice and sultanas to take back to Gorge River. It was also an essential way to end the long, cold, hard winter, with depths of isolation that few people could even begin to understand. When I walked down to Big Bay around the middle of August I became one of the family and part of a small village.

Graeme, better known as Mitch, had been whitebaiting at the Awarua River mouth since the late 1960s. He was also a venison hunter during the rest of the year, and provided for his family by selling whitebait and red deer. They lived at the bay for most of the year, but usually went out during the depths of winter to a place they owned on the Otago Peninsula. Graeme's ancestors were the Webb family, who were the original settlers of Martins Bay in the 1870s, and Graeme had inherited a 20-hectare section there from his mother. He was an experienced man of the bush, and he and Anne had hunted for a number of seasons down in Lake Poteriteri in southern Fiordland. The hardships and trials they endured inspired me as I listened to their stories of the cold, windblown hut at the head of that lake. They had eventually settled at Big Bay in a canvas tent on a wooden-plank base just before their first baby was born. Even 40 years later, the family always come back to the place they call home to whitebait, hunt and surf.

Before each season we would knock up four whitebait stands on the riverbed, built from kahikatea stakes and rough chain-sawn planks from storm-fallen rimu. I would help Anne dig the extensive vegetable garden, where she grew parsnips, potatoes, carrots, swedes and artichokes to feed the many hungry mouths. We would collect trailer-loads of seaweed from Big Bay beach to use for garden compost and fertiliser. Often their meals would be entirely from the land, with the trout, whitebait and venison that abounds in the area.

There is one place in my heart that is filled with indescribable emotion, and a longing to relive an acre of contentment, fulfilment and sense of place that few other memories hold. The time is the early '80s when the whitebait sought their way up the Awarua River at Big Bay. My mind drifts back on the waves of Van Morrison's music to a time so basic in its simplicity, but so complete in its totality, that my eyes fill with tears and my breathing comes short.

Sitting in Mitch's hut on the bank of the Awarua River, the northerly rain is just starting to set in. The winds gusting about the flowering kowhai trees scatter the wood pigeons to flight. Large droplets of rain pound against the glass of the sliding doors on the northern end of the hut.

Mitch and I sit in our respective armchairs, mine beside the glass door, separated from Mitch's by an upturned fish basket that acts as a coffee table. Brew time after a hard, busy day. The warmth of the fire pervading the large, airy, high-vaulted room. The sense of achievement of a job well done after spending the day, and the past days and weeks, wading chest-deep in the river in wetsuits and sandshoes building whitebait stands. Me holding the kahikatea wooden stakes, while Mitch hammers them into the stony, sandy riverbed with a heavy five-kilogram wooden mallet. Mitch is balancing on an old sunken 12-gallon oil drum, while I stand with utter faith that each strike will hit the metal capping placed upon the stake, and not me.

The delicious feeling of escaping the rain and the sodden wetsuit to sip hot coffee amid the glow and security of the shelter. The delicious feeling that a Fiordland shelter offers like no others in this world. Escaping the cold and wet and the wild to a hot brew around a warm stove spitting sparks as the golden resins emit their life's blood to give us hope.

Kelly, Grant and Warrick playing Yahtzee on the floor, oblivious to the raging storm gathering about their home, throwing the five dice with the vigour and enthusiasm that only young children have. Their squeals of excitement and laughter filling the room, as Anne looks on, tending the stove, watching over the hot coals laden on top of the camp oven. The batch of scones will soon be set upon between brews of hot tea and coffee. Van's music drifts on the air as the northerly gales herd the clouds across the hillsides and blast the sides of the hut. We are warm and safe inside; let the storm begin.

By mid-September 1981 it was time to head back to Gorge River. When Peter Plew arrived with the supplies he picked me up off Big Bay beach and flew me back home to the Gorge River airstrip with my box of groceries.

Now was the time to tend to my vegetable garden for a couple of weeks and enjoy some R&R before walking back to Big Bay for the crayfishing season. This time alone was essential to get back to my own reality of my life at Gorge River. My life here was entirely different from that of my neighbours. Much as I loved the time I spent with them, my priorities were quite different, and the only way for me to become totally grounded again was to be back at the Gorge alone or exploring the hills and coastline.

My needs were very few and very basic, whereas others' were usually of a commercial nature. Whether they were raising families or not, their aim was to catch whatever they could to sell for money to buy goods to maintain their lifestyles. Though this was part of my life, the majority of it was spent in awe of the beauty and power of the surrounding land and seascapes. I felt that much of my life's energy came directly from the awesomeness of my surroundings, which were definitely helping to sustain me. My main priority was to remain one with this divine nature. Even today, after nearly 30 years, this is what this place essentially does for me.

The many years absorbing the power and workings of this place are etched within my spirit, my data bank. Now, as I paint and sculpt the elements, I become one with the ocean, the mountains and the trees. I feel a part of what is being created, and I have an umbilical link with the person who has asked me to go there on their behalf to create the artwork. This sustains me, along with the fruits of the garden and surrounding foodscape. I am empowered by the surrounding energies. Humility enables me to endure my work with others.

Dale's priority was to land as many fish as possible. At the end of each day it didn't concern me how many fish we had caught, since any amount was ample to sustain my needs. I was more concerned with a job well done, proud that my work was up to scratch and that I kept up with the demands of each waking day and came out on top, still running. This was the challenge that kept me as first mate on a fishing boat. This enabled me to live and work with others during my first 10 years alone at Gorge River. Once my family arrived on the scene, I evolved to work for myself, directly from the elements and energies about us.

Dale expected 110 per cent from his crew. He is the toughest, hardest man I have yet to know. He has mellowed a little in later years, but during the early 1980s 'mellow' wasn't even in his vocabulary.

As I walked back down from Gorge River the bay opened up in front of me as I gazed south and east from Awarua Point. The awesome power of this seascape was to be my constant companion for the next five months and on into the following years. As I quickly made my way around the point towards Crayfish Rock I was yet to realise just how deeply this workplace would grow under my skin, and the extremes we were to push in order to earn our daily bread.

When I arrived Dale was busy welding up craypot frames from steel he had had flown in onto Big Bay beach. His Massey Ferguson tractor was an essential part of the equation. He used this to transport supplies and gear the six kilometres from the northern end of Big Bay beach, where the Cessna aircraft could safely land on hard sand below half tide with a moderate sea.

I set about stripping the rusty netting off the old pot frames, leaving them ready for a fresh coating of galvanised-steel mesh. Dale fought off the sandflies as he wired up the first pot and then he left me to it. I enjoyed this craft. It was important to end up with a tightly fitting mesh and waste as little stainless steel wire as possible. We didn't bother with doors on the pots since that would use an extra two metres of stainless wire and three metres of steel rod.

After we had prepared the pots we headed out to launch *Sika*, Dale's five-metre aluminium-alloy Shark Cat. Before she had been brought ashore for the off season, an aeroplane wheel had been slipped into the side of each hull to support her, and she had been winched up high and dry in front of the generator shed. Now we loaded her up with half a dozen pots and bore our weight down on the stern, lifting the bow and pushing her until she gathered enough momentum, heading down the sandy strip of beach straight for the gap in the boulders and into the breakers. Dale jumped aboard while I kept pushing her off until thigh-deep in the water, then I turned back up the beach to fetch the dinghy. Dale grabbed the boat's oar and paddled one side after the other until he was clear of the rocks and shallow water. Then he carefully eased the twin 70-horsepower Yamaha outboard motors into the seawater and brought them to life. Meanwhile I launched the dinghy and quickly rowed out to the Shark Cat. We towed the dinghy out and tied it onto the large pink mooring buoy bobbing about 300 metres offshore.

Dale pushed the throttle lever up to full power and away we went from zero to 40 knots in less than 10 seconds. Immediately any cobwebs in my mind disappeared as the blue, blue skies brightened up overhead, the breeze sending my hair streaming back, the thrill of the day opening up before us. As we drew up beside Penguin Rock, Dale eased back the throttle and we began setting all the pots we had on board. Since the weather appeared settled Dale set most of the gear in quite close to the rocky shoreline, just outside the breakers in about five fathoms or less of water. He never used a depth sounder, relying on his prior knowledge of the reef's whereabouts. We ducked in and out between large partially submerged rocks and islets until the six pots were in the water. Dale would simply nod when it was time for me to toss the craypot onto the surface of the sea. While it sank, I would quickly throw the buoy and rope overboard, avoiding any tangles, as Dale sped off to our next mission.

We needed fresh bait so we emptied the bait net onto the deck, then Dale found one end of the net and tied the anchor and buoy rope into the loops and placed this on the stern deck. He fastened another buoy and anchor line onto the other end of the net and then he pulled up the wooden stern door, opening up the back of the deck. As he slowly steamed away from the rocky shoreline I tossed the anchor and then the buoy line off the back deck, allowing the net to gradually feed out off the stern between the two outboard motors. I then tossed the other anchor and buoy away when the entire net had eased into the sea. This was always a tricky business, and important not to twist the net.

As we headed back to retrieve more pots the mountains far behind the bay took on a new light from the seaward vantage. I began to realise that fishing at Big Bay would involve hard work interspersed with scenic pleasure.

Earlier that morning I had rowed out two or three pots at a time in the back of the dinghy and tossed them carefully over the stern. This was after making sure their ropes and buoys were outside the cages. So the local bay was dotted with many buoys. We loaded up 10 pots at a time, and headed out along the south side of Big Bay, around past Penguin Rock and further along towards Long Reef near Martins Bay. Later we flew across to the north side of the bay, chewing up the miles along the waves. I felt exhilarated by the fresh air and salty spray until we neared Big Bay Landing and once again began setting a line of pots parallel to the bouldery coastline, past Crayfish Rock, out to Awarua Point and north around towards the Hacket River. The return journey of about 10 kilometres allowed me time to study the moods and lights of the stunning Southern Alps in all their majesty, viewed from the ocean swells.

By the end of the day we had 50 craypots set. Before heading ashore we hauled in the net. We had caught blue moki, marble fish, blue wrasse, greenbone and some rig sharks, enough to bait tomorrow's pots. Dale filleted the blue moki and greenbone for tea.

After resetting the net 400 metres further along the coastal reef, we whizzed back to the mooring, secured the boat and rowed the dinghy ashore. Time for a brew and to begin peeling a few spuds for tea.

After splitting up some rata driftwood into thin slivers I carefully stacked them upon the glowing embers of the open fire where they gradually came into life. I refilled the blackened billy and placed it above the growing flames, satisfied by our first day at sea.

'Ah well, we'll see what tomorrow brings,' Dale commented as we drank a welcome cup of tea. He then cranked up the diesel generator to run the freezer and lights as the shadows lengthened towards dusk.

Unless we were off to a daylight start the morning ritual began with the lighting of the open fire, boiling the billy for a brew of tea, and then seeing what the day might bring. If the weather allowed, Dale preferred to rebait the pots in the afternoon. Since the crayfish usually feed at night, the bait would then be fresher.

It was important to constantly follow the game plan of each day since Dale rarely verbalised his timetable. He expected you to know and understand. The more questions you asked him, the vaguer he became. The main factor affecting the sequence of daily events was the weather. It was important to listen to any forecasts and read the signs in order to anticipate our course of action. If the wind started to freshen, then we were not likely to linger any longer before Dale would announce, 'I spose.' On many a day over the early years I worked with him, this would be all he would say, all day. This meant, 'I suppose it is time to go fishing.' If you happened to miss this cue you could easily be left behind, wondering why Dale had gone fishing on his own. Anyway, to me this was just another of the challenges, minor in comparison to the daily grind of some of our more demanding days.

We quickly fell into a routine and as the weeks went by the course of action became more logical and apparent. As the weather settled Dale would move the 20-kilometre line of pots in closer and closer to the shoreline, staying just outside the line of breakers. On the north and south sides of the bay he fished his own zone of seabed, always inshore of the other boats.

After three or four days of fine weather and diminishing roll we would be clearing out the crayfish catch, rebaiting the pots, then resetting them shallower and shallower, until we were gazing at the colourful seaweed attached to the rocks and large, rounded boulders of the seabed not far below. An evening would come when the silence of the sea would lull you to sleep. The calm before the storm.

Next morning, before daylight, Dale would bang loudly on the outside of the sleepout wall, waking me out of my slumber. After a quick brew on the gas cooker we would carry the dinghy to the white line of breakers crashing onto the pebbly beach. I would row the bobbing craft out to the mooring where *Sika* lay like a tethered stallion, the tension palpable in the air as Dale focused on the moment and studied the distant smoking coming off Awarua Point's North Reef as the reddish dawning light began making our day more apparent.

After hauling in and clearing the bait net Dale would set out at full throttle across the bay while I knelt down, cutting up the bait on the rolling, heaving deck with a large cabbage knife. Once the bait was sorted the journey across the bay left me time to watch the northerly clouds streaming towards us across the looming hills, the hogsbacks lining up over the distant Alps and the spray peeling off the tops of the large, smooth coastal rollers where they met the strong offshore gales whipping down the valley.

The lack of food in our bellies was offset by the adrenalin that began flooding our bloodstreams as we closed in on the first pot of the day. When we were 300 metres out Dale eased up on the throttle as he studied the state of play, the lay of the gear and the rhythm of the breakers. As each series of waves crashed and broke it left walls of white water up to five metres high flushing through the ropes and buoys.

The moment had come. Dale anticipated the lull, then with full throttle whipped the boat into life and fully committed us. We planed up beside the first rope and buoy, and I whipped them aboard, up and over the pulley as Dale cranked the hauler into life. One, two, the seconds ticked by, an eternity as the next set of rollers began shaping up on our horizon, five and six. The moment the pot broke the surface and was landing aboard Dale was already bringing the engines back into life, whisking us out and away, cresting the massive smooth swell as we gazed down the hollow tube and white water that dominated all the seascape inshore of us. Dale motored on until we were well offshore, then we reset the pot. One down and 49 to go.

As the morning wore on, we would rescue each craypot from inside the breakers, Dale anticipating the lull, easing up, then leaning on the throttle and away inside to a zone, a place where the clock ticked; a time warp where we ran on adrenalin, our senses honed, full of anticipation, where we would grab our goal, often loaded with gold, spiny rock lobsters. Then escape this no-man's-land before we met our maker. Dale's sense of timing was impeccable. I relied on this. He relied on my ability to work the gear with speed and no fear.

As we worked our way out to Crayfish Rock and on to North Point the rollers became larger and we watched the five-metre walls of white water pound through our working area, but we still carried on retrieving each pot. To me these days were the epitome of my time on earth. On a regular basis, with nerves of steel, we ventured forth and returned safely home as if it was just another day at the office. Running on adrenalin.

Each period of fine, settled southwesterly weather was usually followed by an unsettled northerly flow. So after rescuing the pots and moving them out into deeper water, we would have to bring the boat safely back to shore rather than risk losing it off the mooring during the peak of the raging storm. It was important to bring the boat in before the northerly roll developed too high and made it impossible to bring the boat in through the beach breakers.

Occasionally we left it too late to bring the boat ashore, so we would sit in the hut nervously gazing out at the *Sika* being ravaged by monstrous seas trying to rip it off the mooring. Other times Dale would take the boat around to the Hollyford River and leave it tied up in a small creek in away from the sea and river flood.

During the summer holidays, Dale's wife Dana, daughter Lisa and son Craig would come and live at the bay. This was a highlight for me; my first six Christmases in South Westland were celebrated with them. Lisa would run small shore pots and sell the fish to Dale. Craig and Lisa would often come out fishing with us on calm days and help me with the bait fish, and I would spend time building model aircraft with Craig when he received them for Christmas. Dana was always good fun and looked after Dale and me with regular meals and motherly concern. Before Dale built the hut they had lived in a wooden car crate with windows built into it.

Some days Dana, Lisa and Craig would walk halfway down Big Bay beach to meet up with Anne, Kelly, Grant and Warrick to play on the beach. Dana would cook camp-oven bread on the open fire. After mixing and kneading the dough, she would place it in the bottom of the camp oven and leave it to rise by the side of the open fire for an hour or two. Then, after having built up a bed of glowing red embers in the fireplace, she would hang the camp oven so its bottom was about 30 centimetres above the ember base, then shovel some hot coals onto the oven lid. It was important to have the right balance of embers above and below to cook the bread gradually and evenly. Within about 45 minutes a successful loaf would occupy the whole volume of the oven and could be eaten sliced with butter and homemade strawberry jam.

Occasionally when we were out fishing amongst the swells of North Reef a flying fish would fly out off the peaking face of a wave and fly right over the top of us for 200–300 metres, gliding like a bird until landing back in the sea. Dale and I would shake our heads in wonder and amazement.

Once we were fishing on the south side of the bay about 200 metres offshore in about 12 metres of water when we saw a whale. As we gazed at it we noticed another whale accompanying it about 100 metres away. We were busy lifting and resetting pots but spared time to study these intriguing creatures. The southern right whale is massive in its girth, having the dimensions of a large bus, and it has two blowholes amongst the jumble of bizarre whaleskin tissue. But the most puzzling and unfathomable part of this whale is the top of its head, where there is a mass of white and grey crusty-looking structures resembling giant barnacles. It is hard to work out whether you are looking at a whale or barnacles. The second time we saw them, a couple of years later in the same area, their heads were just as strange to observe.

Some time previously Dale had been out fishing in the same place with Dick Jones, better known as Captain Fantastic. They were busy working the gear, as you do, when they spotted a whale nearby. They slowed up and came to a standstill as their curiosity got the better of them, gazing intently across the waters at the large creature swimming sedately by. Then slowly they began to be raised up into the air by some monstrous force beneath them until the boat was right up clear out of the water. They gaped in disbelief as they realised that they were atop a whale that had surfaced beneath them. Being a Shark Cat catamaran the twin hulls sat astride the massive whale's back. Dale and Dick felt totally helpless, knowing that at a whim of nature the whale could flick them off. So Dale slipped the motors into neutral and gave the throttle a slight dose of pressure, hoping to remind the whale that they were perched up there on its back. Following this manoeuvre the whale slowly lowered them and released the boat back into the water.

My word, they had had enough fishing for that day. They made straight for home and drank a bottle of whisky.

During the winter of 1985 a large pilot whale about six metres long washed up on the beach just in front of Dale's fishing hut. I was the first to come across this specimen, as I was heading south to Martins Bay in September. The dead whale had two tusk-like teeth pointing forward on its upper or lower jaw. Already the carcass was smelling rather bad so after a close study I left the whale intact and headed off along the gravelly shoreline towards Penguin Rock and Martins Bay and out to the Hollyford road end.

In mid October Dale arrived back to begin the summer crayfishing season. But, lo and behold, there was a dead, putrid-smelling rotten whale parked right in front of his hut.

Well, he was pretty devastated by this discovery, but being Dale it wasn't too long before he worked out a solution and put it into action.

He managed to tie a rope harness around the whale's tail, then he hooked it onto the back of his tractor and endeavoured with all his might to shift the bloated carcass, but to no avail. Next he poured diesel and petrol all over it and placed driftwood on top. He set this alight with the aim of turning the stinking flesh into ashes, but still no success.

Then Dale experienced a brainwave, as he usually does when the chips are down. He asked one of the local fishermen to bring down some dynamite to fix this old whale. After strategically placing the sticks of dynamite, enough to blow up Fort Knox, they set the charge off. Up the rotting carcass went and down it rained all over Dale's roof and the surrounds of the hut.

Fiordland was hit by a rare drought that month, so most of the stinking remnants lay there for the next two weeks until the rains finally broke and washed the smell away. Later in the month Dale found part of the whale's jaw washed up miles away on the main beach of Big Bay. He and I carved some excellent pendants from this bone.

In late 1983 Dale bought himself a small two-seater aeroplane, a Cessna 150. This enabled him to come and go as he pleased without having to rely on Jules Tapper from Martins Bay Lodge to fly his frozen crayfish off the Big Bay beach and out to Queenstown. Dale then had to learn to fly. I began studying his flight manuals, which lay on the kitchen table as we brewed up between fishing exploits. Before too long Dale had me flying the plane off Big Bay beach as we headed out to Queenstown for some R&R and to visit his family on their 20-hectare deer farm near Dalefield. Of course, Dale was still studying for his flying licence.

One day as I flew the Cessna into the air off the beach there was a strong northerly airstream making its way across Fiordland ahead of a cold front. I was careful not to lift the nose up too quickly, but just nudged the plane into the air and headed for the mountains, climbing at 70 knots at 2500 rpm. It was quite exciting for me, and it gave Dale time to study the landscape sliding along below.

A couple of days earlier we had flown up the coast, swooping down to buzz the local fishermen. As we neared the boats Dale would duck down so that I appeared to the fishermen below to be flying solo. As we flew back up to Barn Bay an Australian Air force F-111 had appeared out of one o'clock at eye level and whisked by before we even had time to think about it.

Anyway, on this day we levelled off through the Olivine Mountains and through the Fohn Saddle, flying along at 90 knots on a level course. Then we upped our speed to 120 knots as we soared down the Beans Burn and out over the Dart River flats, until eventually Dale landed us onto the airstrip paddock of Routeburn Station, owned by Russell Hamilton and his family. We offloaded a live deer that we had caught in one of the dozen deer pens that Dale ran up the MacKenzie Creek flats in the southern corner of Big Bay.

I had helped Dale build many of these pens using wedge-split totara beach logs as corner posts. We regularly checked the pens, and would have to quickly and effectively tackle the deer, dodging their hooves, then we would bring them back in a livey box on the back of the tractor to a shelter near the back of the hut. Here they would acclimatise before being flown out, and we would regularly feed them fuchsia, broadleaf and five finger branches and leaves.

Dale needed more paddock to graze his deer so Russell had offered the use of his farm until Dale eventually relocated his deer farm to Te Puke in the North Island.

During the mid to late 1980s a change came over Dale. One of his best mates had been accidentally shot in the back during a duck-hunting trip. Dale had been standing next to his friend in the maimai when he had been killed. He came back fishing with a different outlook, and must have realised that there is more to life than just work and earning money.

He arranged for the local fishermen to bring up a home-brewing kit, but the over-abundance of instructions were confusing so he gave me the job of simplifying the technique and putting down the first couple of brews. He became much more sociable, and we began inviting the fishermen to come and sample our homebrew which actually wasn't too bad.

We used to bury extra bottles of brewed beer in the sandbar at the mouth of the Hollyford River, and we left a thick flat steel cooking plate there as well. After a successful set of the bait net we would have beautiful fresh blue moki. We would fillet these, save the frames for bait, then moor near the inside of the river bar. Here we would set a fire going under the steel plate, and once it was hot enough we would set our moki fillets sizzling. No need for cooking oil since this naturally oozed out from the fillets as they fried. On a beautiful sunny day the freshly dug-up beer would be just the right temperature to quench our thirsts after a hard day's fishing.

We invited the Hollyford Valley Walks staff to come down to sample our brew, and the crew from Barn Bay would come down too. On clear nights we would enjoy bonfires on the river bar, and we sometimes slept the night beside the fire under the stars.

During the early 1980s we used to tail all the spiny rock lobsters we caught, toss most of the heads back into the sea and bring the bagged-up tails ashore to be frozen down to -18°C in the blast freezer before exporting them to the US. It wasn't until the late 1980s that the Asian market bought the bulk of the fish, and then the crays were sold whole and alive, delivered to seawater holding tanks either at Jackson Bay or Milford Sound.

We usually made good wages throughout our fishing endeavours. In the 1981/82 summer season we averaged about 80 kilograms of tails each day, with a best catch of 120 kilograms. This would equate to about 200 to 250 kilograms of live, whole fish each day.

During the 1980s the catches were diminishing quite rapidly because there was too much pressure on the fish stocks. Similarly, the catches of the 1970s far outdid those of the '80s. Within five years, by 1986, we were catching an average of 40 kilograms of tails per day, less than half the 1981 average. By 1990 we averaged 25 kilograms of tails equivalent per day.

In 1988 the Ministry of Fisheries brought in crayfishing quotas which severely reduced the total allowable catch. This was a difficult period for fishermen, especially those just entering the industry since they faced the added cost of leasing quota on top of running costs and general lack of fish. But by 2005 the fish stocks had recovered brilliantly, to the point where in 2008 they reallocated 25 per cent back onto the total allowable catch. The fish stocks are now better than they were at any time during the 1980s.

chapter 12 journey to the red hills

During my early days on the Coast, especially during the 1980s when I was single, my travels led me far and wide as I explored the regions about me. Gorge River became a resting place between journeys and working at Big Bay and Barn Bay. In those days there was no radio contact with the outside world, which meant there were no news bulletins or weather forecasts coming in. As a result I developed an acute sense of hearing, along with a deep awareness of weather patterns. I relied entirely upon my senses to observe the weather and cycles, and this was particularly important when choosing the best times to travel.

The weather here generally moves in from the west across the Tasman Sea, so that it strikes the West Coast first. The clouds have been relieved of their watery burden by the time they have ascended to the peaks of the Southern Alps. The clouds condense and the rain falls, often flooding the rivers while running back out to sea.

When a rainy weather pattern approaches the coast the winds usually drop to a calm before they gradually come to blow from the north or northeast. This pattern can be seen before the wind is actually felt, in the form of a dark band on the horizon out to sea. Instead of a glassy ocean, the beginning of the prevailing wind ruffles up the water so that it stops reflecting the sunlight. Usually within half an hour the wind, from whichever quarter, will be actually blowing in your face.

In the case of the northerly wind, the speed with which it rises and gains velocity is usually relative to the overall intensity of the approaching storm. This is also reflected in the height of the waves that are stirred up. So the first stage of the approaching storm is the rising of the northerly sea. This can continue for most of a day or two while the sun continues to beat down and the rain clouds are still being herded in towards the coast. Gradually the skies darken, and as the wind and waves begin to peak in intensity the first showers of rain start to fall. This cycle is as predictable as day follows night.

The intensity and quickening of the approach enliven the senses as all this information is taken into account. One remembers that overall everything balances out. For every drop of water that is evaporated from the ocean by the sun's rays, there is one drop of rain that condenses and falls. The intensity of the sun is harnessed by the vortex of the storm as it rotates clockwise and the winds lash their way towards us.

When the rivers are low and due for a drenching an enlivened northerly sea heralds heavy rain. Sometimes I have been packed up and ready to travel overland for two or three days but have quickly changed my plans on sighting overhead clouds beginning to stream in from the north. As the storm progresses the rains get heavier and heavier, and the wind gradually swings around to the northwest, sometimes within four or five hours if the storm is travelling quickly. By this time the river is flooded and peaking.

With each cycle of weather, the overall balance or equilibrium becomes more apparent — dry spells followed by wet; some very wet, some hardly raising a drizzle. When I wanted to go exploring I would try to pick a spell of at least three or four days of fine weather. I would be waiting for an intense windy and rainy spell to pass over, swinging from northwest to westerly and eventually to the southwest as the skies began to clear. The consistent southwesterly pattern would settle in as the wind began to abate.

When the Gorge River is in peak flow it is a sight to see. Rainwater from the entire catchment of the river is funnelled through a narrow gap formed at the river mouth by limestone bluffs. The last glacial period has carved this channel through the main coastal ridge, leaving a gap in the rock about 100 metres wide and 200 metres deep. The current at the river mouth is about 30 knots at peak flood, and possibly exceeds any other river on the coast.

The catabatic wind behaves similarly in the winter months. This wind comes down the Gorge River due to the heavy cold air in the valley, and the temperature gradient between the colder mountains and the warmer sea. It's very strong here since the valley narrows sharply to a high, rocky gorge with 200-metre-high sides just before the river mouth. This squeezes the cold air through a narrow gap, speeds it up and increases the chill factor. It also does a beautiful job of taking the tops off the waves coming in from the ocean, throwing up a veil of fine spray. In the depths of winter the wind lifts the tops of the waves all the way to the horizon. The West Coast fishermen say nothing matches the intensity of the wind that whistles through this gorge.

In the summer of 1985 I had set my sights on a journey to the Gorge Plateau and the Red Hills, which are at the headwaters of the river, and about 1200–1500 metres in altitude. There had been some heavy rain and I knew the river would need at least a couple of days to settle back to a negotiable flow, so as I waited for the perfect day to set off I readied my gear. I had a homemade canvas pack that was specially designed to suit my needs. Being frameless, it acted as a sleeping mat once emptied. I rarely carried a tent on my travels, but usually carried an oilskin sleeping-bag cover. This allowed me to set up camp quickly almost anywhere, and I had a down sleeping bag to ward off the cold.

I had been given several Christmas cakes, including one Mum had sent me, and I had saved most of this for the coming journey. As well as the cake, I carried a bag of mixed oatmeal and wholemeal flour, peanuts and raisins, brown rice, and a mutton-cloth bag full of beansprouts. I had a 500ml milk tin for a billy, an enamel cup and a teaspoon, along with a locking-blade Mercator pocket knife.

The day of my departure dawned perfectly. As the first glimmers of light reached me I was up and about. All I needed to do was eat my breakfast — a pre-soaked cup of oatmeal, wholemeal flour, with beansprouts and watercress mixed in — wash my cup, place it in my pack, and I was ready to go. When I am travelling on my own across country I don't waste time lighting a fire. I always rely on food that doesn't need to be cooked.

The sun's rays were still finding their way above the hilly horizon as I stepped out the door and bid my house adieu. The last of the stars were hiding and my bare feet felt the crispness and excitement of the day ahead. I made my way down the back track behind the house and out onto the sandy riverbed that led up to the limestone bluffs of the gorge at the river mouth. As I crossed the ford between the bluffs my step quickened, and I settled into a loping boulder-hop along the north bank, around the broken limestone cliffs that rose above the large, deep, emerald-green pools between the energetic rapids. After a kilometre the rounded boulders of dunite, basalt, granite and sandstone provide a natural walkway below the podocarp and beech forest terraces that line the river's edge. Above climb the steep sides of the glacial U-shaped valley which then flatten off at about 400 metres.

A golden peachy glow still enlivened the sky as I reached the upper end of the first boulder beach. The glistening orb of the sun was aiming to sneak above the mountainsides and shorten the shadows, warming the cool air. The long day ahead was still an eternity held in the freshness of the morning.

Glints of green reflected off the dunite boulders, which are often mistaken for greenstone since they are born through the same process deep down in the alpine faultline. This stone has small, glassy green windows covering its grey matrix which, once out of the tumbling of the river current, oxidises to a rusty orange or russet brown. This ultramafic stone, rich in iron and magnesium, is perhaps the most common rock type in this water catchment.

The coastal limestone had now been replaced by stones of every colour, most noticeably the white of quartz, reds of jasper, and the green of the elusive jade. As I forded the river my feet slid in and out of clefts between the boulders, which often threatened to clasp my toes as the strong current manoeuvred me this way and that. I flowed through the clear water, thigh-deep, the droplets glistening as I surged towards the sun with each step. I became one with the river, and emerged again freshened by the passing, ready to launch myself upon the next boulder beach.

The water was so clear that in the refracted light the bottom appeared to be near the surface. This is an illusion that must always be taken into account as one searches for a place to ford. Similarly, the apparent closeness of features in the landscape is deceptive. As time passes, when living amid this landscape, one automatically factors this effect in when judging distance and time, along with the depth of water.

Beach followed ford and ford followed beach as I explored my way up the river past Blackwater Creek, which drains the glacial moraine table top between the Gorge and the Spoon Rivers. If a suitable ford failed to appear at the end of a boulder beach I would head into the bush onto a deer trail, which usually led along a terrace of rimu, rata, kahikatea and beech with mossy green carpets in between. The vivid green of the ponga, mamaku and silver ferns enlivened the deeper forest, merging into the shadows.

The dark grey hammer-marked bark of giant matai and kahikatea flaked off as I scraped by them. They towered overhead like sentinels, way above the canopy, their crowns gazing out at the distant snow-capped mountains. Along with the giant rimu and totara, they lorded over the kanuka, beech and rata. The rimu fronds hung downwards as if weeping, an effect that was especially pronounced in the younger trees lining slips and clearings. The mustard-green foliage created a painter's palette along with the bright green broadleaf.

At times the deer trails led deeper into the forest, but they were never far from the trilling, shrilling sounds of the river rapids racing along the edge of the terrace. Up and down gullies, I dipped in and out of hollows brushing aside supplejack shoots and vines that appeared to block my way. The distant roar and heave of the ocean waves had now been

left behind. I was travelling ever further inland up this pristine waterway, through a wonderland rarely found away from these South Westland streams. No roads, bridges or walkways, neither tracks, wires or telegraph poles. From river mouth and upwards, the surrounds are just a magical world of stones, water and trees.

A kilometre above Blackwater Creek found me back once again on the north bank of the river, where the boulders gave way to cliffs of glacial moraine clay. These had been laid down as glacial deposits, once mountains of basalt and schist, ground down by the ice to powder and dust that had settled out in layers of pure blue-grey clay. This clay is ideal for cleansing the skin by laying a mask upon your face, as my sisters will confirm.

I negotiated this slippery surface carefully, especially when wading through waist- and thigh-deep pools around the cliffs. Then once again I was back to boulders and moving onward above Branchions Creek, which spewed like a great rock face of giant marbles into the main river-bed of lovely smooth, flat boulders. As my journey led me on towards the junction with the Jerry River I estimated I was about one and a half hours from home, since I carried no timepiece apart from my compass. After fording the river four times, I reached the distinctive meeting place of the Gorge and its main tributary. I had walked up to the junction once before, but above the Jerry I was in unexplored territory. I continued traversing the boulders, passing by large dunite rocks like house-sized marbles.

As I walked up the true left of the river the whole valley began to close in. My feet gripped each rock like a limpet before letting go and gliding off to the next. I felt like a deer as I travelled. The glow of the sun warmed my body, helping to ward off the cooling effect of the continual immersion of my legs and feet in the waters as I crossed the creek beds and took shortcuts around river banks and boulders.

The energy I was expending warmed my body too, and a glow came from within. I loved the feel of moss and tree roots underfoot; the rocks and shingle massaged the soles of my feet and connected me with the elements as I passed through them. I carried sandshoes in my pack but rarely wore them since they slowed me down. I find another level of energy and enthusiasm when they are removed from my feet. Luckily, many years of barefoot travel had prepared me for this journey. I know no better way of feeling closeness to the landscape than travelling this way.

As the valley closed in I saw the beginning of the main gorge of the Gorge River, and a mighty one it is. The pools became deeper and the emerald-green richer and more inviting, the roar of the rapids more intense as the white water foamed around immense boulders lodged between the limestone bedrock.

It was time to rise above all of this, since the way was becoming impassable. It was obvious that pretty soon it would all be vertical rock and white water leading from one deep green pool to the next. So after finding a marginal ford through the glacial moraine boulders I headed back to the true right north bank and headed up to a terrace high above the gorge. For about three kilometres this forested ledge led me along a relatively easy way, travelling about 100 metres above the shrill that was coming off the river like an orchestra of sound. The high-pitched notes of flute and pipes, with the ever-present bass boom of the mountains, resonated upwards to engulf me.

Eventually from the bush-clad terrace I could look out

over the top flats, the yellow-gold grass and tussock leading off upriver almost as far as the eye could see. From time to time I gazed down towards the river through gaps in the trees. I was about halfway up the U-shaped side of the enormous valley. At one point I startled a red deer that was quietly chewing on the branch of a broadleaf ahead of me. With a leap and shower of hooves the animal headed upwards, disappearing into the shadows of the forest that rises almost vertically to the top lip of the valley.

The going was surprisingly easy along this level area of trees perched precariously above the steep and rocky gorge. Each view of the river revealed a wild series of rapids descending quickly — a no-man's-land.

About three hours after I had left home I set foot on the Gorge River flats. Now, as I continued on my quest, the hustle and bustle of the river had fallen away to a gentle murmur. The grass underfoot was a welcome change, and there was no longer the need to dodge any rocks, trees or rapids, as I had done all morning.

Not far from the bottom of the flats I came across an old canvas bivvy covered with what appeared to be an old railway tarpaulin. I could have spent a comfortable night there, had I wished, but the day still beckoned me onwards. I estimated that it was still well before midday and I had travelled about 15 kilometres.

As I travel overland my map is a constant companion, and I enjoy keeping in touch with where I am and how the journey is progressing. Along with the map comes my compass. This amazing device lets me know when midday has arrived, since magnetic north is slightly to the east of grid north. When the sun is at grid north it is midday.

After I had checked out the bivvy, my compass and the

sun were telling me that the hour was still about 10 o'clock. I was progressing well. The brightness of the sun now contrasted with the dappled light that had filtered through the forest canopy. As well as opening up, the valley floor seemed to have levelled off, as I literally glided along. This is a popular area for venison hunters, and in the '60s and '70s Piper Cub aircraft had worked these flats. They would land in the most awkward of places, where only the brave and foolhardy dared, landing on stony and grassy river flats and moving a log or two to create primitive airstrips where they could get their loads of venison airborne.

Luckily the brush-tailed possum had not then penetrated this remote corner of South Westland, the Gorge and Hope catchments being the last of the last to have this wave of forest munchers. The plague had been moving up from the south via the Pyke Valley. They were already plentiful around Lake Alabaster down towards the Hollyford and were moving in from the north via the Jackson River from the Arawhata.

Even today the Hope River has a line of possum traps stationed every 100 metres along the main ridge around the entire catchment — that's from the coast to the highest point, Mt Delta, and back to the coast again. It takes contractors three days to walk this ridge track, which they do once each month to clear and reset the possum traps and rebait rat traps.

As I travelled up along the edge of the flats, bright red blooms of mistletoe lit up the sedate-looking beech, kahikatea and rimu trees. Although I didn't know it at the time, this catchment was to become one of the last homes of this beautiful trumpet-shaped flower. Once the possums move in, this is the first plant to go. It is a vital energy source for bird life, and kaka will spend most of their time feeding in mistletoe when it is flowering. It was now coming into the peak flowering season, and tui and bellbirds were feeding alongside the kaka. The latter flew high overhead from one side of the valley to the other, their brilliant red plumage flashing with each wing-beat.

Along with the mistletoe the brilliant rouge-red and crimson of the South Island's Christmas tree, the rata, bloomed out from the forest edge and along the sides of the valley. There were also fuchsia berries in abundance. When I picked some to eat they tasted like small purple grapes.

Today, along the south side of Big Bay all the fuchsia have gone, perhaps forever. During the 1980s they were still the most abundant foliage around the back of Dale's hut, and we would collect some of the leaves to feed live deer we had caught in the deer pens. By 2008 these entire stands of fuchsia had perished under the onslaught of the possum, and only the rotten trunks of the massive fuchsias remain. Similarly, between a third and a half of the mature rata at the south end of Big Bay are now massive grey skeletons reaching up through the canopy.

As I made my way up the valley floor I occasionally had to negotiate log jams, skirting around them and back into the meandering river. Sometimes the river would split up, leaving grassy islands with sandy, stony gravel edges.

Luckily, the gentle breeze of the earlier morning was easing to a standstill. An intense heat bore down, energising my soul and generating a considerable thirst. I hardly ever carry a water bottle since there is usually clean, clear water to drink, even up on the tops. Days such as this bring on an unquenchable thirst as my body is working consistently for hour on hour, propelling me onwards. I was certainly making good time up the flats, and I enjoyed having time to observe the bird life and trees.

When I reached the mouth of the Murray Creek I spied a couple of blue ducks quietly feeding on the rocky bottom as they do, looking for small nymphs and caddis flies breeding in the mossy stones and boulders. This was the second pair I had seen that day, since I had also seen a pair at the Jerry junction. They thrive in the fast-running, stony streams of South Westland.

The further I went up the valley, the more the beech trees began to dominate the forest. The tall red and black beech, along with the delicate layering of the silver beech leaves and branches, were like an elfin forest, their mossy trunks and roots framing the grassy flats.

Once above the Murray confluence the Gorge River is noticeably smaller, but the water driving down from altitude demands respect when crossing. Each time I crossed my concentration was focused. The shingle underfoot was comfortable, but the gradient was changing once again as the Duncan River valley came into view.

On reaching the confluence of the Duncan and Saddle Creek, I saw another group of deer grazing quietly. So far I had seen seven deer during the morning. They blended in with the natural surroundings; they seemed to belong here, their beautiful red-brown coats shining in the noonday sun.

At this junction the Gorge becomes the Duncan River, which flows abruptly from the south in a deep valley following the main alpine faultline. This is a deep rent that marks the general landscape north and south of this point. To the south it runs through Duncan, Pyke Saddle, across Big Bay, through Jamestown Saddle and across Martins Bay. It then continues through the Kaipo Slip and out to sea at Anita Bay, Milford Sound, and finally plunges into the ocean depths off Poison Bay. To the north, this line runs through Saddle Creek to the

Cascade Valley. It is the foundation of the Jackson River, and carries on all the way up the West Coast, through Nelson and out to sea, through Tauranga to White Island and the Kermadecs. I was standing on the Austro-Indian tectonic plate, looking upwards and across to the Pacific Plate only metres away. The gradient of my journey was about to change.

By this stage I had walked about 22 kilometres. Apart from stopping to study my map and take quick compass bearings off landmarks, I had taken no rest. I was getting a little hungry. It was probably about lunchtime. Usually my main meal is in the evening since there is more time to eat and you can store glucose, in the form of glycogen, in your liver, to use as needed. After a light breakfast I feel lighter to travel, but by now the idea of a large piece of Christmas cake sounded inviting. After taking more compass bearings I was able to locate my exact position on the map. I cut a slice of Mum's great cooking and gazed up at the leading ridge rising 1100 metres above me to the tussock.

Taking a deep breath between mouthfuls of cake I mentally prepared myself for the ascent. I decided not to stay where I was for any longer than a couple of minutes. The tussock beckoned me. As I forded the Duncan River I left the grassy flats behind and headed into beech forest, which was growing all the way up the ridge as far as I could see. Just here I noticed the remnants of an old track that had been built in the 1890s by Polish settlers from Jackson Bay, part of a government work scheme to connect Westland to Southland which was never completed.

During this part of my journey there was a constant gradient, steep and upwards. The hillside was held together by beech tree and fern roots, which became my hand- and foot-holds for most of the way.

I had an amazing feeling of energy as my blood was flooded with glucose, and I kept my breathing deep and steady as I powered up the hill. By this time I was in shorts and tee shirt, my Swannie and woollen jumper stashed away in my pack as the sweat poured off my brow. I had quenched my thirst at the Duncan, but as time wore on and I gained more altitude a euphoric thirst developed. In this rain-drenched landscape there is usually a string of tarns and streamlets throughout, even on the ridges. Each time I came across water I quenched my unquenchable thirst. On these days when I am travelling large distances overland, especially at altitude, it doesn't matter how often I drink, my body is still thirsty.

Before too long I began to get glimpses to the east of the Cascade Valley and the spires of the Olivine mountain range rising above. To the west, the reddish hue of Junction Hill lay below me.

Soon, after scrambling through the stunted beech trees, which get shorter and shorter with altitude, I emerged out onto the tussock of Gorge Plateau. What an amazing sight I was greeted with. From here onward I was out in the open, high above an endless vista of mountains and large, deep valleys.

From the top of Gorge Plateau I could see large tarns in shallow basins. The rugged Red Hills and Red Mountain lay directly to the south, forming large, open, barren terrain. The afternoon was getting on by the time I reached a knoll just north of the Red Hills. I was feeling elated and also exhausted after the climb, so it was time to fill my billy and set up camp.

When you are out on the tops you are in kea country. If you leave your camp and wander off you give the cheeky kea the opportunity to create havoc with your gear. Already the

Top left: My grandparents, Mabel Long (née Johnstone) and Robert Baskerville Long. My grandfather, a descendant of Auckland's early Fencible settlers, fought in Gallipoli and France during World War One, and was one of only 28 survivors in his company of 200.

Top right: My parents, Bob and Ngaire Long. My father was a keen fisherman and gatherer of shellfish, and many of my childhood weekends were spent on the coast.

Above: Me with my mum and sisters (from left) Annette, Vivienne and Susan, photographed at our home in Papatoetoe around 1962.

Top left: Me aged seven, at the Holy Cross Convent in Papatoetoe. The Sisters of Mercy, who ran the school, dressed in full habits, and all you could see of them were their hands and faces, never a strand of hair, ears or neck.

Top right: Happy days at Brookfield, Brisbane. Me with Wendy Bopp and Nick Moore (behind) at Moggill Creek, 1974.

Above: The prefects of St Joseph's College, Brisbane, 1973. I am third from left in the front row. During my time at St Joseph's I spent four years in the Army Cadets, where I learnt many skills which would be invaluable to my survival when living in the wild.

Left: At the Gorge River Hut, 1985. I was well settled at this stage, making a living on fishing boats and travelling the coast.
Below: With Mum aboard *Kaiawhina Moana*, during Mum's visit to Gorge River in 1990. Mum had an adventurous spirit and loved her ten days staying with us.

Top left: Catherine and
I celebrating our wedding
on November 1, 1992.
We were married by Father
Foote at Whiskey Corner,
overlooking the Cascade
Valley, and held the
wedding reception at the
Okuru Hall, south of Haast.
Top right: This beautiful
portrait of the three of
us was taken by Lynn
Hamilton when Christan
was just a few days old.
Left: The family on the
move. We travelled widely
around South Westland
with the kids from before
they could walk.

Top: Catherine and Robin work with possum fur. Robin is very artistic and is interested in photography and crafts. **Above:** Christan prepares for a game of cricket. When parties of trampers came through Gorge River, he would usually set up his wickets on the airstrip outside the DoC hut, and before too long a game would be in progress.

Top: One of my paintings, of Ric Aubrey's Cessna 185 on the airstrip at Gorge River, 2002. Our home is at right.
Above: Painting has become a major part of my life, and a significant source of income. I sold my first painting to my father but now most of my work is commissioned. Here I am painting the Gorge River valley.

Top: Our home from the air. The DoC hut is to the right, with the airstrip in front.
Above: Our home and gardens, 2009. The large scar on the hillside behind is from a month of heavy rain after an earthquake of magnitude 7.8 in July 2009.

Top: The family on the beach at the Gorge River mouth, 2009: Christan, Robin (with Chooky), Catherine and me.
Above: This is the loveliness we live with every day. Sunset looking south from Gorge River.

kea had me in their sights, so it was necessary to display a little wisdom.

There was a small tarn not far below me, so I had another drink and filled my billy, then I headed back up and laid out my sleeping bag inside the oilskin sleeping-bag cover among the tussocks. I drank in the view and rested. Since leaving home I had twisted and turned for about 40 kilometres and climbed about 1400 metres. What a perfect day, not a cloud in the sky. I thanked my guardian angel for a day well spent.

As I prepared a cupful or two of sprouts and oatmeal, the sound of helicopters buzzing around began emanating up from the hills and valleys below. For a change I was way up above them, where it was too high and barren for deer. They were hunting the slips along the steep scree slopes falling off Gorge Plateau into the faultline of the Duncan River, and the tussock just above the bushline. I could see five or six helicopters browsing the landscape below, then as the sun set away over the distant horizon they carried their loads back to the road ends. I felt in good company, but a little bit closer to the heavens than they were.

At first light the next morning the cool easterly breezes buffeted the tussock and kept me snuggled in my secure little nest as the brilliant stars faded with the new day. As the red and gold beams of sunlight began streaming over the blue-purple mountains, reflecting off the glaciers, I heard the distant whine of a chopper.

As I hopped out of my sleeping bag and stood on the tussocky knoll the sound grew louder. They were scouring the mountainside about 150 metres below. Then, abruptly, the helicopter turned and headed straight up toward me, only metres above the grassy slopes. It circled the knoll and landed, perching on the tussocks, and out hopped Nelson

Thompson and Dane Paul from Te Anau.

'What are you doing up here?' they asked.

'Just having a look around,' I replied.

'We saw your silhouette against the sunrise and thought it could only be you.'

As they prepared to leave they invited me to come along with them. 'We'll take you wherever you wish to go.'

'Thanks anyway, but I've just spent a day getting up here and I don't want to go down just yet.' I told them that I intended to explore the Red Hills and eventually head home via Big Bay.

'Oh well, good luck and take care,' they replied, then they climbed aboard, gave pitch to full throttle and soared away on their mission, descending to the bushline to pursue their quarry.

Well, by this time I was wide awake and brimming with enthusiasm to explore this wonderland. As I gazed north, along Gorge Plateau and the faultline down the Cascade and Jackson Rivers, I could see to Haast and beyond.

To the south the ultramafic rocks and soil contrasted dramatically with the schist. The high concentrations of magnesium and iron adversely affect plant growth, as they are toxic to most plants, so there is a striking transition from mature silver beech forest on the surrounding schistose soils to the serpentine sands and barren herbfields. The Red Mountain belt supports only about 50 per cent of the species that grow on the neighbouring slopes, and growth rates are much slower.

After a nourishing breakfast I packed up and set about exploring, heading south into the Red Hills. This area, with its barren reddish-brown broken rock and dust, is how I imagine the deserts of Afghanistan to appear. Here and there green-blue tarns dotted the basins, and further south stood Red Mountain, the highest point locally. To the west I could see out over Big Bay far in the distance. Usually I would be looking up from the bay, back to this area.

As the afternoon wore on, clouds began drifting in from the north, just high streaming cloud at first, but then it began to thicken. It felt like the weather was closing in. So I headed west towards Telescope Hill and then Bald Hill, perched on a large tussocky knoll. As the cloud continued to thicken I set up camp there, knowing that if it clouded in I was only a stone's throw from the edge of the beech forest and a ridge that would lead me safely to the valley below.

A sketch pad became my centre of attention for the next two hours. I drew the Gorge River catchment with the Jerry in the foreground, then a view of the Pyke Valley, Skippers Range and magnificent Big Bay. I had done the odd sketch since primary school days, and I had also done technical drawing and perspective all through high school. When I began exploring South Westland and Fiordland I carried no camera but still wished to record the beautiful land and seascapes that would literally stop me in my tracks. I bought a large art pad so that I could show my mother these awesome scenes. Often I would put them into my memory bank by dividing the view up into quadrants so they could be remembered more easily and drawn on my pad at a more practical time. I would create songs and poems to remember colours, features and vegetation.

From 1980 onwards this hobby became more and more entrenched since I was continually exploring, analysing and scrutinising the colours of close and distant landforms, the motion of water in the ocean and rivers and the native vegetation. While out fishing I would be totally engrossed by the scenery, taking it all in. Although at the time I had no idea of selling my artwork, in later years I have supported my family with all this data that was stored away in my head.

Many years after this day up on Bald Hill, I was commissioned by Brian McBride, a South Westland-born chopper pilot, to paint this very scene, from a photo of his favourite place in the southwest.

That night a blanket of mist and near drizzle descended, and by the morning I was completely clouded in. So after a quick pack-up I entered the elfin beech forest and began my descent to the valley below. Paulin Creek brought me out to the Pyke, then to an old bulldozer track pushed through by the Kennecott Mining Company, which led me out to Big Bay. By the afternoon I was sipping a hot cup of tea with Graeme and Anne Mitchell at the Awarua River, and entertaining their children with stories of my latest adventure.

Later I headed back up the coast to home, to rest and catch up on weeding my silver beet, carrots and cabbages, and ready for another adventure before the summer was out.

chapter 13 scratched

I n January 1986 I was doing a spell of crewing with Lou
Brown. We were working out of his base at Barn Bay,
and occasionally we would spend a night at Gorge River
when the tides suited for getting in and out of the river
mouth. Lou's wife Elizabeth and their children were having
a holiday out in town, so Lou and I looked after ourselves,
catching crayfish each day as well as cooking our meals and
doing housework.

When some American trampers arrived in from the
Cascade, we invited them to stay. Alan Reigelman and Kay
Berger were from Vermont and were intelligent, energetic
types. We enjoyed their company and invited them out
fishing. After a couple more days another American tramper
from Oregon, by the name of Bob, joined our company. He
loved eating crayfish leg meat and we loved catching it. In
those days we used to tail the crayfish to freeze so the legs
were often wasted unless there were plenty of appetites to
satisfy. While they were all there we fished our way down to
Gorge River and stayed there for the night. Bob helped us
with the bait so that made my job a little bit easier.

Since the weather was relatively calm we had gradually set our pots in closer and closer to the shoreline, taking the opportunity to fish the inshore stocks. These are largely unexploited because of the waves rolling and crashing through this region of the ocean. There is a strip between the breakers and the boulder beaches which is best left alone.

After Alan and Kay had been with us for about a week they decided it was time to move on. They planned to walk back out to the Cascade and head north up the West Coast. Bob was heading south to Gorge River, Big Bay, Martins Bay, up the Hollyford Valley and eventually out to Gunn's Camp.

Lou was looking for diversion to break the cycle of work and fishing so he offered to take Alan and Kay up the Cascade River as far as we could go and save them a day's walk. So off we went. Lou's vessel *Scratch*, a seven-metre aluminium-alloy fishing boat, was moored up the Hope River, tied to a couple of trees against the bank in a deep pool. Lou checked oil, battery and fan belts and fuelled up. High tide was due about midday so we cast off our bow and stern mooring lines by about 9am. We estimated it would take us about an hour to have Alan and Kay safely up the Cascade and that would give us the rest of the incoming tide to work the gear.

The day had dawned bright and clear and already the summer sun was beating down upon us. Bob wanted to tramp this coastline so we dropped him across the Hope River. We would see him that night at the Gorge, where we planned to stay after working all the pots towards the south.

As we approached the channel through the river bar, the glassy sea shone and sparkled. The roll had picked up overnight but Lou planed on down to the river mouth, finding a lull in the wave sets and eased up on the throttle as we thrust up and over the biggest one. We were out to sea and off at 30 knots, powering across the water, the V8 Caterpillar motor driving the impeller of the jet unit, sucking in tonnes of seawater and spewing it out in our wake.

Lou skippered us over to the blue lagoon at the north end of the aquamarine bay to lift the bait net. I grappled the net buoy rope and then we hauled in one anchor, which was a large rock with a hole bored in it. We set about bringing the net up over the side of the boat, retrieving the fish as we went, until the whole net and all the anchors lay aboard. We had half a fish case full of tarakihi, moki, red cod, wrasse and marble fish, enough to supplement the box of frozen bait we had loaded aboard before we had set sail.

Keeping the net aboard, we headed out past the Sugar Loaf Needle guarding the northern entrance of Barn Bay, and sped off north past the bluffs lining the coast towards the Cascade River mouth. In the distance Cascade Point loomed. The motor purred like a pride of lions, accompanying the rhythm, swish and pounding of *Scratch*'s hull upon the buoyant, rushing water. Alan and Kay hung on tight to the boat's gunwales, obviously enjoying the ride.

Before too long we had travelled 10 kilometres and were off the Cascade River mouth. Lou eased back on the throttle and scanned the confusion of waves and sandbars, picked his line, and set off through the breakers following in behind a large wave. We were soon safely gliding up the tannin-stained river.

We halted about 300 metres from the breakers, set the net midstream and carried on up past the whitebaiters' huts. As we cruised up past Old Man Creek the sunlight reflected up off the placid water like a mirror. At times the glare was quite intense as we were heading into the sun. Barn River, heading into the huge Hermitage Swamp, soon slipped behind us, the purring motor helping us to chew up the miles. Up ahead, the mighty Olivine and Thompson Ranges met with the reddish ultramafic hue of the Martyr Spur.

We were about 20 kilometres upriver when all of a sudden we ground to a halt. Lou had taken his eye off the 'eight ball'. Perhaps the glare had hidden it, but we were stranded on a sandbar in mid-river. The river had forked around the obstacle but we had gone full steam ahead. We were still in about 10 centimetres of water, with three tonnes of boat and nowhere to go. Our picnic was over for the day.

Luckily none of us had been bruised or hurt as we ground to zero. We hopped off the boat to assess our predicament. Lou was ready to give up and walk home to radio for help. I suggested that if we could only dig a bit of a channel south towards the stream and dig out under the bow then we could possibly all push and swing the bow around. Most of the weight was in the stern. Lou was doubtful, but what else could we do? We couldn't give up just yet. The tide was still coming in so hopefully we were still just in the tidal zone.

If only we had a shovel. We figured that the Robbie Nolan hut couldn't be that far away. Surely there would be a shovel or two there. I set off and forded the river to the south bank. The hut was not far away across a couple of paddocks, but there in front of me was a good shovel leaning on a fence post overlooking the scene of our misadventure. I quickly hurried back with my prize and we set to work, taking turns to dig away the sand under the bow, around the boat and out towards deeper water. We must have toiled away without stopping for two or three hours at least, then we began heaving away on the bow and pulling on the bow rope, jiggling and shoving. The tide had raised the level of the river by this time, so we began to get some movement in the bow which gradually began to swing towards deeper water. We kept shovelling gravel and sand as best we could until we had swung the bow right around and gained more buoyancy. Eventually we jiggled and rolled the boat until we had the battle won. Wow, we all breathed a sigh of relief.

We figured that Alan and Kay had best make their own way from there, so we gave them instructions on how to find the way and asked them to take the shovel back. Lou climbed aboard *Scratch*, which now seemed aptly named, checked the jet intake and cleared away the sand and gravel with a manual lever on the dashboard. I held the boat off the bank while he checked the oil and fan belts again, making sure our sudden halt hadn't affected anything. The engine started OK and revved up as Lou applied throttle, so I climbed up over the gunwale with Lou's help and away we went back downriver. At least we would get to the river mouth before the tide dropped too much, but we were about four hours behind schedule.

'Well, that was a close one,' Lou exclaimed as we hurried on past stands of green and mustard podocarps, now focused on the day ahead.

'Yeah, that's for sure,' I replied.

The grounding had been a reality check for both of us. Together we had been through many a scrape, in behind big breakers, out in monstrous seas, and crossing wild river bars, but always coming through with literally flying colours. Lou had always made out he was invincible, but I had seen a chink in his armour and now saw him in a different light.

The Barn Islets are massive formations with myriad channels in between them. The three main islets together take the brunt of the ocean swells, and there are numerous pinnacles rising up from the ocean depths 15 to 30 metres high. You can literally reach out and touch these walls and still have five to eight fathoms of water below you. Some of these areas are aptly named the 'widow-makers'. Inside the widow-maker the water always has the appearance of soap suds inside a washing machine, since it never has time to settle.

The same day as our adventure up the Cascade, now running late, Lou and I left the Islets and headed south towards Fox's Point. The tide was by now dropping and the smooth, glassy roll was still making up. As we neared the line of pots we could see the spray and foam smoking off the tops of sets of breakers as they rose up and broke, just inside the orange buoys marking Lou's gear. Occasionally sets would break right through the field of play, sharpening our senses as our adrenalin levels began to rise.

The rollers were peeling off the point so we could see down the tubes side on. They looked like the glassy full-blown waves of the Pipeline in Hawaii. Both Lou and I had been board and body surfers so we related to the sea not just as fishermen but also as surfies. Lou used to refer to us as the Church of the Latter Day Surfies, and he fished accordingly.

It was all a matter of timing as we gradually worked our way through this lot of gear, waiting for a lull in the breakers, speeding in at 30 knots, grappling the buoy, rope over gantry and hauler in one smooth action and winch at full pace. We would grab the pot aboard, ready for a quick retreat back out to deeper water, then reset it at a slower pace, allowing time to feel the rhythm of the oncoming sets.

Waves usually come in sets of seven or eight waves, with one or two larger ones in that octave. Then every three or four octaves there is a larger peak, so every 30 or so waves is a peak wave. These are the ones to avoid wherever possible. Since the roll was continuing to make, Lou was becoming more conscious of the peaks and the lulls.

After Fox's we continued south. We rebaited a couple of pots around Seal Island, then continued onwards to Brown's Refuge. There is a channel through the rocks into a lagoon, and in the old days sealers and whalers used to be able to make landfall here in their long-oared rowboats. Between swells we ducked in behind a large rock and lifted the craypot there. We waited for the next large set of white fury to flow through, taking broken water over the bow a couple of times, lifting us up and down like a beach ball.

We were working hard, and the sun was beating down. I almost welcomed the spray of the waves to cool me down. Working on a fishing boat is demanding work. You're cutting fish on a pounding, heaving deck, holding on to anything solid to avoid being bashed about, often fending for your life as you try to maintain balance and stay onboard. Some days in a southwesterly gale every movement of the day is a calculated risk. You're living in the moment and for the moment as you fight to stay upright and alive.

This day was becoming more demanding by the hour. The tide was below half tide and still going out, and this was lifting the swells up quicker inshore where most of our pots lay. Lou wasn't one to turn away from the risks; he savoured the adrenalin rush and relished the challenge. Together, we were a team.

We made our way back out to sea during the next lull, then around Cutter Rocks toward the Gorge Islets where most of the craypots were in deeper water. The crayfish tumbled aboard as we undid the traps. The catch for the day was mounting up.

I gazed landwards towards the Gorge River, characterised by the deep cleft in the hillsides, looking forward to a cup of tea there after completing the next lot of gear down at Longridge Point.

Before long we were approaching the last few pots. There was a group of four. After the first three we headed straight onto the fourth. We raced over and Lou manoeuvred the bow seawards. I grappled the buoy as I hauled in the pot, noticing how sudsy-looking the water was, like the 'widow-maker'. I laid the rope over the gantry, through the hauler, then as Lou powered the hauler into action all the water underneath us suddenly began draining out. Rocks began appearing from the ocean beneath us. We were dragged seawards and half sideways until we were sitting high and dry upon a flat, house-sized rock. We looked up to see a massive blue wave break onto the rock, becoming a wall of water in full fury rushing towards us, lifting the boat up, up, up and bow over upside down, all in one slow motion.

As we went over I kept my feet on the mid deck and then pushed down once we were upside down, diving down deep and heading out toward the sea. I came up on the seaward side of the stern unit which was still bubbling away. The motor was still going. Luckily, we had been thrown back into the channel and all the rocks had disappeared again. I was bouncing on rocks every now and then as the waves kept crashing through, but I was OK. I still had my gumboots on but I could swim all right and I moved as far away from the heaving boat as I could, since boats, rocks, waves and bodies don't mix.

Looking up, I could see Lou climbing onto the upturned bottom of *Scratch*. Was he crazy? He could be smashed between rock and metal with the next swell. Was he expecting the boat to turn back upright, since the motor was still running? Did he think he could climb aboard, gun the motor, clear the scuppers and away? Was he that invincible?

I yelled, 'Hey Lou, what's the next plan of attack?'

He shook his head, stunned and blinking, and gasped, 'She's stuffed.'

'Well, get the hell away from that boat,' I shouted.

I took one of my gumboots off to get more mobile. Like a couple of pieces of seaweed we were gradually being pushed inshore, with each white wall of water slamming us into and around boulders. The more you relax in such situations the better it is, enabling you to slide around obstacles.

We were both limp, bruised and feeling a little beaten as we struggled to keep our heads above water until we were eventually out of danger and lay like stunned mullets in the rocky pools. Eventually we hauled ourselves up out of the water, and man, did it feel great to be alive. We could get a new boat tomorrow, but if you're dead, it ain't much use to you.

We hugged each other, glad to find we were both alive. Lou was badly shaken. He told me he had been sucked off the wheel and up under the bow section where he had become caught up in cables from the upturned boat. He had been nearly knocked out but had managed to escape the entanglement and swim his way out. He had taken in a lungful of water and had climbed onto the hull of the upturned boat to recover, not realising the danger he was in.

We sat there on the boulder beach watching *Scratch* wallowing in the ocean amongst the rocks and waves. There in front of us lay an orange bobbing in the tide. 'Oh well, at least we didn't lose our smoko!' Lou exclaimed, and we both laughed, feeling a great weight lifting off our shoulders. We had escaped death. The sun shone down upon us. It was a beautiful clear day, one to be alive.

As we peeled and shared our orange, Lou said, 'Do you

realise we could disappear off the face of the Earth? We could skip the country and nobody would be the wiser.'

After pondering this startling idea I replied, 'I don't see that as an option, Lou.'

'Oh well, we'd better get on with it then.'

So we walked north along the sandstone boulders for a couple of miles to Gorge River, cranked up my fire, made a welcome brew of tea, milk and sugar and began preparing a meal to ward off our hunger pangs.

Before long we heard a shout from across the river. It was Bob. We had told him to call us from across the river and we would bring him across. So we headed down to my dinghy, rowed over and picked him up, brought him back to the hut and told him to make himself at home. As we ate supper around the kitchen table by candlelight he told us about the sights he had seen, and how enjoyable the day had been.

As we were finishing the meal Lou said, 'Bob, that's great. We're really glad to hear you had a big day. We had a big day too. We sank the boat!'

Bob gasped. 'You're joking! You're pulling my leg.'

'Did you see any sign of the jetboat on the river?'

'Oh my God! I thought you guys looked a bit ruffled up.'

The next morning we headed back up to Barn Bay. Just north of Gorge River at the Steeples we saw a blatant reminder of how near we had come to disaster — the bow section of the *Empress*, shipwrecked on 1 February 1979, with the drowning of Russell Horne, captured by the upturned boat. Then a further 400 metres on the remnants of the *Coruba*, shipwrecked just a year earlier on 1 January 1985. A couple of miles further on lay the ruined timbers and freezer gear of the *Dolphin*, wrecked in the early 1970s. All these crayfishing boats had suffered the same ill effects of the 'rogue wave', bow up and over.

Once at Barn Bay, Lou radioed out our predicament. The next day a helicopter arrived from Queenstown with an Invercargill marine assessor, Bill Britton, on board, along with two Cromwell salvage experts, Johnny Symons and John Breen. Lou flew back down to Longridge Point to survey the wreckage with the team. They took one look at the remains of *Scratch* and wrote her off, saying, 'You guys are lucky to be alive.' It wasn't worth the effort to try salvaging the wreck.

Later Lou and I went back to Longridge Point to salvage any valuables from the wreckage. We found life jackets and a few odds and ends. The V8 motor had dropped out of the upturned hull and was lying amongst the boulders, visible as the tide was out. We asked Harvey Hutton to come down in his Hughes 500C helicopter, hoping he would be able to lift it out, but he was unable to lift it. Marty Nolan, Maurice's brother, came down in his Hughes 500D model, and with the bit of extra power and lift was able to retrieve the engine and fly it up the coast to Barn Bay. Lou and I immediately stripped the motor down to its pistons, crankshaft, camshaft and engine block, and oiled up all the parts. Lou, being a grease monkey, later managed to bring the engine back to life and sold it to a truckie.

The next task was to retrieve our craypots. George McInroe offered assistance with the *Erynne Kay*, so we rowed out in Lou's dinghy and rendezvoused at the lagoon at the northern end of Barn Bay. Luckily the sea had settled but Lou and I spent an exciting day rescuing pots, some from the white water, hauling them up by hand over the back of the dinghy. Often there was a mad scramble to the oars as cresting waves made their way toward us while we were busy tugging on ropes and struggling with the pots.

George was able to pick up many of the pots which were

in deeper water, so by the close of the day all our pots had been accounted for, rebaited and set amongst George's line of pots. He had generously offered to keep fishing Lou's gear to bring in some extra, much-needed dollars for the Brown family. Lou had had enough and decided to take an extended break with his family, but I was keen to work the gear alongside George and Young George.

So for the next month I had a new boat to work on. I thoroughly enjoyed this period of my life. George was a third-generation coaster whose family had come to Greymouth as merchants during the early gold rushes. Young George was a cheerful, jolly person, and together we worked 130 pots each day, jiving to Classic Hits blaring across the deck.

We worked out of Jackson Bay down to Big Bay, one day down and one day back, camping one night at Big Bay and then back at their cottage at Neils Beach, about six kilometres along the road from Jackson Bay wharf.

Every three or four days I headed back to Barn Bay to feed the chooks and collect eggs and ripe tomatoes from the Browns' prolific vege garden. I managed this by swimming ashore at the lagoon, despite the blue sharks which daily followed our boat. When the sea was too rough to fish, Young George and I walked into Barn Bay and back from the Cascade Road end, a 50-kilometre return trip.

At the end of February we brought all of Lou's pots up to the lagoon and I rowed them into the beach, stacked five high in the four-metre dinghy. I rolled them all back up the beach until there were 50 craypots safe and secure above high tide.

Lou almost gave fishing away after this episode, but eventually decided to rebuild, and *Scratch II* was launched two and a half years later.

chapter 14 the spinning wheel

The winter of 1987 was a crystal-clear one, a time when life stood still and rested during the frozen months until the impetus of spring once again burst out and released the energy for a new season of growth and fruitfulness.

In mid-May, when I had returned to Gorge River, I had come across Marty Nolan and his trainee pilot, Mike, camping at the Robbie Nolan hut on the south side of the Cascade. We had spent the evening yarning beside the blazing open fire, the sparks scattering and singing as the flames warmed us against the chill of the night. The rimu tongue-and-groove panelling of the hut reflected the heat and illuminated the room as Marty's smiling face and his tales of history and adventure filled my mind and heart with an awesome sense of belonging and place. The next morning Marty and I bid each other farewell as I climbed into the Hughes 300 helicopter and Mike flew me down across the paddocks, wetlands and podocarp forest to Barn Bay.

For six weeks I saw no sign of people at all. No boats on the horizon or passing choppers, no aeroplanes or even high-passing jet planes, just the natural world. For all I knew the modern world could have come to an end.

I love the quiet of the winter, when the musical humming of the mountains, ocean waves and river breezes play a constant, clear and crystal song. During this time I once again explored my way down to Big Bay and Martins Bay. I borrowed Neil Drysdale's dinghy and rowed across the Hollyford River, then walked south along the beach to the Kaipo River mouth. The large rocky pinnacles just offshore were clothed in thick layers of bull kelp below the high-tide mark and with each wave their fronds surged in the tide.

A small garden-shed hut provided me with shelter in behind the sand dunes next to the rushing waters of the Kaipo River. In the morning light the beach sands glistened red with the glow of garnet sand stirred up by the overnight tide.

Once again I made my way upstream, following an overgrown track through rolling hills that were covered predominantly in rimu, rata, totara and kahikatea, and ponga fronds hung over my pathway. After about six kilometres I forded the river above a large bend and headed up the true left towards the 'Promised Land'. As you near this open area of landscape you come across massive tracts of forest covered belly-deep in shingle from slips that have come way down off the mountaintops. These are dead standing trees, like skeletons, deprived of their life by the concrete-hard stones and sand. Then, below the Kaipo Slip, a rent in the foothills and mountainside above the alpine faultline, lies a grassy flat of a thousand acres. To me, this is the Promised Land, when after walking through miles and miles of mossy, shadowy podocarp forest I emerge into a valley of sunlight and open country cleared by the forces of nature and clothed in tussock, sedge grasses and coprosma shrubs.

Towards the head of the flat lay Archie's hut, beside a narrow airstrip. I camped here for a couple of nights, surrounded by the sheer faces of rock ascending up the Kaipo face to the Ngapunatoru ice plateau and Mt Parariki. Beyond lay the glaciers and summit of Mt Tutoko, the highest mountain in Fiordland's Darran Range.

During the quiet of this West Coast winter the large high-pressure systems stalled and lay overhead for weeks on end, each day dawning with a pale-blue hue before the sunlight burst forth to warm the frosty morning air. Ice would lie for days in the shadows near the Gorge River hut as the wind raced down through the gorge towards the ocean, lifting the tops off the picture-perfect rows of emerald-blue waves. A veil of spray and sunlight would flare up with each cresting wave, sending a fluted sound across the clear morning air. There is a purity that only the winter knows. The chill of air and ice cleanses the earth, readying it for spring.

Back at the hut, I would light the morning fire to ward off the numbing cold, then set about spinning another bundle of carded merino woollen fleece, releasing the fibre gradually as my feet treadled the wooden spinning wheel into life. As the yarn formed it was drawn through the spindle and onto the bobbin. Each day I sought to complete two bobbins of woollen fibre, which I then plied together, carefully adjusting the brake tension as they twisted together. They were then ready to be wound into balls of wool.

Later the brilliant blue of the winter day would be replaced by the luminous glow of the waxing and waning moon, until the night skies were illuminated by stars that glowed and twinkled like diamonds, each with its own pulses of colour and intensity. At night I sat in my warm bed and knitted by candlelight, until the wool had become part of a garment to insulate me from the cold. Then, as the stars sparkled overhead,

I fell asleep, content with my day's progress towards creating my own woollen Swanndri.

Noel Maitland, a friend of mine who was a woolshed roustabout from Lake Hawea, had saved me a fine, long-haired lamb's fleece. This was ideal for spinning, and I had given her a palm-sized piece of apple-green, translucent pounamu in exchange. After being flown in to Barn Bay with Lou Brown's air freight from Makarora, the fleece came on to Gorge River by jet-powered fishing boat.

I spent many hours carding the 12-centeretre-long fibres with an old plastic comb. Another friend had generously given me an Ashford upright wooden spinning wheel, and later an old steel oven-rack came in very handy for constructing a pair of knitting needles. After cutting them out, I sharpened up the ends and sanded them off to a glistening smooth finish. They became strong, pliable needles, ideal for creating a large woollen garment. My worn-out Swanndri bushshirt became the pattern, as day after day and night after night the new garment gradually took shape.

That winter, while the tomtits and fantails played and fluttered about the window frames in the morning light, I gazed out across the ocean waves, cupping my hands around a hot cup of tea, and began planning my next journey. A friend had invited me to his wedding in Queenstown. Dane Paul, a venison hunter, was due to marry his sweetheart, Jill, in early July. In fact, Dane was someone from my past life, long before I ever came to South Westland. I had known him during my Brookie days in Brisbane and used to compete against his older brother, Brent, in interschool high-jump championships.

We had met up again unexpectedly one day in the summer of 1981 when Ray Nicholson, a venison hunter from Te Anau, had landed at Gorge River in his Hughes 300 and offered to fly me to Big Bay for a night out. Not one to refuse such an offer, I climbed aboard and off we went — it was my first chopper flight. I was positioned in the middle of the three-seater machine, exhilarated by my stroke of good luck, with Ray's shooter sitting to my right. He sat gripping the butt of a semi-automatic rifle and scanning the ground intently for deer as we whisked past steep bush-clad hillsides interspersed with grassy slips and clearings. I looked more closely at the guy I was rubbing shoulders with, and thought to myself, I know him. Out loud I exclaimed, 'You're Dane Paul, but a little bit older.'

Dane looked at me, puzzled, not recognising me under my beard and long hair. The last time he had seen me I was in a school suit and tie.

'I'm Robert Long from Gregory Terrace,' I said.

That night over a bottle of whisky Dane and I caught up with each other, and I also became better acquainted with Ray, who was leaving soon to work in New Guinea. The next morning Ray flew me back home, pretending we were hunting the slips all the way back up the coast. He was completing full flare-outs as we came up to the slips at full speed, showing me the G-forces they work in all the time. He was having as much fun as me as I held on with all my might in the gale-force wind that raced past the doorless chopper as we completed 360-degree turns on a hairpin amid the steep hillsides, surrounded by overhanging forest, the blades whirring overhead.

Then we gradually gained altitude until we were 1500 metres above the Gorge River hut. Ray's grin widened as we dropped out of the sky and he spiralled the helicopter straight down towards the roof of the hut far below. The ground finally loomed up as he levelled the chopper off with larger and wider circuits, then he expertly pulled up on the airstrip beside the hut. After I had climbed out he flew off again, rapidly becoming a distant speck in the cerulean sky.

Dane had invited me to stay with them in Te Anau when I next headed south, and a few months later, in mid-May, I had walked out down the Pyke Valley heading to Bluff. I was off to retrieve my gumboots from Buntie and Ivy's place. After a two-and-a-half-day walk through flaxes and toetoes in bare feet, my shins and ankles below my oilskin overtrousers were a mass of tiny criss-cross cuts. These were a source of fascination as I shared a few brews with my newfound chopper mates in Te Anau.

That was the first time I had walked out after a prolonged spell of three or four months in the bush, and I experienced a kind of culture shock, especially when the first car came rumbling down the Hollyford road. Nowadays I am more used to the change, except when we arrive straight into town from total isolation, as happens when we fly out.

Now Dane and Jill's wedding was drawing near, and I intended to complete the woollen Swannie and wear it on that occasion. It was soon time to head south to the Hollyford. Already the garment was in the form of a vest with hood, and I had enough wool to carry with me to knit the sleeves as I stayed at huts along the way.

The sense of isolation in the middle of winter is total, and no one who hasn't experienced it can begin to understand the sense of loneliness I have endured at times during my years living at Gorge River. I usually work through this and come out feeling positive about it. I weigh up the situation and feel that my destiny is to follow this path, and this gives my life meaning and direction to aspire to. In other words, I just get on with it. I never actually feel totally alone since the spirit of creation fills my being and is my constant companion. The vast vistas that I daily gaze across give me strength and perseverance.

At the same time, my feelings of isolation have made me essentially aware of the true value of human company. Now, as I filled my backpack with food, oilskin, bivvy bag and down sleeping bag, I could already sense the joy of seeing my friends along the way, the celebration we would have, and the experiences we would share.

After heading south along the sandstone boulders and around Longridge Point I came across my bivvy at Ryan's Creek. This was my true home, where my own expression of shelter from the storm existed. In a natural clearing created by a windfall in the forest I had constructed a shelter from driftwood totara and silver pine logs. I had used an old homemade chisel and a handsaw, a wooden mallet for a hammer, and rata wedges to split the timber when necessary. Old craypot ropes tied the logs and beams together, with a tarpaulin spread over them to ward off the rain. Bundles of dried ponga fronds provide a mattress on the ground, covered by a large folded canvas tarpaulin to sleep on and a fully enclosed sandfly net to ward off mozzies and other blood-sucking marauders. Each time I stayed I would collect more large, flat beach stones to stack around the lower walls, line the floor and lay about the hearth.

At night-time I would sit beside a blazing fire on the nearby sandy beach and watch the moonbeams dance upon the waters of the sea. With my back to the fire to warm me, I felt the wealth of gifts that the natural world gives us, though they are not necessarily for the taking. The silver and gold light is ours to behold, as beautiful as any jewellery we could ever own; the blazing embers provide warmth against the chill of the winter night. This bivvy allows me to break my journey between Gorge

River and Big Bay. It is situated between two streams, the Ryan and the Hacket, which are always prone to flooding. This place provides my closest connection to the primeval world while still having a roof over my head. It is the place I go to really get away from it all, since there has never been any modern-day settlement here.

So on this night I watched for hours as the rushing waters merged with the ocean, then I lay down to slumber, ready for the long journey ahead. The next morning as the sun finally rose over the coastal ridges and struck the sandy beach I was already close to the Hacket River, heading towards the beginning of the 10-kilometre stretch of boulders around Awarua Point. The north point of Big Bay fell away behind me as the picturesque beauty of the snow-capped mountains rose above the vast stretch of sea. It is a view to live for, never failing to lift my spirits and urge me on towards the bay's long, sandy reaches.

As the afternoon wore on the welcome sight of Dale's hut appeared around the flaxes above the natural harbour at the southwestern corner of the bay. That night I was once again warmed by the clicking of the knitting needles, along with the boiling of the billy above the split rata blazing in the open fire. Outside the windows, the brilliance of the Milky Way was still obvious above the glow of the candle flame. The sleeves of my Swannie took shape over the next two days.

Over the winter the odd tramper had left their name in the hut book at Long Reef, but there was no sign of human life as I sewed the sleeves on the Swannie and headed onwards to Lake McKerrow and up the Hollyford Valley. The pristine nature of the lake was highlighted by the Darran Mountains, which were bedecked with snow down to the bushline, from the latest skiff of cold sou'westerly weather that had brushed the far south of

Fiordland. Way up the valley where I was heading, the mountains disappeared into a blue mist. The icy blue water of the lake lapped briskly upon the loose shingle at its edge and brought a quickness to my step as the sea breezes threatened to numb my skin.

My pack wasn't too heavy, but I was carrying a wooden picture frame made from some milled timber driftwood off Big Bay beach. I had cut it into shape in Dale's workshop, and would reassemble it once in Te Anau. The frame was for a painting I had done looking north to the Steeples and Cascade Point from the Gorge River mouth. It would be a gift for Jill and Dane.

After a couple more days of wandering through podocarp forest, across creek beds and rushing streams, over hundreds of mossy logs, windfalls and rocky screes, the end of the track began to appear as a glow of light through the trees. As I neared Gunn's Camp the shadows were lengthening. Now that I was nearer the upper reaches of the valley the sheer mountains were dominating the skyline. The elfin forest was quickly giving way to tawny tussock, and the peachy golden glow of the sinking sun reflected off the basalt and granite turrets of rock rising out of the snow. I began to dream of a warm hearth where I could rest my weary bones and boil a billy of hot tea.

Murray Gunn met me with his quizzical smile and warm handshake, but had some startling news. Marty Nolan had been killed. The previous evening he and his shooter, Mark Cust, had crashed into the power lines across the Arawhata River. Mark had survived but Marty was gone. I was devastated.

The next morning Wayne Curran, who checked the Milford road early each day for windfalls and avalanche danger, drove me down to Te Anau. Marty's funeral was to be held in Hokitika. A contingent of helicopters from Te Anau was to fly up there, and Nelson and Dane invited me to come with them.

During the previous seven years I had become used to Marty flying by, sometimes during the middle of the night, spotlighting his way down the coast, giving me a blast of his light as he passed by. Often he would circle above me like a guardian angel if he came across me during the day, and wave as he flew on. He had been keeping an eye on me.

Marty Nolan had been a people's hero, involved in numerous search and rescue operations, always willing to lend a helping hand, a true farmer's son and the salt of the earth. He was always ready to offer a smile, some words of wisdom and a humorous remark as he took to the skies where he now belonged. We celebrated his life, and then as we paid our last respects his favourite song, Dire Straits' 'Coming Home', played while overhead, helicopters filled the air.

Life turns difficult corners, but it goes on. After a couple of beers at the local pub we took to the sky once again and found our way back south, following the beaches and rocky headlands along the rolling blue waters of the West Coast. By the end of the 1000-kilometre journey my mind was humming, and I arrived back in Te Anau feeling as if another threshold had been passed. I had entered a new dimension, with clearer meanings.

Little did I know that I was going to more than Dane and Jill's wedding. I was also on my way to meet my future soulmate, the mother of my children, Catherine Stewart.

Lou and Elizabeth Brown were spending the winter in Queenstown, working on a film set, and it was while I was visiting them that I met Catherine and Cathy Mountier. They wanted to undertake a tramp through the Pyke Valley, north of the Hollyford, but they weren't confident walking the Pyke without someone experienced. So they invited me along.

That same year I had begun a naturopathy course, and after the wedding I had planned to travel up to Nelson for some tutorials with Phillipa Rutherford, who practised up there. My neighbour at Barn Bay, Elizabeth Brown, had told me about her interest in this course, which was run by the New Zealand Naturopathy College at Himatangi Beach, in the North Island. When I read some of her books I finally realised that there was a name for the philosophy I had adopted as I had moved away from my conventional medical studies to one of natural healing. I had been a naturopath since 1975, and now I wished to continue my medical studies in this New Age form. The tutorials with Phillipa Rutherford were part of my diploma course.

I had arranged to get a ride with Steve Pullock, a helicopter shooter from Murchison, who was also in Queenstown for the wedding. After talking to Catherine and Cathy, however, I decided I might as well take the shortcut to Nelson via the Pyke, even though it would take me an extra two weeks.

During the wedding I became acquainted with Lewis Brown, a possum- and deer-hunter based at Gunn's Camp. He was heading back to the Hollyford in his van the very next day, and he offered to give the three of us a ride all the way back to the Hollyford road end.

What a stroke of luck. I informed the girls, so next morning they were packed up and ready for the journey around to Te Anau, then north up the Milford road, over the Divide Pass to Marian's Corner and down the Hollyford Valley road. We called into Gunn's Camp for a brew with Murray, who showed us some beautiful pieces of polished tangiwai. But the day was moving on and we planned to reach the Hidden Falls hut by evening, so Lewis drove us the last eight kilometres to the beginning of the track and away we went. We were reasonably loaded up since the journey through to the Cascade via the

Pyke and Gorge River would take us about 10 days, though I knew there were extra supplies at home to see us through. Cathy had walked most of the journey before, but this was Catherine's first tramp through this part of Fiordland and South Westland, although she had explored some remote parts of the Milford Sound region on previous occasions.

We made good time to Hidden Falls, and reached the hut by nightfall. Next morning we set off early through the elfin podocarp forest, over Little Homer Saddle, past Homer Falls and the Pyke-Hollyford confluence, arriving at Lake Alabaster by late morning. The pristine nature of the lake was stunning. On this clear, crisp, wintry morning the edges were shrouded in mist which gradually burnt off as the day progressed.

We carried on past the DoC hut beside the lake edge, since we aimed to reach the Red Alabaster hut, on past the head of the lake. We followed the lake edge most of the way, climbing and scrabbling around windfalls that disappeared into the tannin depths of the shingly bottom. We occasionally took to the forest to avoid wading in too deep around log jams and steep rocky ledges and outcrops. Luckily the winter high-pressure systems were still holding, so there was no rain. The shadows had a sharp crispness to them, but the blue skies and shafts of sunlight warmed us. Anyway, carrying a laden pack is always guaranteed to keep you warm.

After reaching the head of the lake we headed over towards the Pyke River mouth and up the dry shingle bed. Here the sun was blazing down. We were out in the open valley floor, surrounded by grassy clearings scattered between shingle river braids. The walls of the valley rose up steeply, bush-clad up to tussock, then giving way to upthrusting rock and snow.

In order to reach the Red Alabaster hut we needed to ford the Pyke River. The crossing was usually quite deep, so

Catherine, who was the lightest, took the centre position as we forded together. She actually floated while Cathy and I held her through the deepest stretch. Dodging mossy, sunken and half-buried logs focused our attention, and once across we scrambled up the bank to the grassy airstrip which led straight towards the old hut.

By the time we had collected some dry firewood and set it alight the hut's welcoming character had sprung back into life, and we settled in for the night. The numbing cold of the river crossing ebbed away once we had whipped up a hot brew, and we soon had a meal bubbling away in a billy hanging from a blackened cast-iron hook above the flames.

Next morning the sun had already found its way through the frosty window panes before we ventured forth. This is a place that harbours a special feeling that emanates from the burst of sunlight that beams in from the north to brighten up the shadows on a fine frosty morning. It is a feeling that allows one to head off into the freezing outdoors knowing that the sun's rays will thaw out the numbing cold of the shadows. The Pyke Valley harbours that particular light when tramping north from Alabaster through to Wilmot. I once again experienced a profound connection to this inspiring place. Catherine was developing a strong connection with the area too, and we felt a great sense of adventure as we made our way up through the Pyke Valley and out to Big Bay.

Our first task was to walk north to the end of the airstrip, clamber through the ice-coated toetoe grass and wade across the river. This was a shallower but log-infested crossing, so we once again linked together for safety as we made our way to the north bank. This diversion, involving twin river crossings, was well worth taking since we had avoided the notorious 'Black Swamp' — a pathway that involved 600 metres of leaping from one grassy clump to the next, immersed in a field of sticky black mud that was thigh- to waist-deep. Having avoided this ordeal we found our way back to the overgrown Pyke Track and headed on towards the Olivine.

Cattle were once grazed through this country, and were mustered from the Kaipo through Martins and Big Bay then run down the Pyke Valley to the road end. This has left a track etched in the ground, although it is mainly overgrown above ground level, and Catherine and Cathy were finding the toetoes and flaxes a bit thick at times. We managed to stay on track most of the way to the DoC hut, which is situated in a beautiful glade of beech forest at the mouth of the Olivine. Here the Pyke's rushing waters lap beside sandy banks, meandering across the vast valley floor. The track often cuts out loops of the river, setting off through the podocarp forest, then once again following the grassy river banks where washouts have reclaimed much of the original track. I remained alert, since windfalls also added to the general confusion, and the need to read the way ahead.

The only noise here was from the meeting of the two streams. We were miles from anywhere, immersed in a vast wilderness. The remote hut welcomed us as we cranked up the wood stove to ward off the damp and chill of the night air.

At daylight the dawn chorus echoed throughout the valley as we set off. The tui and bellbirds were almost deafening. We had a big day ahead of us to reach Big Bay; otherwise we would need to camp in an old freezer, the remains of Dobbie's venison-hunting bivvy.

The elfin glades of beech forest opened to shingle scree as we neared the Barrier River. I showed the women Davy Gunn's old hut, now half buried in sand, stones and mud as the stream sought to reclaim an old river flat.

We scrambled around the rocky shores and bluffs along the eastern edge of Lake Wilmot, and then set a steady pace through the flax and toetoe on the valley floor alongside the Pyke River. Trout darted across deep pools and back eddies. The brilliant sunlight burnt off the frost and penetrated the emerald-blue waters, though many a side puddle was still caked in layers of ice that gave way underfoot. The weather was holding up well, with only faint wisps of cloud slowly drifting from the southeast.

Once above the overgrown Pyke airstrip we headed for Paulin's Creek where we met the track that led for two or three hours out to Big Bay. Nightfall was descending as we reached the bay. We forded the Awarua River and quickly found the trampers' hut nestled in behind the sand dunes.

Cathy had visited us at Dale's hut the year before, so we decided to make a detour there for a couple of nights and enjoy a rest day. We then tramped up the coast past Crayfish Rock, Awarua Point and up to Ryan's Creek, to camp the night in my bivvy there. An open fire beneath the brilliant night sky was a highlight of the journey. Moonlight sparkled off the gentle ocean waves, while we warmed our backs at the fire.

After eight days of fording rivers, bush-bashing and boulder-hopping we finally reached my humble home, a haven from the storm. We settled in for a few days.

Catherine had been working in the field of auto-immunity research at the Dunedin Medical School at this time, but she was about to leave for Europe and the US for a year or two with her sister, Alison. I enjoyed her company and we were compatible in many ways, but it was up to her to decide whether she would want to return. I knew it would require a unique person to actually live here for the long haul.

chapter 15 a family visit

S ince settling at Gorge River I had not returned to Australia, and neither had my parents visited me, so it was a significant occasion when I met them at Haast in October 1984. They had travelled by car from Auckland, with Uncle Jack and Aunty Doreen, and I had walked up from Big Bay where I had been helping Mitch set up his whitebait stands. I had made contact with them by talking to Graham Scobie in Wyndham via Mitch's single sideband radio transmitter, and Graham had spoken by telephone to Dad in Auckland.

Over five years had drifted by since I had seen my parents, so it was a rather emotional gathering at Des and Jackie Nolan's motels at Okuru, where I finally tracked them down. The first thing they noticed was that I had grown two inches.

I was especially glad to see Jack and Doreen since they have always been my mentors, and having them there was great for the family dynamics. Luckily Jackie and I had caught a couple of kilograms of whitebait on the river nearby, so before too long all the family were sampling the mouth-watering patties made from this local delicacy. We also managed to buy some fresh crayfish off George McInroe, with Geoff Robson's help on the radio transmitter down at Neils Beach, and later we visited the wharf at Jackson Bay.

We spent a wonderful day driving up the Jackson River, the nearby Monkey Puzzle Gorge and into the Cascade Valley for a picnic at the old Martyr Homestead, where we cranked up the fire and boiled the billy for a welcome cup of tea. After staying in Haast for a couple more days we travelled across the Haast Pass together and stayed a number of nights in Wanaka, Queenstown and Te Anau. Uncle Jack then drove us all the way to Milford Sound, where I managed to pick up a ride with Dave Mackie, the skipper of the *South Seas*, who was about to steam up to Big Bay to work his crayfishing gear.

It had been an enjoyable week, and I was sad to see my parents leave. They appeared much more accepting of my lifestyle, maybe realising that time moves on and you have to adapt or be left behind. Deep down their views probably hadn't changed, but it was better to settle our differences and enable our family dynamics to move forward in a positive way.

Later, in May 1988, I flew to Brisbane and stayed for six weeks with Mum and Dad at their Mooloolaba home on the Sunshine Coast. Now that I am a parent myself I realise how hard it must have been to see me drop out of medical school and literally head for the bush, for many years having little or no contact with them. But I needed this time to establish myself and gain new momentum, which was usually disrupted by their challenges to my new lifestyle. Despite the longing to share my parents' company I needed time away so they would take me seriously and realise that my destiny was sealed. But it is not until we are parents that we become aware of the hardships and sacrifices our own parents made for us, the joys, expectations and disappointments they bear on our behalf, along with the deep sorrow when a child has departed for a new life. Even though we wish them well, we long for their company. All the young person sees is the world and the opportunities that lie ahead. They don't look back to gauge their parents' longing and sorrow.

In late 1989 my sister Annette also visited, staying with me at Gorge River and meeting many of my friends. She was amazed by the beauty of the place, and it was great to catch up with her since we had always enjoyed a lot of fun together during our childhood. People had often mistaken us for twins.

Two years after our tramp through the Pyke, Catherine and I met up again in Queenstown. It was now July 1989. She and her sister, Alison, had boated down to Gorge River in February with Lou Brown but I had been away. Catherine had left a phone number, and a note asking me to contact her again.

We headed up Lake Wakatipu and tramped through the Greenstone Valley, which was a winter world covered in hoar frost. The following year Catherine began spending more time at the Gorge, sometimes walking in and out by herself, although we usually walked together. During this time she lived in Christchurch for six months, taking courses on carpentry, meditation and naturopathy.

Previously Catherine had studied at the University of Western Australia, gaining an honours degree in immunology. Her grandparents, Robert and Peggy Stewart, had migrated from Scotland to Western Australia during the depression days of the 1930s, looking for a better life for their young family. Robert had been an artist in Scotland and worked as a signwriter in Australia. Catherine's father Ian is a diesel mechanic, and worked in the iron ore mines in Goldsworthy and Geraldton in Western Australia.

Her great-great-grandfather on her mother's side, Herbert

Allen Giles, was a British diplomat in China, compiled the first Chinese–English dictionary (using the Wade-Giles system of transliteration), and became the second professor of Chinese Studies at Cambridge University after Sir Thomas Wade. Catherine's great-grandfather, her grandmother, and her mother, Rosamond Stewart, were all born in China during their family's service in the British Diplomatic Corp from 1869 through to 1949, when the Communists formed a government.

I think Catherine has inherited her determination and perseverance from her Stewart Scottish ancestry, and her academic side from her mother's family.

During this time, as well as my usual activities I was busy studying for my fourth-year naturopathy exams. To me, naturopathy is a way of life rather than just an ambulance waiting at the bottom of the cliff. Moderation is the key to health and happiness; our mind and body tell us when enough is enough. A basis for health and well-being is growing your own vegetable garden. This will provide you with the freshest food available to nourish and heal your body, along with exercise and a connection with the earth to soothe your soul and spirit.

I did most of my study for the naturopathy course at home, but attended classes for two weeks each year at the college at Himatangi Beach. During the fourth year students attended the college twice. The course fees and college expenses amounted to about $7000 for the four years, plus travelling expenses. Usually, my monetary needs were very minimal, but this commitment brought out a reluctant drive to come up with the goods. By fishing with my neighbours north and south of me, I managed to save this much in two and a half months.

My earlier medical studies were very helpful since we covered detailed anatomy, biochemistry and physiology along with natural healing modalities such as massage, herbal remedies, nutrition, homeopathy and iridology, to name a few. We were trained in naturopathy as a form of complementary healing, alongside conventional medical therapy.

By 1990, I had completed my thesis on 'The Healing Power of the Wilderness', and in August Catherine typed this up. It was 180 pages long, and Catherine's friends Robyn and Graeme Kennerly generously invited us to stay with them in Christchurch so she could use their word processor.

Earlier that year, in January, my mother had visited again, meeting Catherine for the first time. We met her in Christchurch, and after staying the night with Robyn and Graeme we caught the train through Arthur's Pass to Greymouth, then a bus to Haast. With a little encouragement and a few dollars for petrol, Roger Ramjet, alias Batman, drove us down from Haast in his Chevvy pickup, all the way across the Arawhata, up the Jackson, and into the Martyr Homestead. Mum rode in the cab with Batman while Catherine and I enjoyed a breezy ride in the back watching the podocarp forest cruise by beneath a clear blue summer sky. After a stop for a chat and a cup of tea at Maurice Nolan's hut we headed off down the muddy, puddly track towards the Cascade River ford. Much of the way was shingly, as we passed through the grasslands lining the banks of the mighty Cascade. A cleaner, clearer river would be hard to find, coming as it does off glaciers and snow-capped mountains into a pristine West Coast valley wilderness.

Mum was 62 years old at the time, and had kept in good shape playing tennis, swimming and walking on her local beach. Catherine and I carried most of the heavy gear, enabling Mum to concentrate on her footing and enjoy the landscape. Flocks of paradise shelducks launched into flight as we tramped across the tawny brown terrace above the wide, even-flowing waters. Occasionally the river would converge and plunge quickly down into a rapid then come hard up against the following bank, cutting and eroding it before mellowing out to a more even flow. Luckily the West Coast rains had eased for four or five days, so we were hopeful the crossing would be reasonable. Even so, I was continually studying the river flows and shingle bars, judging the depths and distances and mentally preparing for the upcoming challenge.

Eventually the ford lay before us, looking to be about thigh-deep. The idea is to stay well above the spillway of the ford, where the current picks up dramatically, but not too far up where the waters are slower but deeper. We picked our line, with me upstream holding Mum in the middle, and Catherine downstream of her. The waters were cool and clear to the shingly bottom. We crossed at a steady pace, ensuring we kept our legs and feet moving reasonably quickly to maintain our momentum and balance, and leaning slightly upstream to counteract the current. Before we knew it, we were once again leaving the shallows and the southern beach was won.

After stopping briefly to reorganise our gear we headed off towards Cascade Hut, one of Maurice Nolan's musterers' huts. The evening light began to glow in the western skies and the northerly flow of clouds already loomed across the top edge of the Cascade Plateau, auguring the arrival of more rain. Hogsbacks streamed high above the mountain ranges as the corrugated-iron hut came into welcome view. Jumping from sedge grass clump to clump, we crossed the last swampy

200 metres to the hut.

The open fire burst into life with a hiss and a roar as the first heavy droplets of rain pelted down on the tin roof and found their way down the corrugated-iron chimney. Flickering flames lit up the classic rimu tongue-and-groove lining of the old hut. For more than a century the pioneering Nolan family had made a living from breeding cattle across the flats and clearings of this valley. The heavy cast-iron camp ovens and pots were still in constant use, despite being from a bygone era.

Once the comforting fire was established we raised the kettle above the flames, looking forward to a hot cup of tea, a meal and a cosy night's sleep. Overnight the drenching rains eased off to a drizzle. There was no need for us to hurry off since the creeks and streams would need time to subside before our tramp on to Barn Bay. At least there were no rivers to negotiate along this section of the journey.

Mum's father had been stationed in various country towns during his time in the police force, so she was used to rural life and always enjoyed a bit of adventure. So a few muddy puddles and slightly swollen creeks weren't daunting enough to hold us up. She was happy to rely on my judgement as we walked in the drizzle through the moss-covered beech and podocarp forest, all the way to Lou and Elizabeth Brown's house at Barn Bay. The Hope River was still flooded and would require a day or two to subside before we headed down the coast to the Gorge. A rest day would be good, and would prepare Mum for the coastal walk.

So the following day we had a picnic and explored the sand dunes, and while I went fishing for blue-striped wrasse to eat Mum and Catherine made a batch of my favourite peanut brownies. Lou, Liz and their family arrived back at the house that afternoon, via the Cascade, and the next morning, after a breakfast of Lou's famous sourdough pancakes, Mum and I packed up our gear and headed off towards Gorge River. Catherine, meanwhile, was heading out to the Cascade and back to Christchurch, where we planned to meet in a week or two's time.

Mum and I always got on well and travelled with the same adventurous spirit. She was always interested in my friends, and enjoyed conversing with them and exchanging ideas. She really enjoyed staying at Gorge River, finding it a place where she could really relax, away from all the pretences one usually needs to keep up when living surrounded by people. During the 10 days she stayed there a number of friends dropped in; Dave Saxton landed in his Hughes 300 helicopter accompanied by Martin Abel, a DoC ranger from Haast, and Lou Brown and his crew, Victor, stayed three nights while they worked the crayfishing gear between Barn Bay and the Gorge. Mum enjoyed dining on freshly boiled spiny rock lobster each day.

When it was time to leave we decided to travel back up to Barn Bay by boat with Lou and Victor. Mum loved being out at sea, so we enjoyed a great day while Lou and Victor whipped through the gear. Lou planned to take us up to Jackson Bay the following day since the weather was looking favourable. That morning we spied the *Striker* out off the Sugarloaf Needle at the northern end of Barn Bay, so we radioed up her skipper Brian McKerr, alias Spacey. He was heading south to Big Bay, so we arranged a rendezvous with him out off Barn Islets, and headed back south again. The sea was a beautiful blue-green and the skies a clear blue with the odd fluffy cloud bank as Spacey skippered us past the Gorge Islets and our home, nestled among the trees below the steep hillsides and bluffs. Spacey had radioed through to Swag, on the *Chinook*, who had spotted Dale Hunter out working his pots. He asked Dale to pick us up off Lone Rock, near Ryan's Creek, about eight kilometres south of the Gorge.

The second rendezvous of the day went successfully as the *Striker* slowly pulled up alongside Dale's Shark Cat, the *Sika*. After thanking Spacey for his generosity, Mum and I carefully disembarked and boarded our new sea taxi, bound for Big Bay. We were greeted by the smiling faces of Leigh Joyce and Henrietta, a visitor from Holland, who were also out fishing with Dale. Luckily Dale had just completed his craypots, so he quickly brought the boat up to a plane of 40 knots. Our hair streamed back in the breeze as we steamed around Awarua Point and Big Bay opened to view in all its majesty.

Over the next few days Dale played a fine host and looked after Mum and me well. He and Henrietta worked the craypots while Leigh, Mum and I kept the open fire burning, cooking biscuits and camp-oven bread.

One afternoon Peter Meisch, skipper of the *Kaiawhina Moana*, and Jeff Buckley, skipper of *Solitaire*, came ashore to soak up a couple of homebrews and meet Mum. Peter and Jeff were working out of Milford Sound, and Peter kindly offered to take Leigh, Mum and me there the next day. Leigh worked as a track guide at Milford, and needed to get back there.

So on Sunday 4 February we once again headed out to sea. Dale rowed us out to the *Kaiawhina Moana* and we headed out around Long Reef and past Martins Bay, lifting craypots as we went. As we reached the mouth of Milford Sound the mountains rose up out of the sea, disappearing into the high cloud overhead. Some of the solid rock faces climbed vertically and appeared to overhang us. Before too long we pulled into the fishermen's wharf at Deep Water Basin, surrounded by bush-clad cliffs. Far distant mountains disappeared into a bluish-purple mist far up the Arthur and Cleddau Valleys.

We farewelled Peter and his crew, and a couple of days later Mum and I caught the Intercity bus to Te Anau, then on to Queenstown and Christchurch, where we met up with Catherine again. Mum flew back to Brisbane and home to Mooloolaba. We had had a great adventure, and Mum had gained an insight into my life on the Coast, and met many of my friends. These are memories I cherish.

chapter 16 walking the coast to milford

When you explore upriver while watching the rapids bustle and chirp, or travel along the coast and ridges, there is an indescribable energy. You feel a pitch, a fever of electric vitality, on a southwesterly day when the sea breeze is dominant. The rapids whistle and turn while the skies become bluer, clearer and the clouds disperse. There is a sense of euphoria as this energy enhances your spirit, as you drink in the sheer delight of a domain so clear, clean and wild. It becomes, of its own accord, a total entity complete in its balance, the forces giving and taking, lifting and sinking, pulling at your clothes and hair, as your body traverses the terrain.

On these days my spirit travels back, remembering other journeys taken years ago when the energies seemed even stronger. Perhaps my connection with these elements was more complete, my naïveté a characteristic of my personality and soul. I now envy the spirit once possessed by a being so intent on connecting with all this and little else. Barefoot on boulders, the cool emerald waters, the mossy dampness underfoot.

During their peak these days seem invincible. They are charged and defiant with infinite energy, until the shadows lengthen and I yearn once again for the shelter of hut, tent fly or bivvy bag to ward off the inevitable cold of the night. Then to wake and gaze out upon the distant whitecaps on the ocean, heralding another day of heightened energy. The sense of belonging and being alive is a delight.

Such was the feeling the day I set out down the coast for Milford Sound in early March 1985. The southwest sea breeze was on the rise as I set off down the airstrip and onward to the coastal boulders on this memorable day. The shadows were drifting off the coastal bush ridges and faces as my feet and legs propelled me from one rounded boulder to the next. The tide was abating, perfect for negotiating the full range of rocky options along the coastal way. The hazy horizon was beginning to clear as the wind began lifting the tops of wave crests far out to sea, presaging that a strong headwind would develop by early afternoon. But an invigorating one at that, no need to slow down, just a breeze to lean into as each boulder was won.

As I negotiated the irregular sandstone boulders around Longridge Point, the salt air and sea spray moistened the intense sunlight beaming towards the lingering shadows beneath the haphazard bluffs. The clarity of the day was increasing as Awarua Point grew on the distant southerly horizon. My intention was to reach the Martins Bay hut at the mouth of the Hollyford River, so I loped steadily along the sandy beaches to the Hacket and took up boulder-hopping again on my way out to Awarua Point.

What a magnificent day. The view from here never ceases to amaze me. The white-capped ocean waves lunge their way into the biggest bay of New Zealand's western coastline,

Big Bay alive in all its glory, with a backdrop of distant blue mountains. I gazed across the bay at Long Reef, the south heads eight kilometres away as the crow flies but 24 kilometres around the foreshore of the bay. The Fiordland coastline lay south of here. Martins Bay, the Kaipo and Milford Sound were visible as the vista stretched all the way to Sutherland Sound in the far distance. Mt Madeline and Tutoko, the highest Fiordland peaks, topped off the view.

With renewed vigour and enthusiasm I headed around the large boulders towards Crayfish Rock then on into Three Mile Beach, the fastest section of this coastline. Next I tramped around Penguin Rock and on to Martins Bay. This hut is perched overlooking the Hollyford River bar, with podocarp forest behind, and boulder-strewn river bank in front. The first reach of the lower Hollyford extends south from here just inside the sandy river bar.

Next morning the outgoing tide enabled me to walk quickly south along this reach to the private huts just south of Jerusalem Creek. No one was home so I left a note and borrowed a dinghy. I rowed across to the south bank and left the boat near the mouth of the McKenzie Lagoon. From here I set off out across the sandy river bar and headed down to the Kaipo River mouth. Along this beautiful stretch of coastline large limestone pinnacles rise up out of the sandy, bouldery beach. They are bedecked by heavy fronds of bull kelp that surge and sway with the passing of each wave.

As I reached the south end of Kaipo Bay the terrain began to alter and the going became tough. But I was carrying words of encouragement from Nelson Thompson and Dane Paul, who had recently called in to visit me at Gorge River in their helicopter. Despite the fact that the South Island *Moir's Guide* advised trampers not to negotiate this section of coastline except in case of emergency, Nelson and Dane had a rough idea of my capabilities and declared that I should make it. I had previously studied the lay of the land by boat and from the air, and considered it worth having a go.

Anyway, I was met by steep bluffs as I worked my way around the south heads of the Kaipo towards Ruby Beach. There were a few tight spots but none dangerous enough to make me turn back. The limestone rock was a little bit soft in places but generally provided good footing. With four possible contacts, two feet and two hands, I try to insist on having at least three firm contacts before shifting one onto the next new connection. I then ensure that is a firm contact before my next move.

My adrenalin was pumping as the smooth boulders of Ruby Beach lay ahead of me. The outgoing tide stirred me onwards since this increased my chances of access around the bigger bluffs up ahead. A smooth, lazy roll of about a metre surged up the beach from time to time, but generally the deep blue sea looked inviting as the sun streamed down and sweat lay upon my brow.

After an enjoyable boulder-hop, the headland at the south end began to loom closer. I began boulder-hopping beneath the rocky bluffs. Occasionally I waded through pools and crevasses, dodging the odd waves amongst the bull kelp and seaweeds. After a kilometre of climbing past colonies of paua I came back out onto a bouldery beach which quickly ended in a sheer wall of rock dropping into the sea. I headed into the windswept scrub at the end of the beach and began scrambling up through the stunted koromiko, mahoe and flaxes growing in a steep gut. Eventually I crawled on all fours or stomach up under intense thickets of kiekie, all the time gaining altitude but slowly working my way south around the back of the headland, until eventually I scrambled over a rise leading into a creek bed dropping through the bush onto the next beach.

Good to be back out in the daylight again, even though the next headland looked worse. The height of the next hill scramble looked like a major. The gnarly, windswept headland rose up as far as the eye could see with no end in sight. The beach quickly petered out as the boulders disappeared and I began scrambling around rocky limestone outcrops and ledges. I inched my way around the water's edge, coming to small, secluded coves beneath the steep, looming cliffs, my bare feet gaining good traction on the small crustaceans layering the smooth, water-polished cobbles and boulders. I often waited for waves to surge and retreat before heading onwards, ducking across narrow guts through waist- or chest-deep water, swimming amongst the seaweeds, climbing through the bull kelp and back up to higher ledges as larger waves moved back shorewards again.

Now it was time to rearrange my gear. I had arrived at a point where ahead lay a deep seawater gut extending up into a sea cave that went way up inside the cliff. Perching on a ledge of rock I stripped off my nearly dry clothes and wrapped them tightly inside my oilskin sleeping bag cover along with my down sleeping-bag and other dry gear. I donned my oilskin coat and overtrousers and tightly tied a gooseneck around the top of my pack, sealing it off. I had recently oiled and waxed the canvas to prevent seepage.

The gut was about 10 metres across to another rocky ledge. Waves were surging in from the oily-surfaced ocean, up the channel and into the sea cave. Every now and again a lull would appear and the swim across the deep blue trench appeared negotiable. I waited here for a rest knowing that timing would be essential. Then away I went, scrambling off the rocky ledge with my pack on my back, and began swimming breaststroke as quickly as I could across the gap.

As I began to climb back up out of the sea towards my destination my overtrousers came loose and began to slip off. As I fought to retain them, the next large surge caught me, wiped me off the rock and tossed me up into the sea cave like a piece of flotsam. I was sucked back out to sea past the point where I had just swum the gap. Then back up into the sea cave again. Then out again. This went on for about seven waves. During this time I had absolutely no control over my fate, being at the mercy of the surges. Eventually I managed to hold fast to my target as a wave tossed me up high enough, and then there was a lull.

As I rested up and gained my breath and composure once again, I surveyed the next stage of my journey. There was total bluff, sea cave and no end in sight around the corner. The surprising thing was that even though I had just been at the mercy of the sea for a number of waves, I never actually struck rock. I just seemed to zip past everything as I relaxed and went with it, until the opportunity for action arrived once again.

So this was my best option. After waiting for a lull, I scrambled back off the limestone outcrop into the blue-green sea, swimming as fast as I could and staying about 10 metres from the bluff's face. When I had swum about 20 metres a large breaking wave lifted me up towards the rocky, seaweed-covered cliff, where I swirled and spiralled around, but without any actual hard contact. As the wave struck me I had totally relaxed and succumbed to its power and intensity. Succeeding waves carried me in a similar direction and pathway until a lull arrived. I then swam quickly south until I was taken over by the power of the next large surges swirling me up and twisting me around again. Each time the large waves abated I kept heading south, swimming breaststroke. Luckily, my sealed-off pack remained firmly strapped on my shoulders and provided me with buoyancy, so I continued to ride high in the seawater.

This went on for quite a while, perhaps 10 minutes or more, until eventually I could see a boulder beach around the corner. Before too much longer I washed up into waist-deep water and crawled out through the seaweed into the sunlight.

To journey onwards was my quest.

After I had dried out and changed back into my clothes, the sand and boulders drew me southwards once again. Luckily the hot afternoon sun was still beating down, and it warmed up my bones as I quickly lengthened my stride. The secluded beaches were pretty much untouched by man, paradises between headlands and bluffs, with plenty of sand and driftwood, and backdrops of hills rising steeply up to 600 metres. Not far inland, the foothills rose to rocky turreted mountains three or four times that height.

After an easy kilometre of progress another headland and sea cliff stood before me. There was a slip heading up behind the headland so, without further thought, I set about climbing, clinging to toetoe and mahoe regrowth on the steeper sections. Eventually the slip petered out and above its lip I crawled into another three-metre-deep tangle of kiekie. The only way forward was at ground level on all fours and stomach, dragging my pack along behind me as I gained altitude.

After I had reached about 150 metres above the picturesque coastline I could see the sun was quickly dropping towards the horizon. The oily blue sea reflected the golden rays upwards to the crest where I stood in awe but with no time to linger. I once again found myself dropping down into a creek bed that I hoped would lead out to the next beach.

My confidence was building since the way was now easy going. I could already see the sandy beach ahead, far below. But then, with just 30 metres of altitude to go, the creek bed dropped away and its waters became a torrent that tumbled over a sheer rocky face and disappeared out of view.

I was bluffed. After studying the steep rocky face of the creek bed that rose to the south I could see a chance to climb up and along above the bluffs. The further I traversed, the higher I became, to stay above the cliff face below me. The sun was beginning to set. No Man's Beach lay below me, inviting with its golden sand. Massive rata gave me secure footing and handholds, but I had been forced back up to about 150 metres again, and had scrambled about 500 metres south of the creek bed with no end to the bluffs in sight.

Just as I was about to give up on reaching the beach and set up camp in a rata tree for the night, a steep gut opened out in front of me. I quickly descended, to find myself safely on No Man's Beach just as twilight set in.

What a relief, what a day. I was totally drenched in sweat, but still buzzing with adrenalin and excitement. The surrounding abundance of dry driftwood soon provided me with a warm, blazing fire above which I set up a frame of wooden sticks. I stripped off most of my sodden clothes and lay them over the frame, then set a billy boiling for my first feed since a quick breakfast many hours before. This was one of the best campsites I had ever come across. It was many hours before I could wind down. The calm, clear night was lit up by the stars and moon shining brilliantly above. Glowing embers warmed my spirit as the lazy ocean swells eventually lulled me to sleep.

After an early start the next morning, I was soon scrambling up and over the next headland without too much difficulty, dropping into a small creek that led out to the northern end of Madagascar Beach. Ahead of me stretched sand and boulders all the way to Yates Point six kilometres further on. I breathed a sigh of relief and set to a steady boulder-hop, remembering comments that the worst of the journey to the mouth of Milford Sound was between the Kaipo and Madagascar Beach. The late summer sun beat down. The day had dawned crisp and clear so as the morning wore on the sand and boulders underfoot began to heat up. A lazy roll continued to surge in off the ocean and a beautiful day lay ahead.

After fording Wolf River I noticed a fishing boat offshore. By the time I reached Musket Bay, just north of Yates, the boat lay about 100 metres away, just out past the breakers. The crew were waving at me, and motioning me to come out. So after waving back, I motioned to them in sign language that I would swim out. I stripped off my gear down to shorts and donned my oilskin coat and overtrousers as I had the day before. After stowing my gear carefully in my pack I began swimming out through the breakers. I again swam breaststroke style, keeping my chin just above the water with my hands and arms reaching out forward just beneath the surface. The pack helped to provide buoyancy as I gradually made my way out, bracing for each wave as it came through.

With a sense of achievement, I finally arrived beside the boat where the skipper, Dave Edmonds, and his son Tony quickly hauled me aboard.

'Dale said you were coming down this way,' they exclaimed, smiling. 'So we've been looking out for you.'

'Great,' I replied, relieved. 'Thanks for picking me up.'

They had a few more craypots to work, up towards Martins Bay, then they were heading back to Milford Sound for a Saturday-night bonfire with the hotel staff and other fishermen. Sounded good to me.

Dave had been fishing these waters for many years in his eight-metre jetboat, *Resolution*. As they expertly worked their gear I was able to survey the lay of the land I had travelled the day before. From Martins Bay we motored south to the entrance of Milford Sound, where we were met by the stunning views of the Sound on a clear blue day. The walls of the glacial valley rose up vertically from the sea.

I was exhilarated once again to be heading towards the tiny enclave of humanity that exists near the head of the fiord, and was looking forward to catching up with friends and acquaintances there. That night around the raging bonfire there were staff from the hotel, the boats, and also from the Milford Track. Complementing them were the local Milford fishermen, who are always ready for a party or celebration.

In those days the Milford Track guides could invite one friend or family member each month to visit them along the track and be catered for by the Tourist Hotel Corporation. I had been invited along twice, flying or walking up to the Quentin Hut then over MacKinnon Pass to Mintaro and Pompolona huts. Both times we climbed Mt Hart, looking out over Lake Quill, which is drained by New Zealand's highest waterfall, Sutherland Falls.

This night we partied around the bonfire beside an old macrocarpa, nicknamed the Steinie Tree, until the early hours, warmed by the sense of humanity nestled in such a vast region of incredibly powerful wilderness.

Next morning, as I was catching up with some mountain climbers at the 'White House' on the fishermen's wharf, I heard a chopper land at the airstrip nearby. I jogged over to see a Hughes 500D parked beside the fuel pumps. It was Nelson Thompson's machine. He and Dane were heading back over to the Hollyford, then hunting their way up to the Skippers Range behind Big Bay. They invited me along and offered to drop me home at Gorge River.

Wow, what a buzz. I quickly retrieved my gear, and before you knew it we were hunting our way up through the Darran Mountains, over the Homer Saddle, past Mt Talbot and Christina, scouring the bush and tussock all the way. We hunted Falls, Marian and Moraine Creeks, all hanging valleys that drop dramatically into the Upper Hollyford river valley.

We hauled onto the Hollyford airstrip to load up a batch of jet-fuel jerrycans, then set off north searching for any elusive red deer that happened to be unfortunate enough to be feeding out in the open. We mainly stayed up at tussock level just below the rocky buttresses of the mountains, with the glaciers disappearing upwards into the brilliant blue sky.

Above the Skippers Range we spotted a couple of stags which sent Nelson into a flurry and flutter of whirling blades. We banked and manoeuvred so Dane could secure a series of shots and then we landed briefly while he gutted the two deer, before setting off north again across Big Bay. In a short space of time I was looking down on the Malcolm Ranges leading to my home. After landing safely I thanked Nelson and Dane and bade them farewell, looking forward to a quiet Sunday afternoon before setting off south again to Martins Bay to relocate the dinghy I had borrowed.

This didn't turn out to be as easy as it sounded, since there was a strong southerly screaming up the lake and setting up a sharp wind chop on the Lower Hollyford Reach. After rowing another dinghy across I rowed a long way up the side of the river, towing the second boat, to get above the worst of the wind. Finally I got back across successfully and once more returned home to the quiet of Gorge River.

chapter 17 in a family way

By 1990 Catherine and I had developed a strong relationship, and we decided to become engaged. Catherine's sister, Alison, who lived in Edmonton, Canada, was planning a home birth late that year, and Catherine was keen to go over to assist her. Since our relationship had reached an important stage she offered to pay my airfare so we could both go. I had been looking forward to a quiet summer and felt no strong urge to travel overseas, but how could I turn down this opportunity? The fact that we both decided to go was a form of commitment, which was reflected in our engagement.

Our journey to Auckland coincided with my graduation from the New Zealand Naturopathy College, which took place at Himatangi Beach in the Manawatu. Mum and my sister Annette were there as well. The college was run by Melva Martin and Joy Wauchop. Out of the 50 students who had begun the first year of the course, 12 had completed the fourth and final year. I gained the best pass and was awarded a silver tray and cup for best all-round naturopath, along with my diploma.

From Himatangi, Catherine and I hitchhiked up to Auckland. I had raised some cash for the trip by catching whitebait as we had passed through Big Bay, but I needed more for spending money. So when we arrived in Auckland I did some labouring for Catherine's brother, Andrew, who lived with his partner Jenny and their daughter Madeleine out at Bethells Beach.

I also sold a painting for the first time, to Dad. He was always talking about investing money, so I suggested to him on the phone that he could invest in some of my artwork. He agreed, and my mother, who was in Auckland visiting family, surveyed my work and chose a painting. This was the first painting I ever sold. I also sold some jade carvings to friends and family.

Soon we were off to the US. After we hit LA, Catherine flew straight on to Edmonton to be with her sister, while I flew across the Grand Canyon to New York. By the time we neared the Big Apple night had fallen across the city, which was sparkling like a diamond tiara.

After stepping off the airport bus in central New York I began searching for some budget accommodation. Every policeman I approached was too busy chasing crims to answer my pleas. Eventually I spotted the Penthouse backpackers, 40 storeys up. As I gazed out the window of my bunkroom I could see the moving electronic lights of the bulletin board atop Times Square and read the fluid news: 'US declares war on Iraq'. There was a palpable tension in the air.

Despite arriving late, I broke all the rules and went roaming the city streets of Manhattan until the early hours. It was funny how transvestites kept popping up everywhere I went. I spent most of the next day atop the World Trade Center, 110 storeys up, with views of the Hudson River, the

Statue of Liberty, and the busy streets and harbours of Manhattan Island. The sound of police sirens drifted up from the streets below.

Somehow this place seemed to portend something very significant in the history of modern man. The architecture struck me as exceptional as I looked down absolutely vertical walls over a thousand feet to the street below. When I returned to Auckland the buildings there seemed like shacks and shanties compared to these.

That evening I hit the streets again, taking a shortcut towards the Empire State Building. Before I knew it I was in a shady part of town — no lights, just vacant lots, people lingering and following me, propositioning me, trying to sell drugs. So I just kept walking, hands deep in my pockets, and gradually did a U-turn straight out of there and back to my hotel. The pressures of the concrete jungle began to dawn on me. My energy levels were waning after about 30 kilometres of strolling the streets of Manhattan, Wall Street, Greenwich Village and Central Park, and I began to feel vulnerable. Over coffee back at the hotel, half the people I spoke to had stories of personal muggings, robberies and uncomfortable incidents. As I checked out next morning a transvestite appeared at the door to the lift just long enough to survey the area for any unattended baggage.

From New York I flew to Salt Lake City, where I slept in my bivvy bag among the snow drifts at the end of the runway. Luckily Catherine had sewn me a gabardine down jacket with a sheepskin-trimmed hood. I awoke the next day to screaming jet aircraft taking off every three minutes. After leaping out of my sleeping bag I hit the highway and hitched a ride to Reno, a tinsel town in the Nevada desert. The driver handed me a very welcome cup of hot coffee which helped my circulation get back to normal.

In Reno I stayed with my friend 'Mark the Miner', who had worked on a gold claim in the Hope River at Barn Bay in the early '80s. Later his father Dave drove me across Highway 51, 'the loneliest highway in the USA', to visit his niece in Moab in the state of Utah. We drove 1100 kilometres that day, over seven mountain ranges that rose up between desert and salt flats stretching as far as the eye could see, passing through the ghost towns of Eureka and Eli along the winding way. On leaving Moab, I hitchhiked for a few more days, sleeping freezing nights in woods or abandoned sheds surrounded by snow, but I soon tired of the cold and headed back to Salt Lake City. After another night at the end of the runway I caught the first plane to Edmonton to meet up with Catherine again in time to celebrate a white Christmas. Alison's daughter, Elena Piere, was born on 27 December.

While blizzards swept off the arctic wastelands across Alberta and the temperatures dropped to -37°C, our son Christan was conceived in Edmonton, Canada. A new era in our lives had begun.

We spent another month in North America. Alison's husband, Darrell Piere, was an American truck driver who travelled the interstate highways from Texas to Canada. In early January I accompanied him on his next trucking expedition, transporting a single mining drill bit on the back of his long semi-trailer. This 'hotshot' was needed urgently, so it was the quickest trip south Darrell had ever made. We did a round trip of 6400 kilometres, south through Montana, Wyoming, Idaho, Utah, Arizona and Nevada to Los Angeles in California, stopping only for a bite to eat and a few hours' sleep. On the return journey we travelled in convoy with five other trucks, all stopping at the same diners along the way.

Finally, it was time to travel back across the Pacific Ocean to the wilds of South Westland. So, on January 28, Catherine and I flew back to Auckland via Los Angeles and Hawaii and then hitchhiked south to Haast.

When we reached the Hope Hut, a mile short of Barn Bay, I discovered that I had left my passport, money and greenstone carvings back at Bill Barclay's house near Neils Beach. So next morning at daylight I raced back along the forest track, through the mud and puddles, out to the Cascade River and road end, arriving just as a chopper-load of venison was being dropped off on a truck. The truckie drove me out the Cascade–Jackson River road to the Arawhata, and dropped me at Bill's. After picking up my gear I walked back into the Cascade, arriving back at Barn Bay by 8pm, having walked 80 kilometres that day. The sun was still an hour away from setting and I arrived in time to help celebrate Jennifer Brown's eighth birthday, but I had worn out my jandals along the gravel stretches of the Cascade–Jackson River road.

By the time we arrived home to the Gorge, Catherine was six weeks pregnant. We settled back in to tending the overgrown garden and netting fish in the river mouth. We collected firewood, worked on the hut, and I carved greenstone and whalebone. We were both looking forward to raising a family, so as the pregnancy progressed we dealt with the hardships and joys together. Since we intended to have a home birth we had to secure the services of a midwife, and also a place where Catherine could bear our child closer to medical aid. We went out to town a couple of times during her pregnancy, and she had check-ups to ensure the pregnancy was progressing well.

Despite the challenges involved in assimilating another person into my life after being only accountable to myself for so long, I became a more balanced, contented and healthy person thanks to Catherine sharing her life with me. I had known my life would never be complete without a family. I had prayed and hoped that dream would come true, that my soulmate would arrive one day, and in due course our children would grow fine and strong.

In that dream, I always saw our children walking along the beach for mile upon endless mile to reach town, as a family travelling together through the vast untamed wilderness, not by vehicle, but on foot. What individuals these children would grow up to be, what sheer determination and survival skills they would develop. Surely they would be an asset to all of us in today's world.

Now that our expenses were due to climb I poured more energy into producing my carvings and paintings, since these were beginning to sell. I still had work lined up fishing with Dale, but my artwork was a practical way to supplement our income when there was downtime from fishing. I sold most of my work to interested people as I travelled along the way, but occasionally I would be invited by friends or acquaintances to display my jade and bone carvings in their shops to sell on commission.

One day in March Lou Brown arrived down at Gorge River out of the blue, coming in off the ocean in his jet-boat. He carried sad news. My youngest sister, Vivienne, was critically ill with cancer. Dad had asked me to come home.

So Catherine and I returned with Lou to Barn Bay, caught a ride to Jackson Bay with Spacey, then hitchhiked up to Christchurch. Catherine stayed there while I flew to Brisbane to see Viv.

Vivienne had had a successful career as a nurse, and before she began raising her children she had been the matron of a convalescent home. I had last seen her two years before, and had stayed with Viv and her husband Guy Waterman at their home in Brisbane. Viv and I were very close, and Guy had been a friend of mine for many years.

Viv was still hopeful of a recovery, and we all prayed for her and helped her in any way we could. But in July, three months after we had returned to South Westland, Vivienne died, aged just 33, leaving behind three young boys all under the age of five. We received the news of Vivienne's passing by radio while fishing with Dale at Big Bay.

By now Catherine was seven months pregnant. She had undertaken the arduous journey down from Gorge River to Big Bay, where I was going to work a stint of winter crayfishing with Dale before we headed out for a home birth at Sue and Ian Todd's farm near Arrowtown. The baby was due in late September.

On 9 September, after six weeks of fishing, Dale took Catherine and me in his boat around to Martins Bay, across the Hollyford Bar, then up the river to Neil Drysdale's hut. Russell Baker of Fiordland Air then generously flew us out to the Upper Hollyford airstrip, after tightly circling between the mountains above Gunn's Camp. By the time the Cessna 185 landed and taxied up the airstrip, Murray Gunn was waiting with his van to drive us up to the camp. Over a welcome brew of tea and chocolate biscuits, Murray bought $800 worth of tangiwai pendants off me. These were eight fish-shaped carvings, which had been hand-carved on sandstone with water and the holes drilled with sharpened flint.

Later that morning Murray drove us up to Cascade Creek Lodge on the Milford Road, where he had the managers, Owen and Doreen Payne, in a panic by stating that Catherine was already having contractions and going into labour. By the afternoon we had a ride to Te Anau, where we stayed the night with Gordon and Debbie Kane, and from there we hitched a ride to Queenstown then on to Sue and Ian Todd's farm near Arrowtown. Sue, Ian and their children, Willy and Casey, were heading off to Big Bay for their annual whitebaiting holiday, so Ian left me a list of chores to do while they were away. There were lawns to mow, chooks and cats to feed, trees and deer to water, along with gardening and landscaping to keep me busy and help pay the rent.

We had arranged for Denise Black, from Alexandra, to be Catherine's midwife. They had met once before, at Denise's home, and now she was touching base with Catherine in readiness for the birth. Then before too long, and much to our delight, Christan Robert Long was born on 26 September 1991 in the upstairs bedroom of Eagle Rock Farm. From that moment on all our priorities changed. I felt I had entered a time warp. We have never ceased working, and loving every moment with a passion.

Anne Mitchell, in transit from Big Bay, was our first visitor, and took the first photograph of Christan with his full head of dark brown hair. Alan, Dot and Lynn Hamilton were next, with Lynn taking black-and-white portraits of all three of us.

After Sue and Ian arrived home from Big Bay, I became a stonemason's apprentice, keeping Ian and his partner Ray supplied with building stone. This involved breaking up 25 tons of schist with a sledgehammer, stone chisel and mallet, as well as mixing mortar for a two-storeyed building project across the valley from Toddy's home.

After a few weeks Catherine and I had our sights set for home. So on 25 October, after loading up the Cessna 180, Roger Monk flew us from his Arrowtown airstrip up the Shotover River, across the Southern Alps and back out to the

West Coast, landing us on the Gorge River airstrip right outside our door.

Once Christan had arrived we focused all our energies on supporting him as best we could. Catherine became a 24/7 mother, never relinquishing her role to anybody else or letting any other pastime encroach on this role. I worked on honing my carving and painting skills to help pay our way in the world. Life became a constant learning curve. With an extra mouth to feed we extended our vegetable garden, and devoted more time to collecting seaweed when large drifts piled up on the beach. I also set about renovating the hut, making it more weathertight and letting more sunlight in to warm and brighten up the living space. I had already begun clearing the airstrip, knowing that we would need to fly Catherine and Christan home. It was also important to make the airstrip safer for future use.

Catherine's main priority, apart from feeding Christan, was to get his dozen or so nappies washed and dried each day. During rainy spells we relied on the old copper hot-water cylinder that fed off the wood stove to get them dried out each day.

There was a period when one episode after another brought me to a gradual realisation of how our future travels and adventures would have to be undertaken. For many years now I had roamed this territory at will, summer, winter, rain, hail or shine, during calm or storm, flood or tempest. Naturally I usually chose the better times to travel, but it was not unusual for me to push the limits of my endurance when fronting up to the natural barriers that had been bestowed on this wild country.

In the case of large rivers and rocky coastlines, the potential dangers were usually overcome by care, consideration and application of sheer physical, mental and spiritual energy. Sometimes this involved being immersed, one with the elements, for short sustained bursts, and at other times for prolonged periods of time. Fishermen would often retrieve me or drop me off on rocks out at sea, leaving me to swim ashore through the breakers. I used to ford the Cascade River when it was over my head and in half flood, or swim around sea cliffs and sea caves. I had not considered that with a whole new set of conditions and responsibilities my future approach would be altered for good.

After Christan was born we still had the same paths to travel, the same ocean to negotiate; our journey to town crossed similar terrain and obstacles. But there was now a major and profound difference. We had the responsibility of maintaining the life, safety and well-being of another human being, one who was totally helpless, couldn't walk or swim. Catherine and I were at his beck and call. He became our sole responsibility. His livelihood became paramount.

But it took a series of events to bring home the extent of the changes we needed to make in our thinking and planning. In hindsight, these events often pushed us into states of shock when we reconsidered the dangers and possible repercussions of episodes that we had, luckily, successfully undertaken.

I remember one time in particular when Catherine, Christan and I were heading out from Barn Bay, walking to the Cascade River and Martyr Homestead. There had been recent rain and the streams were still running reasonably high. As we travelled along the muddy, soggy track we focused upon the fact that there was a canoe on the south side of the Cascade. So we had the option of using this, since fording the river would have been out of the question. As we tramped the showers of rain continued to fall and the southwesterly squalls persisted.

On arriving at the Cascade we realised that it was to be a marginal crossing. As usual I had prayed to my guardian angel for most of the journey, psyching myself up for the crossing. By the time we launched the small canoe we had about 3–4 centimetres of freeboard. Christan was travelling in a canvas pack on my back, with Catherine sitting in front of me. I focused all my concentration on the crossing, not looking at the log jam downstream but keeping my eyes locked on a pathway just upstream of where we would actually be going. This naturally provides a stronger sense of balance. The river was a powerful entity but we never faltered, and the canoe arrived safely at the northern bank.

It was not until that evening when we were sitting beside a warm fire, describing the journey to our friends Johnnie Hewer and Claire Easterbrook at their house in Neils Beach, that the shock hit me. I suddenly realised that if even the slightest mistake had been made we would have ended up in an uncontrollable situation that could have wrecked our lives forever.

During that first year of Christan's life I experienced a number of similar incidents, which eventually led to higher levels of responsibility and caution. You can never predict what lies around the corner, and that is as true today as it was all those years ago.

Catherine and I considered ourselves to be well and truly married once Christan was born. Organising a wedding seemed a daunting and expensive project, since we were now flat out supporting our newly arrived son. But we had become engaged before Christan became a reality, so in conversations with my father the question that always arose was: 'When is the wedding?'

Mum had come over to visit Christan soon after his birth, but whenever we asked Dad when he would come over to see his grandson, he would reply, 'When is the wedding?'

So eventually we set a date and invited our friends and family, including Dad. At the same time, I told him: 'This wedding is all very well, but I am about to become financially deficient.' This inspired him to send me a large donation which, along with all the beautiful and generous gifts we received from our friends and family, actually brought us way out ahead.

On a previous journey up the coast we had contacted Father Foote, the Catholic priest stationed at Whataroa, and asked him to be our marriage celebrant. We have both always felt a connection with the divine nature of existence, so we wanted a celebrant who would enrich our marriage with that spiritual connection. Before the wedding Father Foote actually made the effort to come and visit us at our home at Gorge River. Maurice Nolan took him by sea from Jackson Bay to Barn Bay in his river jetboat, and after spending the night with Lou and Liz Brown he bravely walked the 20 kilometres down the coast to see us and discuss our intentions regarding our marriage. He also celebrated Mass on our living-room table.

The following day as he headed north again, Father Foote gave us a blessing at the Steeples, two large limestone pinnacles about two kilometres from our home, which resemble a cathedral.

Sunday, 1 November 1992 was our chosen day. About 250 friends and family members from near and far converged on Whiskey Corner, overlooking the Cascade Valley. From then on Bruce Buchanan, a whitebaiter at the Cascade River mouth, called this area The Altar.

We held the wedding reception at the Okuru Hall. Gary McCormick and the crew of the *Heartland* television programme also attended the wedding, and donated 12 bottles of champagne for the reception. Locals contributed legs of venison, crayfish and whitebait, as well as four kegs of beer, wine and spirits.

The next day Murray Bowes and John Kerr flew us in their Cessna aircraft back home to Gorge River, with Mum and Dad, for our honeymoon.

chapter 18 the long way home

My dream of having a family and helping them to grow into strong, self-reliant individuals was now coming true. Being at Gorge River provided me with the opportunity to live my dream, and I can honestly say that this has been one of the most profound and fulfilling aspects of my life.

Before a child can walk on its own two feet it must be cared for, nurtured, fed and bathed. Initially they are helpless and rely entirely upon their parents for their well-being. And as we parents all well know, we must carry them until they are ready to make their own way through life's journey.

And so it was with Christan and later Robin. Before they could walk we carried them for hundreds or even thousands of miles along beaches, across rivers and through forests. Even when they were able to walk themselves, they could not cover the distances between huts or shelters that involved a full day's travel. Many years went by while we carried first Christan, then Robin, until they were both fully mobile and capable of going the full distance.

In May 1993, when Christan was 21 months old, we planned to travel to Eagle Rock Farm to celebrate Toddy's fortieth birthday. Sue and Ian's home holds a special place in our hearts, being our son Christan's birthplace.

Two DoC carpenters had been working on the hut next door, and were due to fly out in a few days. One ended up walking out a couple of days early to meet a family commitment, so they offered us the spare seat in Dave Saxton's three-seater Hughes 300. Catherine thought it would be a good idea if she and Christan had a ride to Barn Bay. I could catch them up on foot later that day, beating an incoming storm. When Sax arrived I told him I was happy to walk if Catherine and Christan could get a ride to Barn Bay, but he declared, 'No, we'll be right. I'll fit you all in.'

So we all climbed in, Sax, Sproulie the carpenter in the middle, and me with Christan in the front pack. Catherine sat on the floor against the bubble with our packs. Dave cranked the machine up to full revs and the blades were pelting overhead as the northerly wind gusted headlong through the flaxes at the end of the airstrip. As he applied pitch to the blades Sax yelled, 'Lean back!'

We all obeyed and the helicopter lurched up and over the flaxes, and out over the riverbed. Buffeted about by the strong headwind, we gradually climbed and climbed until we were at 1000 metres, high above the white-capped blue ocean. With the doors off, there is an eerie feeling of exposure to the wind and altitude. Dave was struggling to keep us on a stable heading, and I could feel Christan beginning to sense the tension when Sax declared above the turmoil, 'It gets worse up here, over Sandrock Bluff. You know, the updraught, the wind!'

We were now perched like a pendulum, swaying precariously under the stability of the blades.

'I'll have to drop one of you off,' Sax announced.

So we descended 1000 metres within a distance of about

a kilometre. Towards the end of the descent the ground was coming up very fast, and we were all holding on very tight. Were we going to crash-land, I wondered as we swayed downwards. In the last 30 metres of descent, Dave flared the blades with red-lining full throttle, pulling us up, as the skids finally made contact with the beach. We were just south of the Spoon River mouth.

I hopped out and handed Christan to a white-faced Catherine. 'I'll come back and pick you up,' Dave yelled as they took off again, then they disappeared north into the gale-force wind.

Twenty minutes later, Dave landed in exactly the same skid marks, then he flew me back to Barn Bay. Sax has flown tens of thousands of hours, but he still motions Sproulie over at the local pub to verify his description of the worst flight he has ever had.

The journey to Arrowtown was less eventful, and Toddy's birthday was celebrated in grand style. We spent a few days catching up with Queenstown acquaintances, since we would be heading back in for the winter, then we planned to complete the round trip and walk back home via the Hollyford.

Our friends Steve Harvey and Andrew 'Buzz' Grant had walked down the Cascade coastline the previous month and stayed with us, and now Buzz showed us some flakes of jade he had picked up on the day they had headed south from Gorge River to Big Bay. He commissioned me to carve these pieces for him. One in particular impressed me, a bright emerald-green, palm-sized flat piece. It looked like a bird, which is what I eventually created: a 10 x 12 centimetre falcon. I delivered the finished pieces to Buzz in November that year.

Soon it was time for us to hit the road again. Time to

experience some real adventure, head to the Hollyford and walk home. The morning we were due to leave, Christan was a little off colour, so Steve dropped Catherine and Christie Boy at the depot to catch a bus to Te Anau. He then dropped me off south of Frankton to begin hitching a ride.

As I walked the highway that snaked out towards the Remarkables Range, Catherine and Christan passed me in the bus, waving out the window as they went by. I spent the morning and early afternoon cadging rides down the lake, through Kingston, Five Rivers, then across the Mataura River towards Mossburn, arriving at Bev and Ian Thorne's home in Te Anau later that afternoon.

Ian was away up the Routeburn, where he managed the area for the Department of Conservation, but we stayed a couple of days with Bev and her boys. Then Bev lent us their car to take up to the bottom of the Deadman's Track, where Ian would pick it up on his way back out. Deadman's comes out on the Hollyford road just above Gunn's Camp, so after parking the car we walked down to catch up with Murray Gunn and stay the night in one of his warm and cosy cabins.

Murray was his usual chipper self, full of jokes, anecdotes and words of wisdom. We loved to go into Murray's shop and browse around his stock of grocery items. He had postcards, locally written books, and odds and ends that only he could have come up with. His museum was a goldmine of local history, with relics from the MacKenzie Homestead at Martins Bay and the building of the Homer Tunnel through the mountains to Milford Sound.

When the time came to tally up the cost of whatever you had purchased he would lay the change out boldly on the countertop, but when you went to retrieve the coins and notes they would disappear into thin air. With a calculated grin on his face Murray would ask, 'What are you waiting for? I gave you your change.'

After a stunned silence from his astute customer, he would laugh and pull the apparently evaporated money back out from behind the counter, attached to a strong rubber band.

Never ask Murray for a hut to stay in.

'We only have cabins, no huts here,' he would smartly respond.

Murray was a man with a heart of gold and a character to match, and we always enjoyed staying at Gunn's Camp. Later, as Christan and Robin grew older, he would invite us over in the evenings to watch *Mr Bean* videos. We often wondered who was funnier, Murray Gunn or Mr Bean.

We bid Murray farewell early next day as he dropped us off in his van at the Hollyford road end. We set off into the crisp morning air with Catherine and I loaded up to the gunwales. With a 120-kilometre journey ahead of us, we needed enough food for the tramp, plus some for wintering at Gorge River. Usually we fitted Christan into our packs on top of the other gear, but this time there wasn't any room. So we set off with Christan in a front pack strapped onto my shoulders. Christan had the best view, since he was facing forward and could see clearly ahead. His arms were free, and his legs were suspended out the bottom of the canvas pack.

This set-up required extra care and attention to balance on my part, since Christan partially restricted my view of the track ahead. I don't know what weight I was carrying but it was about the maximum I could take.

As we made our way along toward the Alabaster Hut, Christan kept up a playful commentary on the birds, trees and scenery along the stony, mossy track. I gained pleasure from the knowledge that he was taking this all in, his young mind seeing a kaleidoscope of natural beauty as Catherine and I trudged along the track. Christan kept in time and was coordinated with my movements, the swaying and motion of walking, keeping balance, leaning around trees, rocks and obstacles, keeping us working as a team. From time to time he would nod off to sleep, lulled like a baby in a cradle.

As you walk under a heavy load, the physical burden becomes numbed by the rhythm of your stride. Your intense concentration leads you into a space where gravity is merely a sensation to be accepted and allowed to pass on into another reach of your mind. Once free of this attachment to the physical I can be thinking of other things or just drift off into a restful state as my 'machine' does the hard work. Fuel it right, keep it well oiled and let the body find its own pace and rhythm. Let the pain find its own place after you have worked through it. Often my eyes, body and coordination function on autopilot while I drift off for sustained periods of time. The path ahead flows under my feet unconsciously, my full attention returning from time to time to keep in check. Still, each step is still taken with the utmost care, since I can't afford to slip or stumble with my delicate load aboard.

During the seven years that I carried my infant children for thousands of kilometres, I never faltered in my stride. Every slippery or loose boulder, every river or stream, log or overhanging branch was negotiated as best I could for the sake of their safety.

After journeying through beech forest, crossing many dry creek beds and the occasional stream, we stopped for a rest at Hidden Falls. This mighty torrent comes off the mountain through a solid rocky cataract, roaring into a foaming pool below. Then, carrying on past the first hut, we headed on to the Alabaster, eager to get a good day's walk under our belts. As we climbed up to the Little Homer Saddle the views of the nearby Darran Mountains began to delight us as occasional windows through the trees opened up to reveal their hanging valleys, walls of basalt rock and glistening glaciers.

On this brilliant day, 22 May 1993, there was a large high-pressure system moving onto Fiordland. The recent snows lay fresh upon the towering peaks under a deep blue sky. Mt Madeline and Tutoko moved in and out of focus as we came over the low saddle and descended towards the confluence of the Pyke and Hollyford Rivers.

There is a wonderful quality about this place. When the breezes blow there is the constant bustling music of the river, combined with the crystal light scintillating down as shafts through the forest canopy, all this energy creating a tangible magic. The mossy roots of the beech trees and the russet-brown leaf litter reflect the sun's warmth off the forest floor. Pongas and blechnum ground ferns bristle and rattle, dry in the chill wind. This energy enthrals me, captures my spirit, and I carry these memories always.

Now, as the winter shadows began to lengthen, the shores of Lake Alabaster appeared and the hut came into view. The golden glow of the late afternoon sun shrouded the distant peaks and continued to warm the inside of the hut as we thankfully released our packs onto the welcoming bunks. Time for some rest, then the chores to ready us for the coming night.

One of our main tasks each day was to dry Christan's nappies. When we were tramping we used a light gauze nappy which we would stuff with dry sphagnum moss for absorbency. At each change we could throw away the moss and only have the gauze cloth to wash and dry. This worked well, but each evening I would have to collect a good supply of firewood so we could dry nappies and other washing while cooking our meals. We never carried gas cookers until Christan bought one when he was about 15 years old. You need a Tiwai aluminium smelter and a Maui gasfield just to run a simple gas cooker.

We heated up water in the washbasin on top of the large pot-belly stove for Christan's evening bath. We also baked flat damper bread on the stovetop, along with thick slices of potato. We usually carried brown rice to cook, oatmeal, milk powder, wholemeal flour, sugar, whole potatoes and onions, oranges and apples and, of course, some seed sprouts. For greens, I would collect supplejack shoots and the young tips of tree ferns.

As the candlelight flickered around the inside of the cosy hut Catherine and I decided to spend an extra day here and take the opportunity to become better acquainted with this wonderful area. We had plenty of food and our packs would be lighter after an extra day here. As we rested up, Christan was busy pulling billies, pots and pans off the shelves. After his day's 'walk' he was a bundle of energy and ready for action. He loved exploring the woodbox and bouncing his way across the bunks. We had the hut to ourselves, so he could go about his activities uninhibited.

After a welcome night's rest we were out of bed early and ready to explore the lake edge. Plenty of driftwood lay in flood bands along the perimeter, and it was amazing to see the flood levels relative to the lake at rest. Sometimes this body of water would reach almost to the front steps of the hut, indicating the unimaginable amount of rainfall that could fall in these parts, up to 800 or even 1000 centimetres a year, a deluge that could wipe out the valley without the forest cover to buffer the onslaught. The Pyke Valley above the Alabaster, towards Big Bay, is difficult to negotiate during a wet spell since the river meanders across a flat basin most of the way.

As the sun rose crisp and clear we searched for flat, round pebbles to skim across the mirror-like surface of the lake. Christan was already adept at achieving a bounce or two.

This journey was not just a means to an end, but a lesson in itself. A time to learn more about the region we called home. We played by the lake between collecting driftwood to fuel the stove. I also took the time to sketch the vista across the inland sea towards the Skippers Range, rising up to sheer rocky bluffs and tawny tussock-covered ridges. Sixteen years later, I can study the sketches I made that day and see again the living character of the old Alabaster Hut, with its table, stools, stove, broom and washbasin, long since demolished to make way for something bigger and better.

Being well rested, we hit the track with renewed vigour. Home was calling, though it was many days away yet. After a short stroll, we carefully made our way across a swingbridge over the Pyke just above the confluence with the Hollyford. We looked down from mossy river banks into deep pools of aquamarine water swishing and bubbling, then settling out again before the next set of lively rapids shrilling out into the sharp, crisp air.

Christan was still perched on my front as we leaned into corners, dodging fallen logs and fern leaves, powering through small stony creek beds and back up onto the terraces that led through a flat wooded wonderland towards the head of Lake McKerrow. For about two hours we were totally immersed in the tall podocarp forest, the trunks of rimu, kahikatea and totara defining the way until we burst out upon a lake that stretched as far as the eye could see. Lake McKerrow stretches for 20 kilometres towards the coastal region of Martins Bay, a massive body of water formed from unimaginable forces that have carved out the surrounding mountains. It was more like an ocean surrounded by rocky bastions, the tallest of the Fiordland mountains, the Darrans, with Mt Tutoko rising up between the clouds that were whisking by.

The weather was holding well, with brisk southwesterly breezes billowing about the turrets that defined the skyline as we began our assault on the Demon Trail. The track rose and fell again in a succession of arduous climbs and descents, but gradually the going fell into an enjoyable rhythm, bare footfalls upon dried beech leaves, fern, tree roots and mossy carpets. Our nimble-footed paces to gain maximum comfort from the natural pathway led us ever onwards.

Finally, as the mid-afternoon allowed the late autumn sun to reach over the high ridges, we reached the Demon Trail Hut, perched upon a peninsula. Again we thankfully accepted the chance to rest up and see what the morrow would bring. Catherine and I were both feeling the need to lighten our loads. Now that there was more room in my pack, Christan would ride jockey upon my back. His baby pack was connected to my pack frame and supported him, with holes cut in appropriate places for his legs to hang out against my sides. After spending two nights at the hut we moved on once more. Christan loved riding in the pack, and was usually impatient to start again when we stopped for a necessary rest. He was very keen to get moving that morning, and now that he was on my back I had better visibility.

From the Hokuri Hut we headed off again along the edge

of the lake, which opened up into a wide beach of gravel for a two-hour walk, followed by a forest walk down to the hut at the Hollyford River mouth. Here we managed to catch fish on handlines off the rocks to supplement our diet. This place has seen many shipwrecks, especially in the days of the pioneer settlement in the 1870s, and as the tide surged in and out we could see the rock partially hidden midstream in the channel waiting for its next unwary victim.

On the seventh day, we finally hit the coast as we made our way from the Hollyford around Long Reef to Big Bay. Christan was still chattering continuously, giving us a running commentary and his observations. We passed the seal colony on the reef, taking care not to disturb or corner them. Hundreds of New Zealand fur seals dwell here amongst the large granite and sandstone boulders. If you cut off their exit to the sea, they can charge right over you in their pursuit of safety.

Big Bay is a truly magnificent place, the jewel in the crown. We could see to Awarua Point, the north head of the bay, six kilometres across the rolling sea. Inland rose a chain of snow-crested mountains with distinctive peaks and colours — the Red Mountains, glowing in the morning light.

Our spirits lifted as we entered the expanse of the bay, boulder-hopping for many miles until the gravel and sandy beaches were underfoot. We passed Dale's fishing hut, a place of many memories, the sights and smells taking me back to adventures, thrills and hard toil. Then onwards to Big Bay beach, a welcome five-kilometre stretch of wide open sand. Our loads had been getting lighter with the passing of each day, and it was great to whistle along this beach, singing songs to Christan, calling out to the birds and the mountains.

Northerly gusts greeted us as we neared the north end of the beach, and clouds were streaming in across the mountaintops. The weather was now closing in as we made our way to the small settlement of whitebaiters' huts. Terry Fisher, a whitebaiter from Balfour, had shown us where his key was, and we welcomed the opportunity to camp in his hut since the DoC hut at that time had no stove. Overnight, the rain began lashing the tin roof; bucketing down, in fact, and being blown up under the tin, finding ways in. We ended up sleeping in the only dry patch left, near the cosy warmth of the open fire. The deluge continued all the next day, until in the evening the wind and showers ripped on out of the southwest as the skies began to clear between squalls.

Once again we had managed to dry all of Christan's nappies, and he had spent another day exploring the pots and pans and ins and outs of the hut. The next day was 4 June, day 12 of our journey home. We planned to walk as far as our bivvy at Ryan's Creek, eight kilometres south of the Gorge.

Despite our lighter packs, it was still a long haul out of Big Bay around Awarua Point. This coastline is strewn with large glacial moraine boulders, and has been the home of many jade boulders. We fossicked our way out past Big Bay Landing to Crayfish Rock then out to Awarua Point. I pointed out the landmarks to Christie Boy as we went. From the point we enjoyed the stunning views of the Fiordland coastline down past Milford all the way to Sutherland Sound, along with views to the north of the Gorge Islets and up to Cascade Point 50 kilometres away. The mountains behind Big Bay glowed in the light captured by the sullen-looking cloud that hovered around the peaks, the sunlight highlighting the hanging valleys in between.

The southwest wind hustled us along the beach. Often, squalls came racing up behind us. As we looked over our shoulders rain and hail burst down upon us. We usually relied on our bush bivvy at Ryan's Creek to break our journey, and Catherine had never walked the whole way between Big Bay and the Gorge. But with the weather brewing we decided to press on after a welcome rest. We sheltered out of the showers and rain in my home away from home, where I had spent many a day and night living as close to the earth as I possibly could.

The shadows were already lengthening as we climbed through the jumble of sandstone boulders around Longridge Point. There were the Gorge Islets again but closer now, only an hour away.

As the twilight became the night, we finally made it home, thankful, tired and worn. We hadn't seen a soul since farewelling Murray at the Hollyford road end. But as we neared the northern end of our airstrip we noticed candlelight and smoke billowing from the chimney of the DoC hut.

Before too long there was a gentle knocking at our door. Our friends Julia Bradshaw and Pete McIntyre had arrived earlier that afternoon. We ushered them in and cooked up a brew, enjoying the opportunity to chew the fat. It was a good welcome home.

chapter 19 how the other half live

At this time I was developing my work as an artist, but still working on the boats from time to time to make ends meet. The previous Christmas I had been doing a spell of fishing with Dale, and we all stayed down at Big Bay for a couple of weeks.

On Christmas Day we were out off North Reef, heading into a freshening northerly breeze, lifting crayfish, baiting and resetting pots up towards the Hacket. At one point we heard the thumping and beating of blades, and looked up as a large yellow and red Westpac Rescue helicopter cruised by heading south, then disappeared around into the bay. We thought nothing more of it, as the breeze and developing wind chop demanded our attention, and soon our line of pots was complete. We turned and headed back around North Reef, finding more sheltered waters as we sped back across the wide expanse of Big Bay.

Dale's hut was a steadily growing speck away in the distance across the leaping waters. A vital energy pervaded the atmosphere, as the wind, the spray and the clarity of the light heightened our senses. You could smell and taste the salt in the air. Before too long we were nearing the mooring, as I continued working on the manual bilge pumps, clearing out the leaking hulls. Dale eased up on the throttle, dropping from 40 knots to a standstill, so I grappled the mooring rope and carefully fastened the shackle onto our leaping bow. We lowered the holding basket, full of live crayfish, into the lively sea and secured it against the side of the boat then hopped in the dinghy and rowed towards the breakers.

Catherine, holding Christan, came down the beach to meet us as we hauled the dinghy up above the high-tide level.

'Robert, a chopper landed half an hour ago looking for you. They want to buy some of your greenstone carvings.'

'Oh, OK,' I replied, surprised. 'Where are they now?'

'They're off to Milford for lunch,' Catherine answered. 'They said they would be back in a while.'

Our first priority was to head inside for a brew. It was Christmas Day, after all, and it was time to whip up a few festivities before the day was over. Catherine stirred the open fire into life, and Dale and I were soon sipping a brew of steaming hot tea and munching on a feed of Christmas cake.

Just as the bottom of my cup came into view, the heart-racing whine and thump of helicopter blades began to dominate the airwaves, the unmistakable sound of a seven-seater Squirrel. By the time we reached the generator shed the pilot was deftly landing his skids on the gravelly beach head amid a whirl of dust, sand and seaweed. As she wound down, out popped a group of people, among them Peter Matich from Taupo, his familiar large, toothy grin prominent as they headed over towards us. Peter was a regular visitor to Gorge River and Fiordland during the 1980s, and had often given me rides in his Cessna south to Big Bay, Martins Bay, the Kaipo, Milford Sound and the Hollyford when I happened to be heading down that way.

It turned out Peter had met these people while he was driving a taxi from Auckland airport, and before long had become their guide to New Zealand. After he had greeted us he introduced us to the group, four men and a boy. 'These gentlemen are from Boston,' he said. 'They'd like you to show them some greenstone and are interested in buying some of your carvings. We flew especially from Christchurch to Hokitika to buy some greenstone souvenirs but being Christmas Day all the shops were shut. So what could we do? We thought we would fly down and find Beansprout — so here we are.'

I felt a wee bit stunned as I took this all in.

'Well,' I replied, 'we'll have to head up to Gorge River. Could Catherine and Christan come with us? Some of you would have to stay here.'

As a family we usually stick together, and when you fly off in a helicopter you never really know when you are going to get back. It would also give Catherine and Christan the opportunity to water the garden.

'That's fine,' the men answered. 'Let's go.'

So before I knew it I was sitting in the front seat of the chopper alongside the pilot. Catherine, with Christan strapped into a front pack, was in the back with two men and a boy of about 12. We flew north straight across the bay, the white-capped waves below us familiar as we cruised around North Reef. I was busy spotting our craypot buoys as we soared past them, then I turned around and, through the headset, asked, 'What do you guys do for a living?'

'Oh, well,' one of them answered. 'We have a company that makes tools and spare parts. But we bought ourselves an aeroplane and now we're on holiday, just like you. But we haven't got the same sparkle in our eyes that you've got.'

'Oh yeah, OK,' I chuckled, taking this as a compliment, or maybe they were just trying to butter me up.

As we travelled north of Awarua Point I pointed out my wrecked dinghy lying abandoned amongst the boulders and flaxes far below. I explained how my brother-in-law had recently been flushed out of the Gorge River mouth as he was attempting to cross while it was in flood.

'We'll send the chopper back to fly it home for you,' one of the men offered generously, an offer I accepted gratefully.

Soon the helicopter was settling down on the northern end of the Gorge River airstrip, just outside our hut. We all went in and I started to show them some of my work. They were also interested in my methods of carving the stone. At this stage of my development I was still working the pounamu by hand, cutting and working with abrasive sandstone and ample amounts of water. I showed them a 25 centimetres adze I was finishing, one that I had already cut out with a sandstone saw and was bevelling on one end to bring up a sharp wedge-shaped edge. Another one had been made by breaking a large flake off a stone using a piece of hard, heavy hydrogrossular garnet. This had been ground into shape on a flat piece of sandstone. They were particularly intrigued by the fish-shaped pendants made out of tangiwai greenstone, and keen to buy some of these as well as a palm-sized floater from the beach.

They also commissioned me to carve a logo for their Learjet club, named the 'Go Go Club' because they get in their Learjet and go go go — around the world, that is. They had apparently been around the world three times in the last four months. I showed them a flat piece of jade, 30 centimetres long, 8 centimetres wide and about 6 millimetres thick, which was ideal for the job, and agreed to carve the Go Go logo and send it to them in Boston. The lead man handed me his business card: Mr David Goldman, President, Goldman Financial Group.

I had seen that name before, among members of a cartel of international financiers.

It was soon time to head back to Big Bay, so we all climbed aboard the helicopter and headed south along the coast until we were once again landing in a cloud of sand outside Dale's freezer shed.

The gentlemen thanked us for a great day out, and told us just to let them know if we ever needed anything. Then they shook hands, boarded the machine, and away they went, disappearing into the blue where they had hailed from.

Over the years many interesting people from all walks of life and many different countries have visited us, stopping in for a brew, to exchange ideas and share cultures. People of all ages, including those well into their seventies, have tramped through. On average about 50 trampers pass through each year either travelling up or down the coastline, usually starting out from either the Cascade Valley road end or the Upper Hollyford valley. The tramp right through takes about eight to 10 days and is weather-dependent, especially between Martins Bay and the Cascade River since most streams are unbridged and need to be forded.

During a good spell of weather the scenic wonder of this journey is hard to beat. The terrain includes river, forest, coastal and lakeside walking through low-altitude country, with awesome views of the snow-capped mountains. I can honestly say that I never tire of the privilege of walking this beautiful place.

I have been 'caretaker' here for 30 years now, and though DoC has replaced the old Forest Service not much has changed. I still take care of the huts and airstrip at Gorge River, as well as maintaining a short bluff track one kilometre south of the river and around Crayfish Rock in Big Bay, one along the north bank of the Gorge, and a two-kilometre-long track eight kilometres north of Gorge River over Sandrock Bluff.

During the last 30 years I have ferried many hundreds of people across the river. When the tide is low it is easy enough to ford, but when the tide is in, the water backs up to the limestone bluffs along the southern river bank. You can still ford further upstream, but then you have to spend an hour scrambling back over a high ridge to pass above the bluffs.

I keep a dinghy and canoe by the riverside to ease the crossing and I am always happy to row people across, except in high flood. If people are coming from the north they just need to call out. If we are not home we usually leave a dinghy or canoe on the north bank. The six-bunk DoC hut on the south bank has recently been renovated and painted, and two kilometres north of the Gorge River mouth is a 'bivvy rock' under a limestone cliff, just above the beach head.

Some trampers return again and again. Veteran trampers Engelbert and Beatrice Artho from Switzerland have tramped through here eight times in the last 15 years. This is their favourite place and they love to stay in the DoC hut for a few days while in transit. We always enjoy their company and gaining insights into their European culture. Recently they commissioned me to do a painting of their beloved Gorge River hut, which will be the fifth painting I have done for them.

One time Blair and Alvin, two very keen surfers from Haast, tramped through from the Cascade heading for the break at Big Bay, complete with wetsuits and surfboards.

Blair carried his surfboard all the way through to the Upper Hollyford. They had timed their trek well, and were rewarded with some great waves.

An interesting party of trampers arrived from the south back in the spring of 1987: a Maori lad, Walt, his girlfriend Cass, and a Pakeha youth by the name of Paul. Walt's name was unmistakable since it was tattooed in bold letters across his throat. Their first comment was, 'We've heard you have a rabbit problem.' They were toting a shotgun, and immediately offered their services.

'Oh yeah, good one,' I replied, since the rabbits were gradually grazing my garden to ground level. I didn't have the heart to deal to them.

I invited them in for a cup of tea, then they settled into the DoC hut for a couple of days, just like neighbours. Walt was from Ruatoria on the East Coast. He seemed like a high-spirited lad who might attract trouble, but he was a playful, friendly type all the same. When they left I rowed them across the river and bid them well as they headed north up to Barn Bay and out to the Cascade.

Well, a couple of days later a Robinson 22 helicopter landed and out popped Stewie Fever, a venison recovery pilot. 'Did a Maori guy and his girlfriend pass this way lately?'

'Yes,' I replied.

'Well, they're on the run.'

At that moment an aeroplane buzzed low over the airstrip and banked tightly, indicating an imminent landing. Stewie's chopper was buzzing away at the north end of the runway, near our hut, but this didn't stop Russell Baker landing. He glided over the top of the helicopter, pulled up halfway down the airstrip and quickly turned around. Stewie jumped back into his chopper and by the time the plane had taxied up the runway he was airborne and gone. After turning the aircraft around on a pinpoint opposite me and letting the propeller come to a standstill, Russell jumped out and introduced me to Lloyd Matheson from Te Anau and two detectives from Queenstown. Well, from their questions, it did appear that Walt, Cass and Paul were on the run. They had jumped bail in Queenstown and headed to the West Coast via Glenorchy and the Routeburn Track. Their shotgun had been stolen from Dale Hunter's hut at Big Bay. I suggested that by now they would probably be near the road end at the Cascade.

Over the next few months I heard rumours of the group's fate, and they were eventually picked up by the Haast policeman, Roger Millard, on the Cascade–Jacksons River road. And that was that.

Well, several years later, in May 1991, Catherine and I walked south from Gorge River through Big Bay, Martins Bay and up Lake McKerrow, eventually arriving late one afternoon at the Hidden Falls hut in the Upper Hollyford valley.

Catherine was five months pregnant, and we were glad to reach the hut as a Fiordland rainstorm was about to set in. This was the eighth hut we had stayed in since leaving home and all had been empty. As the first powerful gusts of wind and a heavy downpour began, I commented to Catherine, 'All we need now is a tramping club to walk in.'

Not more than five minutes later a procession of weary, uniform-looking trampers entered the hut. Soon there were nine busy people emptying packs, tossing sleeping bags upon bunks and generally turning the previously quiet hut into a circus. Eventually they settled into a quieter routine, and over a common brew we began a conversation. We were happy to chat and answer their questions since two or three weeks had elapsed since our last contact with anyone.

Eventually one of the blokes said, 'You must be Beansprout. I had a cup of tea with you when we tramped through your way a couple of years ago.'

I couldn't place the guy, and asked, 'Was that in my hut?'

'Yes,' he replied.

Still curious, I asked, 'Were you with someone else?'

'Yes, I was with Walt.'

The penny dropped. OK. My brain went tick, tick, tick. These jokers were possibly all prisoners. And they were. 'On holiday, courtesy of Her Majesty the Queen,' they all chorused.

Paul had been inside since I had last seen him. The group were about to go on parole and were undertaking an Outdoor Pursuits course. One of them was a prison warden. Freddie Angel, the notorious bird smuggler, was among them and provided continuous entertainment all evening. The next morning we had porridge with them and then we were on our way.

The 'Roar' is the busiest time of the year, with the South Westland landscape being divided up into hunting blocks from late March through to late April. Each party is allocated one week of exclusive hunting on their appointed block, which in our case is bordered by Brown's Refuge in the north, Longridge Point to the south, and up the Gorge River to the Jerry junction.

We generally lay low, stay out of the forest and keep to the coastline. This period is our festival time of the year, when we meet new faces and catch up with regular visitors and friends.

Most hunters fly in by chopper. Dave Saxton and his son Morgan have flown in the majority of the hunters over the years, with Jamie Scott from Fox Glacier and his pilot Ken Hutchins taking up the slack in more recent times.

For as long as I have lived here Sax has always been very

generous to me. He is always concerned about our welfare, and always asks whether we are in need of any help. He has spent enough time in the bush to understand the hardships of isolation. Apart from Roger Monk, who has been like a godfather to us, David Saxton has been the most generous pilot in all the years that I have lived at Gorge River. If you stacked up all the apples, potatoes, oranges, eggs, loaves of bread and butter, cabbages and lollies that he has brought us there would not be any spare room in the hut. You wouldn't get in the front door.

We were totally devastated by Dave's loss of his son Morgan, who died in 2008 when his helicopter mysteriously crashed into Lake Wanaka. We all know how much he loved his son, and Morgan's death has been a great loss not just to their family but to the whole Haast and Central Lakes district community.

The helicopter pilots and their crews have been constant friends in this quest we call life. They have watched over me and my family, and I hold them in the highest regard. Some have passed on to greater ventures but they will never be forgotten since they are all legends in their own time. We live out here amid the hunt and see them operating *in extremis*, carrying out manoeuvres and risks unmentionable as they set about their tasks of securing another goal, whether it be a load of venison or a cargo of hunters and their mountain of gear. They wind their machines up to get pay dirt to a road end. Their lives appear to us melded with a machine magic that defies all laws of gravity. They appear from nowhere, anywhere and disappear as quickly as they came.

As we yarn with hunters who are new to the area we often offer them advice concerning the terrain, river crossings and where the deer are likely to be. We pore over maps together and chew the fat. I've never shot a deer, but probably would if need be. I prefer to fence them out and leave them to the hunters, sometimes swapping a feed of fish for a feed of venison as a change of diet. One year the last chopper left excess baggage in the form of four back deer legs. Over the next month we managed to chew through two of them and buried the rest in the garden.

In 2009 the hunters ended up sharing the DoC hut with a crew of carpenters who had come down from Fox and Haast to renovate it. Three loads of DoC building supplies and three workers were flown in, followed by two loads of Danish hunters who had flown direct to New Zealand for a week's deer-hunting.

The carpenters were expecting to replace one floor joist along the rear of the hut, but after a closer look they realised that all the floor joists and bearers were rotten and would have to go. So while the four Danish hunters and their Kiwi cousin occupied the hut, the DoC workers proceeded to replace every joist, bearer and many of the floorboards without removing the kitchen bench, wood stove, bunks or dining table. I was amazed by how well both the hunting party and the DoC staff coped. Once the rain stopped the Danes shot three deer for the week, then returned home covered in welts from the bites of affectionate sandflies that had swarmed up through the gaping floor.

chapter 20 providing the essentials

I n 1994 Catherine became pregnant with our second child. As the time for the birth drew near we flew from Gorge River to Neils Beach with Roger Monk in his Cessna 180, then hitched a ride with a friend to Queenstown. From there we caught a bus down to Lumsden, where Celia Bowmar was waiting patiently to take us to the picturesque Waikaia Plains Station where she and her husband Peter farmed. We had arranged to stay in their farm cottage for the birth, with midwife Terryl Muir to assist Catherine.

On 22 November our beautiful baby girl, Robin Grace, entered the world 10 minutes before midnight. We spent a month on the farm while Catherine was adjusting to Robin's birth, becoming involved in the work of the farm as well as Peter and Celia's busy social life. My mother also came over from Mooloolaba to help us, staying with us in the cottage for three weeks.

When we were ready to go home we loaded up Peter's Cessna 185 and he kindly flew us west across to Te Anau then north up through the Eglinton Valley, across The Divide and down the Hollyford to the coast, finally landing us home at Gorge River.

We quickly settled back in with our newly extended family, Christan, now three, and Robin, just a month old.

Naturally, having a family has meant certain practical arrangements have changed over the years. For the first five or six years, when I lived alone at Gorge River, I had no showering arrangement so I used to bathe in the river. On a winter's morning, leaping out of a nice warm bed, I would grab a towel and soap, then head straight down to the water. When I reached the crystal-clear river I would gaze up the valley, my eyes blurring in the numbing wind that was steadily whistling through the rocky gorge on its determined journey towards the sea. It was mind over matter as I splashed enough water from the shallows to raise a lather, then plunged into deeper water to get the rinse-off over and done as quickly as possible. I would then gather up towel and clothes as a rosy glow permeated my body.

This was ideal in summer, but during the winter the catabatic easterlies that blew down the valley kept the water rather chilly. I used to keep the old wood stove going to boil water for cups of tea and to cook meals, but it was too much trouble to heat water for washing, so bathing in the river was necessary all year round.

Some mornings after a river bath I would emerge feeling rosy all over since my skin would be numb. But after I had thawed out by the stove the cold would seep in until I managed to warm up once again. In winter I washed my hair down by the river separately from taking a bath, since I needed about three lathers and rinses.

Anyway, it was all character-building, and it inspired me to eventually rig up a hot-water tank supply from the roof spouting. This was joined up to the hot-water cylinder that was already in the hot-water cupboard, connected up to the old Shacklock range.

It was tricky getting enough pressure through the hot-water cylinder to come out the shower nozzle in the old bathroom. The previous occupants had pumped water up to a high-level tank by means of a generator or a petrol-motor-driven pump. The best time to shower was when the rain was descending from the skies onto the corrugated-iron roof, topping up the 44-gallon drum suspended on its side on the rata tankstand. When the drum got down to half to a third full the pressure would not run the shower's hot and cold water supply, but water would still come out the hot tap over the kitchen sink.

During the early 1980s I had to replace the old 44-gallon drums. Dave Saxton had left some drums when Dobbie was fishing out of the Gorge, and Lou Brown also brought down some empty jet-fuel drums from Harvey Hutton's hangar at Mussel Point. I also used Dobbie and Sax's old freezer box, which held about 100 gallons of water.

Once Catherine and later young Christan arrived it was a continual struggle to keep the water supply up. The tanks were rusting away as quickly as they were being replaced. When Christan was a baby Catherine would wash and dry 12 nappies a day. She would soak the washing in buckets of cold, soapy water, rinse them a couple of times, then carry it down to the river for the final rinse, laying out the clothes on the stony riverbed with a rock on top of each article. She still uses this method today, allowing the surge in the tide to rinse the clothes, though she now wears freezer gloves to protect her hands from the cold. Occasionally she has to dive to retrieve clothing that has been ripped away by an unexpectedly large tidal surge.

During dry spells, which do often occur on the West Coast, we would be reduced to bucketing up water from the river. Elizabeth Brown had given us an old hand wringer to help dry out the clothes.

All this changed unexpectedly in July 1993. Paul Cooper, from Southern Alps Air in Makarora, had flown in a party of four hunters who had come for the week. Then out of the blue, a couple of days before they were due to fly out, Dave Saxton dropped in two more hunters. They were father and son Bruce and Sidney Kershaw, dairy farmers from Paeroa in the Waikato. Both parties had permits to hunt on the DoC estate, and at that time of the year you couldn't book a block. So both groups of hunters had a right to be here.

Anyway, the first party were not too keen on the idea of sharing the DoC hut with other hunters, so we offered to put Bruce and Sidney up in our spare room-cum-workshop until Paul had flown the first group out. They refrained from hunting during this time, but were keen to help Catherine with any chores that needed doing.

Well, they brought us in a load of driftwood off the beach, then Catherine asked them to carry up some buckets of water from the river, since our tank was near empty. They were happy to help, but that evening Bruce, a concerned look on his face, stated, 'Surely you can do better than this. We have 15 kilometres of alkathene pipe on the farm. Pace out the distance to your nearest water supply. Next year we'll bring down some coils of half-inch pipe.'

He was serious about this, and a few days later when I went over for a brew with them in the DoC hut he asked me again how much pipe I would need. I had paced out the distance through the supplejacks and kiekie up to a limestone waterfall that came off a natural spring up on the steep hillside.

'600 metres,' I replied.

Well, they were true to their word, and nearly two years later they arrived down with 600 metres of black alkathene pipe, plus taps, joiners and fittings. This event led to a quantum leap in our standard of living. Since then we have enjoyed the benefits of a constant supply and good pressure of water, thanks to the generosity of the Kershaws. And since we burn driftwood in our stove for most of our cooking, we have plenty of hot water for all our washing and showering every day.

Luckily, Eion Wylie had installed a concrete septic tank and flush toilet back in the early 1970s, and this system still works today with periodic maintenance. So our bathroom, along with the shower and washbasin, provides us with the comforts of any household.

In 1992, not long after Christan was born, I began to extend the hut. Firstly I pushed the front wall of the house out and windowed in the verandah to catch the sunlight and let more light into the living room. Then I moved the kitchen bench and sink into the side of this new space. After Robin was born in November 1994, I built on more room at the back of the house which eventually became her bedroom, and rebuilt the entire bathroom in the process.

After this I systematically replaced all the floor from the ground up in the rest of the house. After pulling up the floor- boards I discovered that there were no stumps holding up the floor joists. No wonder the floor waved up and down as you walked across it. The joists had been laid down across two large beech logs which had since rotted away, so all that was left was a hollow shell of thick bark half full of wood mulch and dust. It looked like gravity was the only thing holding up the hut. All of the floor joists, bearers and most of the floorboards and the walls up to one metre from the ground were full of huhu grubs and rot.

The house became a building site over the next year as I replaced one section of the floor and walls after another. Our living space moved about the constant hole in the floor. Christan, at three years old, helped me nail down most of the floorboards while Robin, who was still crawling, was avoiding falling down into the abyss.

Over the previous years I had combed the beaches for any milled timber. As long as it had one flat surface on it and was longer than about 60 centimetres it came in useful. Much of the timber had been washed out to sea off whitebait stands and ended up strewn along the coastline. Since the advent of metal stands less milled timber has washed up.

Timber salvaged from the old shed plus leftovers from the Forestry and DoC work on the hut next door were all put to use. By the time Robin was 18 months old we had rebuilt the main living area. Later I rebuilt the workshop and guest-room area.

Before we laid in new totara stumps we dug out another foot of soil to increase the space between the ground and the floorboards. I also dug trenches around the outside of the hut to allow better drainage and keep the ground dry beneath the hut. Huhu grubs take advantage of any moisture and move in accordingly.

In May 1993 DoC workers Bruce Sproul, Martin Abel and Steve 'Lightning' had replaced the tin roof of their hut. The old tin had rusted through at the nail holes but otherwise was in good condition. The corrugated-iron roof on our hut was beginning to leak in several places, but the corrugated-iron walls were still reasonably sound.

So I hatched a plan and took the good tin off the outside walls. I replaced this with the old tin off the DoC hut, cut in half across where the rusted-out nail holes were. It was easy enough to thatch the walls with the shorter lengths of corrugated iron, and then I was able to replace the roof iron with the good stuff off the walls. This has worked out well. Some of the old roofing iron was OK for some of the walls also. As we recoated the roof and walls we firstly stapled on silver insulation paper, and we also put this down before we replaced the floorboards. This made a great difference to the ability to retain heat in the hut. Previously the walls dripped with condensation continuously during the winter months. Since installing the silver paper this tiresome problem has largely disappeared, much to our relief.

I persevered with the old Shacklock Orion 501 coal range for many years, then in March 1989 I bartered with Lou Brown and got a 12-gallon oil drum for wages owing. The old Shacklock was so totally stuffed that I was able to pull it out, steel plate by steel plate, until all that was left was the wetback jacket still connected up to the copper hot-water cylinder in the cupboard nearby.

This wetback is still there today. It has never been moved or disconnected from the copper cylinder. To install the oil drum I merely cut a hole in one side to allow the drum to slide down and around the wetback. Then I cut a slit to allow for the connecting pipes, cut another square hole for the steel hotplate to sit on, all with a certain amount of panel-beating to the required shape, and a rectangular hole in one end of the drum for a door.

To finish off I stacked large stones and cemented up underneath and around the drum to seal off any gaps, and installed a stainless steel flue pipe through the roof. This basic stove has served us for the last 20 years, though I have had to replace rusty drums from time to time. The last heavy steel drum has seen 12 years of service and we're due for a new one now. But they draw well, having the kettle boiling in 10 minutes from woe to go. We can use any firewood the length of the drum.

On many occasions I have sat and watched the glowing embers, heating the hut and warming our souls, burning a seemingly endless supply of driftwood from the nearby river mouth and beaches. Torrential rains continually scour the surrounding forest-clad hillsides and valleys, so there is never any lack of wood.

From 1980 through to the mid-1990s, paraffin wax candles provided most of the lighting in the hut, along with a kerosene lamp, and later, a pressurised Tilley lantern. It was always a challenge using the methylated spirits burner to preheat the cloth Tilley and set it to a radiant glow.

It was a massive improvement when we finally spent the $500 Mum had given us as a wedding present, to buy our first electric solar panel and deep-cycle battery to run a night light. The deep-cycle battery can be discharged to a greater degree than a normal car battery and still be brought back to full charge again, so it is ideal for use with solar-powered electrical systems, providing lighting overnight. During the long winter months we would, and still sometimes do, light up our candles if the weather was overcast for sustained periods, but we have largely done away with smoky kerosene and candle-wax fumes.

As the years have gone by we have kept adding to our solar panel bank, and now we have five panels generating together 200 watts of power on a sunny day. We can usually run two nine-watt fluorescent bulbs for four to five hours in the evenings. During the day this power is used for running the 12- and 24-volt electric motors I use for carving greenstone.

About four years ago we invested in a wind generator to harness the prevailing gale-force winds from the northeast, southwest, and the catabatic easterly. During the winter the breeze from the valley charges up the batteries overnight and in the early morning before the sun comes up. We can generate about 400 watts of power with 30 knots of wind velocity. This is invaluable for keeping my workshop going. In the early days, if I leaned too hard the grinding wheel would stall to a halt.

Nowadays I often spend one day a week or more maintaining the hut and workshop. Sometimes I might spend two or three days redesigning an electrical or mechanical system so that I can get back to work after a breakdown, but I always find a way to get the systems running again, sometimes with the help of friends who are suppliers and engineers scattered throughout the South Island. The more technology you use the more time you have to devote to keep it running.

During the 1980s and early '90s the fortunes of Barn Bay and Gorge River were interlinked. Most of our supplies during that period came via Barn Bay, with Lou Brown and his sea-going jetboat.

We could go to Greymouth, Christchurch or anywhere for that matter and spend a day or two accumulating groceries and hardware supplies then parcel them up into a large cardboard box labelled:

> Robert Long, Beansprout,
> c/o Lou Brown, Barn Bay,
> c/o Makarora West via Wanaka.

I would carry this parcel to the local Rail and Road Services depot, which in those days always had a freight service, though this eventually disappeared once they became Intercity.

This box of goodies would eventually reach Gorge River, usually aboard *Scratch*, while Lou was working his gear down to Longridge Point. Lou and Elizabeth Brown were always a great help to me, and to us all later on when Catherine and I began our family. Lou and I usually tried to better each other in the favours we worked for each other. I often crewed on the boat and worked around their homestead, to barter for the services and favours that Lou and Elizabeth brought our way. The Browns moved away in the winter of 1994, though they never actually made their departure official until about seven years later when Lou flew in with Harvey Hutton in his Hughes 500 helicopter and retrieved his favourite tools and precious gear.

During the 1980s I would often run out of food, and would usually only head out to town once the cupboards were bare. Once we had children to support this was no longer an option. For the last 15 years we have had a regular supply drop in from Arrowtown every four to six weeks. Over the years we have had a standing order with Roger Monk, and each time he came he would ask us when we wished to see him next. If we wanted to change the dates or add other items to the list we would send out a letter to be posted to Roger with a passing tramper or visiting aircraft. The only time this didn't work so well was in 1999 when Roger's plane was out of commission for six months. We had supplies sent in which saw us through for a couple of months, but when there were unexpected delays in the repairs to the aircraft our food stocks dropped to a very low level. All we had left was rice, sugar, sultanas, milk powder and split peas, and we were living on rice pudding. During this month or two I spent most of my time catching fish and gathering shellfish and bull kelp to feed the family. When the sugar and sultanas ran out and we had only enough rice to last one more week I went up to the Spoon River and brought back our food stashes from there, and later I brought back our food stash from Ryan's Creek.

I was about to do a runner down to Big Bay to ask Mitch

to radio a message out to get supplies in when we heard via a passing Milford-bound boat that Roger was due in on the following Monday. This period was character-building, and it sharpened our ability to survive and live much closer to the land.

Today our extensive vegetable garden provides our greens, beans and peas and most of our spuds. Since the deer numbers are quite high I have fenced off the garden with old trawl mesh off the beach held up by driftwood poles. I have never shot a deer and haven't the heart to do so, and we rely on hunters and chopper crews to keep the numbers down to stable levels to maintain a healthy forest.

Catherine does most of the planting and digging, and each day I bury possum carcasses once they have been skinned or plucked. This, along with fish frames, helps to feed the garden. Possums break down very quickly and are an excellent source of nutrients. Catherine burns most of the mussel and paua shells that we have collected, and once turned into lime by the heat of our wood stove these help to neutralise the acidic soil, enabling a greater range of vegetable plants to survive. In the event of large deposits of seaweed arriving on the beach we drop all tasks to retrieve and stockpile as many bags of this valuable nutrient as we can before the ocean takes it back again.

When I first moved to Gorge River there were no possums to be found in the river catchment. Since the early 1990s there has been a slow but steady influx of the brush-tailed possum. They have moved in from the north via the Jackson and Cascade Rivers, and from the south via the Hollyford, Pyke and Big Bay.

Each morning I check a trapline of 10 to 20 traps set along the river bank, the airstrip and the base of the hill. As each wave of possums moves in we attempt to keep the local numbers down to prevent them destroying the local rata, fuchsia trees and our vegetable garden. We also have a trapline of about 25 traps on the north bank which we set each month for three to four days to tackle the next wave moving in from the north. Possums are caught in up to 60 per cent of the traps overnight with each recent influx, dropping off to next to nothing before the next wave moves in.

Christan usually manages the trapline when he is home, but the rest of the time I kill the possums and either pluck the fur or skin the larger, better-quality black-brown skins. Later in the day Robin resets and baits the possum line to earn a half-share of the profits. We sell the fur and send the better-quality skins away to Dunedin to be tanned.

Of course possums are not the only pests in the area. In 1998 John Meads, a DoC ranger based at Fox Glacier, asked me to take on a contract as part of a gorse-eradication project. He explained how they intended to eradicate the gorse plants that grew in profusion in various places along the coastline, and asked if I would mark and map all the gorse along the coastal fringe between Awarua Point and Cascade Point, a distance of 50 kilometres. I agreed, and looked forward to the opportunity to get paid $100 a day to explore and map the coastline further.

John posted me aerial photographs and maps to mark the gorse on, and I began by surveying from Awarua Point back to the Gorge. The ocean tides must have spread most of the seeds, while the birds and wind had spread some inland, 200–300 metres across very swampy ground. Most of the bushes were taking advantage of gaps between sedges and flaxes that had been knocked over and salt-poisoned by rogue waves. Later, while Catherine, Christan, Robin and I walked out to town, I surveyed up through Brown's Refuge, the Spoon, Barn Bay and up to Cascade Point, mapping and marking gorse bushes all the way.

Our main source of protein is fish caught in the river. When the weather is suitable I set a 10-metre-long net in the river mouth at low tide. Each end of the net is marked with an orange fishing buoy and weighed down with a stone anchor.

When I build the net I use herring mesh to target the yellow-eyed mullet which travel upriver at high tide in schools. The fish are usually captured in the net overnight, so each morning I haul it in, clear it and if need be reset it. We often catch up to eight to a dozen fish which we usually fillet and eat as fish and chips.

Occasionally we catch kahawai and sea-run trout, which we often cook up in the wood smoker. Often the local eels come overnight and take fish, leaving a mass of tangles and half-chewed fish for us. When they become too much of a problem we catch one or two on handlines and smoke them up as well.

You need to be very cautious working around the net since the stone anchor and rope often jams on the boulder-strewn river bottom. If this happens I have to launch the dinghy to use as a platform to lift the net. Sometimes if the net is set and the rain develops overnight I have to get up at all hours and don my wet-weather gear to haul in the net before the river rises to flood. This can be extra tricky if the anchor jams as well in the black of the night, though by use of torchlight and dinghy I can manage to retrieve it.

One time we lost the net in a large flood overnight but managed to find and dig it out from under two metres of logs and sticks on the main beach. Amongst the wood pulp we also found spiny rock lobster, freshwater lobsters and the brilliant blue-purple giant kokopu, all freshly washed up. The kokopu inhabit a 200-metre-long pool in a flat saddle at the head of the river.

Come whitebait season it is great to have an excuse to spend time down by the river watching the waters flow by over the myriad colourful stones and boulders. Grey warblers sing their spring fishing songs while the sunlight dapples through the shade of the overhanging fuchsias and mahoe. We don't get catches like the other nearby coastal rivers but we usually catch a feed or enough to make the effort worthwhile. Most of the migrating whitebait are koaro, which inhabit the fast-running mountain streams. They are slightly larger and fatter than the more common inanga that inhabit the swamps and lakes.

As life progresses your family become more precious to you than anything else. After Robin was born Geoff Robson gave us an emergency locator beacon off his fishing boat, so we have had that at Gorge River. And once Christan began going out on his own possuming and roaming off to Big Bay whitebaiting we bought him a personal emergency locator beacon, which we have since upgraded.

For the first 10 years of my life in South Westland I could have disappeared without trace and no one would have been the wiser for up to six months, until people in Haast or Te Anau wondered why I hadn't turned up. Even today, I regard my health and safety as primarily my own responsibility. But the safety and well-being of my family are the most important things in my life.

chapter 21 disaster

One evening in early December 1995 we were just sitting down around the living-room table for a meal of fried fresh yellow-eyed mullet fillets and chips when there was the unmistakable whine and hum of a chopper. The sound quickly rose to full volume as a Robinson 22 helicopter emerged from out of the Gorge.

Stepping out the front door, we saw the machine veer sharply and make a direct line for a large slip that exposed the steep, bush-clad limestone bluff on the opposite side of the river. There was a quick succession of gunshots, not more than 250 metres away, as the chopper boys had obviously got onto a deer. We all watched in excitement, waiting for their next move, while the helicopter continued to hover above the slip. Then the pilot turned the machine away and landed on the gravel beach 100 metres north of the river mouth, just below the slip. They were nearly out of sight, but we could still see the whirl of the blades while they prepared for their next manoeuvre.

The engine's revs increased again as the machine gradually lifted off, revealing a chain dangling beneath the chopper. As it gained more height we could see a person hanging from the 15-metre chain. Suddenly, when the shooter was about 10 metres off the ground, the hook gave way leaving the chain and its burden to plunge to the gravel beach below.

Robin was just one year old at the time, but she still remembers this moment when time stood still. I gasped to Catherine, 'He'll be a hospital case.'

Not knowing when I would be back, I raced inside, grabbed my Swannie and coat and sprinted down to the river bank, dragged the canoe into the water and quickly paddled down the river and across to the opposite bank. After lifting the canoe up above the high-tide mark I ran past the flaxes and up the beach.

As I arrived the pilot was trying to tie the shooter into his seat. I hadn't met him before, and he was surprised to see me. His first comment was, 'I was being very careful not to touch the button.'

He was obviously very shaken by the turn of events, as in the fading light he asked where the nearest hospital would be.

'Queenstown,' I replied, 'but it will be dark before you get there.'

'I'd better head back up to Jackson Bay,' he said, as he continued to secure the severely injured shooter into his seat. The R22 helicopter with its doors off is more like a motorbike with rotors, and there is very little room in it. The pilot then hopped in, belted up, and applied pitch to full throttle, but as he attempted to become airborne his passenger kept groping blindly for the controls, obviously in pain and panicking. The aircraft once again came back to an idle. Together we tied the unfortunate man's hands to his sides.

Eventually they became airborne and headed off north up the coast, flying just above the beach. Less than a kilometre away the chopper landed again so I loped along up the beach to lend a hand. But before I reached them, the aircraft took off again, leap-frogging north once again. I was just regaining my breath and composure when the machine appeared from out of the north and landed on the sandy beach beside me. The pilot was now alone.

'Can you stay with Andy?' he shouted above the whirl and whine of the blades. 'I can't fly with him, he keeps grabbing the controls.'

I jumped in, belted up, and next thing we were airborne, heading quickly up the beach past Kelp Rock and the awesome Steeples, thrusting upwards like a couple of sentinels from the bouldery beach. On up past the limestone bluffs of Bivvy Rock rising from the sea, until after about four kilometres I could see the outline of a body clad in a red jumpsuit lying on the sand just below the flaxes.

We descended, hovering above the beach, then quickly bounced to a landing.

'Can you stay with Andy?' the pilot repeated. 'I'll go for help.'

'OK, good as gold,' I replied, hopping out head down, eyes jammed tight behind my hands as the sand blasted me, the blades clawing the air, until the chopper had disappeared once again.

Andy was in severe pain, his gravel voice barely audible through the frothy blood in his throat, mouth and running down his cheeks. It is difficult to describe these events, but he basically held me by the chest of my Swannie with a vice-like grip, never relenting while life remained in his veins.

I realised that we had met a couple of weeks prior to this

unfortunate day when he and a different pilot, Ken Hutchins, had stopped for a cup of tea and a catch-up. Andy had previously worked for DoC but had always had a burning desire to work on the choppers. He was fulfilling his dream when this mishap took him in full stride.

As the sun set behind me over the ocean and a thousand sandflies chewed holes in my feet, I held Andy and he held me. He kept talking to me right up to the end, his bruised and battered face showing no resemblance to the Andy I knew.

After half an hour of constant struggle and writhing pain, life left him. Andy departed and his body lay still and serene. After attempting cardiopulmonary resuscitation on him for 20 minutes I closed his eyelids and said a prayer, asking his maker to look after him.

As the darkness fell and the stars began to blaze above me, I rustled through my pockets and found a cigarette lighter, then I gathered up some kindling and driftwood. As the flames flickered into life I breathed a sigh of relief. My mind still felt numb as I tried to work through what had happened.

Soon after that Ian, the pilot, found his way back, his spotlight beam searching through the darkness. I extinguished the fire and he landed, to be confronted with the shock of the news of Andy's death. He was devastated.

Search and Rescue were on the way, so we relit the fire and waited.

Once again we doused the flames as another larger chopper, piloted by Jamie Scott, appeared over the horizon, landing beside us with paramedic Natalie Wynn. The blades of the powerful Hughes 500D buzzed overhead as we lifted Andy's body onto a stretcher and in through the back doors of the machine. Then, as quickly as they had come, they disappeared into the night.

Ian, who was severely shaken, elected to fly his machine back to our house and stay the night there, rather than flying out in the darkness. We would both head up to Haast in the morning to be interviewed by the local policeman and the Civil Aviation Authority investigator.

I would rather have walked back since the smell of death was still in the air, but once again I hopped in and Ian cranked up the machine. The windscreen was misty so Ian found an old rag under the seat to wipe it with, which left a thick smear all over the Perspex bubble. I was supposed to direct the way, but I could not see through the bubble or ahead of us, since Ian had the helicopter flying half sideways, hanging his head out his doorway to see. We needed to stay close enough to the gravel beach so that with the spotlight we could avoid running into Bivvy Rock and the Steeples, which were in our flight path. As we flew through the pitch-black darkness there was a burst of red, yellow and white light through the oily bubble, first ahead of us, then above us.

'What the hell was that?' we both yelled, blinking.

It was around midnight when we finally landed safely on the airstrip at Gorge River, ending the worst flight of my life. Catherine solved the mystery of the light. She had observed another helicopter fly past Gorge River spotlighting its way up the coast. It had flown straight over the top of us as we were heading down the beach between Bivvy Rock and the Steeples.

After a brew and a feed there was no use trying to sleep. I had some paintings that needed taking up to Haast, so I began packing them in tubes for the journey. I finally hit the sack at about 3am, to toss and turn for the rest of the night.

Next morning Ian and I flew up to Haast and landed at Hannah's Clearing. I dropped off my paintings and we drove up and reported to Roger Millard at the Haast police station.

After an intense interview, and signing a witness statement, I waited for the CAA investigator to arrive from Christchurch early that afternoon to repeat the process. I emphasised that in my opinion the unfortunate pilot of the fateful machine had been flying carefully and steadily as he lifted Andy Marden up off the ground. The CAA's eventual finding was an electrical failure of the cargo hook, though that would have been little consolation to Ian.

Later Ray Paulie, the owner of the Robinson 22 helicopter, offered to fly me back home to Gorge River in his other machine. After flying up the Cascade Valley through Saddle Creek and into the head of the Gorge we flew down the river valley, emerging out over the river mouth and the sea, before I was set back down with Catherine, Christan and Robin.

We watched the machine fly away, knowing that the last 24 hours had put life into a whole new perspective, one to contemplate, assimilate and file away forever.

chapter 22 creative energies

W hen I was on my own I earned my income from the boats, and I didn't need to sell my paintings when people expressed an interest in buying them. They, along with my carvings, were too sacred to actually turn into money, though I often gave them away to people as a show of friendship or in appreciation for favours.

By the time Christan was born my hobbies of the previous 10 years had become our main source of income. Since then I have been self-employed. We remain members of the fishing and whitebaiting community, but with an alternative income.

My work is an inspiration. I keep myself motivated by following the pathway that occurs each day. I have many projects on the go at the same time, and follow the one that I am inspired to do. My inspiration and subsequent motivation finds a pathway through all these projects so at the end of each day I feel something of significance has been achieved, and eventually a batch of works is completed.

Ideally I will have thought out in the evening the projects I will work on the next day. They can be brought up in my mind's eye to concentrate on as I go to sleep, and again in the morning before I physically apply paint to canvas or pounamu to grindstone. This approach works well and little time is wasted. To be at work all I need to do is roll out of bed and get into it. My painting workspace is in my favourite chair in our living room at the end of our bed, next to the radio and CD player. I prefer to share my workspace with my family, to stay involved with the events of the day, though in my own bubble of activity. This bubble actually stays with me wherever we go, winter and summer, even when we are on the road. A selection of tools and projects always travels with me so there is no such thing as downtime, unless a rest is the order of the day. Being totally self-motivated, I love my work and relish this momentum with a passion. After my family, it is my primary focus.

During the last few years I have been very focused on improving my painting and carving ability and techniques. I work most days, unless there are maintenance jobs that need attention or I feel like exploring upriver or coastal beachcombing. Using the natural light for painting and sculpting is important. In summer I usually keep painting until the light fades, though sometimes, if a certain area of a painting needs more work before the oils set, I will use our solar- and wind-powered lighting and keep going until midnight.

For the last six years nearly all my work in jade and painting has been commissioned or pre-ordered. Of the last 80 paintings I have done, all but three have been commissioned. This means I can focus on each work with that particular person in mind. It provides a great social contact with people since each work draws out the personality of the client, and it places particular demands on my approach to the work. I enjoy recalling my interaction or relationship with the person, which gives each work more meaning. This also helps friendships to develop over the years, which lessens the isolation in which we live.

I work with focus and discipline, putting my time to good use. I contemplate and plan each work but don't procrastinate or waste time trying to get in the mood or the right headspace. I usually just get on with it. Having a good range of different projects on the go means I can always be keen and inspired to get into a particular work with enthusiasm and gusto.

Some of my paintings are of nearby scenery. When undertaking these works I carry my easel and other gear to the spot, either down the river, along the beach or on the airstrip. This can be quite demanding since I am often chased home by developing gale-force winds, squalls of rain and hailstones. I usually spend 20 minutes or so picking the wriggling sandflies out of the oil painting's surface after I return home.

Usually I start a batch of six or seven paintings, with the aim of completing them over the next five months. I rarely work on a particular painting for more than two days before I put it down and pick up another one and apply my enthusiasm once again. Finishing up a work can be very demanding. The finer points of each work require attention, and you can't walk away from them since there is always a deadline. As a painting finally emerges into life I am often struck by the energy and vitality of the scene, since each one is an integral part of my home and experience. Tears of relief and emotion often flow as I am captured by a completed work.

In my development as a carver I have literally begun in the stone age and worked my way forward. My carving was inspired by the greenstone floaters, the tangiwai and pounamu chips and flakes along with adze blanks and adzes that lay strewn by the winds and the tides. Originally all my pounamu works were completed by hand, with the use of sandstone cutters and grindstones, with water as the lubricant and muscle as the power source. For the first 15 years this was all I used, picking up on the techniques used by the early Maori settlers and inhabitants of the region. As time went on I began using carborundum sharpening stones as working abrasives, along with sandstone, greywacke and flint. I used the flint to drill holes in each pendant I made, and the greywacke or basalt to mark out a starting groove into which the sharp sandstone cutting edge can work. I have cut by hand through pounamu four centimetres thick and 25 centimetres long using sandstone cutters and water with sand thrown into the groove to increase abrasion.

From an oval piece of pounamu 25 centimetres long, 18 centimetres wide and four centimetres thick I made an adze. I completed two full cuts, working from each side to create a groove which meets up with an identical groove coming through from the other side until the side piece breaks off. Once two side pieces have been cut off you are left with the basic adze shape, which then needs to be rubbed on a large flat sandstone surface with water and sand grit to bring up the sharpened blade of the adze.

This enriching technique consumes many days and months of work, and I envy the commitment and drive of early Maori to complete their works. As you work at a carving you enter a meditative state that takes you on a unique journey.

Today I still use this technique, but most of my energy is melded with diamond tools to release the spirit lying waiting within the stone. Over the years I have gradually increased my capacity by using solar and wind power via batteries to drive the 12-volt, 24-volt and 240-volt motors that power hand-held drills, diamond grinders and cutting blades. Malcolm Hendry, an electronics engineer from Rangiora, comes in hunting every Roar, and he and his mate Dave Hill from Christchurch along with Geoff Robson from Neils Beach have helped to set up and maintain my gear.

Another development that occurred early on was the discovery of the shapes of fish and birds within the smaller shards of tangiwai and pounamu. Many such shards or flakes would have a pointed end with a splayed-out tail, forming the natural shape of a fish with its head and tail. All I needed to do was run the shard along a sandstone cutter to create the fins and there you had a fish. I used flakes of flint in my hand-drill to make a hole, and presto, there was a pendant.

I found tangiwai (bowenite), down at Milford Sound, and also bought shards from Murray Gunn who had worked a claim at Poison Bay, south of Milford. I completed many of these fish, along with the occasional bird. As time went on I evolved towards using diamond gear, mainly so I could produce more works and explore other dimensions in the crafting of pounamu.

The first pounamu dolphin I made, a three-dimensional figure 15 centimetres long, was all done by hand. I used a large sandstone in the sand dunes overlooking the river mouth, along with a carborundum sharpening stone held in my bench vice and narrower sandstone cutters to work around the dorsal and pectoral fins and tail.

Within my being I have a passion for finding the dolphins in all media that are able to be carved. The liveliness and spirit of these creatures has captured me, so I devote much of my life to releasing this essence within pounamu, whalebone, coral and timber. Dolphins are a common sight around the river mouth. Sometimes there are hundreds of them chasing schools of pilchards, herring or kahawai. They leap and frolic, emanating a spirit of cooperation that we humans would love to emulate. As a family we feel a strong empathy with the dolphins that swim close to our home.

On a sunny, windy day, I'm in my element. My work day is governed by the prevailing wind and lack of cloud cover. On a sunny, windy day I will be carving. On a cloudy, still day I will be painting oil on canvas. The two modes of work balance out over the long term as I am continually studying the whims of the weather. I love this since it keeps me in constant rhythm with the climatic forces about me. Once upon a time the wind was just something to blow my hair around. Now it is my work partner.

Part of my work routine involves delivering my craftwork to various places on the coast such as Big Bay, Okuru, Moeraki or Greymouth, or further afield to Wanaka, Queenstown, Dunedin, Christchurch or Picton. We usually send out the rolled-up paintings, carvings and a change of clothes on a passing aircraft before walking up to the Cascade or down to the Hollyford. Some works have been sent as far as Australia, Switzerland, Britain, Germany, Malaysia, the US, China and Colombia. Some people, of course, prefer to fly in and pick the work up themselves.

The many years I have spent exploring this magnificent landscape have all come into use in my artwork, and I enjoy being asked to paint scenes that I haven't yet visited, since this leads me to new and wonderful places that I may never otherwise have experienced.

In 1987 I made a discovery that has dwelt with me ever since, even though I gave it release.

If you can imagine finding a treasure trove, an old wooden

casket full of gold doubloons, with one's own hands, then you can come close to feeling the thrill I experienced the day I met with a chapter of my destiny.

It was the happiest and the saddest day of my life, creating a mixture of emotions for my spirit and senses. This event has connected me with the long-distant past, the present and the ultimate future of us all, the knowledge, relationships and insight to a time long gone by, representing an encyclopedia of understanding and a key to tomorrow. The ancestors had also been waiting for this day, sure in the knowledge that their hard work and their story would not be lost.

I had been working with a spade in my garden, not more than three metres away from where I sleep, when a sound emitted from underground struck my attention — a high-pitched chink from a hard, durable material. I knelt down and pushed my hand deep into the earth. As I brought it out I drew forth pounamu adzes and adze blanks that grated slowly one upon the other.

They were of varying sizes, some 12 centimetres long, others 20–25 centimetres, and some up to 40 centimetres, two or three of each size. Some were rough adze blanks, some hammer-dressed, and others ground out to a beautiful smooth though heavily oxidised finish. Time stood still until they had all surfaced. Eventually 23 pieces lay on the ground and in my arms. All were created from local South Westland pounamu.

The adzes were later gifted to the West Coast Historical Museum in Hokitika by the local Maakawhio people, but before that the DoC had local Maori midden remains dated at the radiocarbon dating unit at Waikato University. These middens had been exposed by ocean waves surging up into the beach head. About one month later, a DoC archaeologist arrived at Gorge River, inviting me to come up to Barn Bay where they were working. I showed him the cache of adzes which they took with them in the helicopter. Three tests were done, and each came up with 1700 years old, plus or minus 100 years. But of course this was documented as 'at least 500 years of age'.

The ancient heritage of the Maori people has been an integral chapter of my life in South Westland, along with the presence of pounamu in this region. My life and pounamu are intertwined, and it is part of my life blood. In a way, the ancestors have been enhancing my intimate knowledge of the formation and distribution of pounamu. The ancient Maori who lived in these parts have left evidence of their habitation in the form of worked pounamu, be it as chips and flakes, adzes and adze blanks, hammer stones, pendants or broken boulders. These workings are directly related to the formation and distribution of pounamu, and add another dimension to my intimate knowledge of this stone. Its origin and pathways are revealed, along with the early use of this resource by the Waitaha Maori who have inhabited South Westland from 1600 to 1800 years ago to this present day.

In my mind's eye there exists a map of the living and working sites. Early Maori in their canoes made landfall in various places which happen to correspond to the safest places to land; hence the campsites and artefacts buried in the tide. Tangiwai was carried on sea voyages up from Milford Sound and Poison Bay and accidentally dropped in the rolling surf. Antiquities of industrial use were crafted from pounamu, to carve out an existence in this harsh land.

According to oral tradition, in the South Island the Waitaha were the first people to impose a genealogy upon this land,

and they are recognised as the first tangata whenua. The Waitaha were a people of peace who had migrated across the South Pacific to escape extinction, and they had dwelt in Aotearoa in peace for 1000 years until the warrior tribes arrived and took the Waitaha women and healers, did away with their men and became the Maori we know today. In New Zealand most of the genealogy and place names descend from Waitaha whakapapa. One thing you can't change is your ancestry. You also have to acknowledge it because that is who you are.

The Waitaha families, the Ruka and Te Maiharoa among others, have handed down their story from grandparent to mokopuna for many generations. Until recently they kept their history secret to preserve its mana. Now they have published two beautifully bound books, *Song of Waitaha: History of a Nation*, alongside *Whispers of Waitaha*. These treasures are revealed by kaumatua and kuia.

Some of the warrior Maori have openly acknowledged their whakapapa, though grudgingly, since the subjugation of a nation of people is a dark period in their history. But once they acknowledge their heritage and embrace the spirit of peace, it will strengthen their mana and that of all the people of this land.

After finding the cache of adzes I visited Kelly Wilson, the kaumatua of the local Maakawhio people, a number of times to discuss matters. Later my journeys led me to the door of Kelly's brother, Bob Wilson. Bob was the Maakawhio tohunga, and after Kelly's passing he became the chairman of the Maakawhio Runanga. At the time I was deeply immersed in my naturopathy studies, so Bob, sensing my receptivity, began to share his knowledge and natural-healing techniques with me. Each day that I spent with him in his humble home in Haast revealed more aspects of his role and his connection with the ancient past. He spoke of his role as tohunga and ti ha, along with the use of the baton, a 30-centimetres-long wooden whakapapa stick.

This ancient implement, which resided in his home, possessed a notch for each tohunga of every generation of his iwi, since they had first settled in Aotearoa. When two tribes met, the tohunga representing their people would come forward facing each other, to protect their people. While standing at a reasonable distance from each other, the tohunga would begin twirling their batons in a prescribed manner and in unison with each other in front of their solar plexus, their stomach. Each tohunga in his turn would describe and relate many or most of the characteristics of his respective tribe's lineage back to the landing of the canoe that had brought them to this land.

The synchronised twirling of each baton showed that each interpreted the other's story to the letter, and as time passed they grew more at ease with each other. From time to time a grievance or challenge could be slipped in to catch the other unawares. But the ever-vigilant tohunga would be ready to deflect and fend off this unexpected threat with a sideways wave of his hands and twirl of his baton, protecting his tribe and their mana from harm. Bob described how he would go into a trance as his ancestors spoke through him and told their story.

Bob also related his concern about the danger that his and other tribes could become divided as they sought to share their new-found wealth as the Crown tried to right the wrongs of yesteryear. He felt that during the 1960s and '70s everything was falling into place, and New Zealand had become a good place for Maori and Pakeha to live alongside each other, despite the turmoil and strife that had obviously occurred a century before.

He felt there was one result that had made up for all that suffering and pain. This was that the previously warring Maori tribes of Aotearoa had become New Zealanders and hence one people, despite their differences. Now they were free to travel the land at will and without fear. The way of the warrior is self-defeating. The battlefield is a sad, desolate and polluted place.

Some recent policies have helped to unite us, some to divide us. With that division comes pain for all parties. Pain brings the desire to heal. To heal we need to remain at arm's length, look at the bigger picture and maintain neutrality. Pain brings the ability to heal for those who can rise above the tension and work towards a brighter today and a better tomorrow, for all our families.

chapter 23 our life, our children

Though my father and I have had our differences over the years, and we walk different pathways, over time we have become reconciled. Having my own children has made me more appreciative of the sacrifices he has made and the generosity he has displayed to me over the years as a parent. He, in turn, has given Catherine and me credit for the time and effort we have devoted to Christan and Robin, and can see that despite the fact that we live in such an isolated place we have ensured they have grown up to be balanced people.

Over the years we have made six trips to Australia as a family. We would generally stay for about six weeks at my parents' home in Mooloolaba, giving Christan and Robin the opportunity to get to know their grandparents and experience how the other half live. They usually adapted quickly to the change in lifestyle, getting on well with my parents and seeming just as at ease as their cousins, who have enjoyed all the opportunities that city life has to offer. My father has often said that if he ever went into business with any of his grandchildren, he would choose Christan.

For many years now Dad has been involved in advising us on some of our monetary affairs and managing a large proportion of our savings. This has given him the opportunity to become more involved in our welfare, and we have benefited from his wealth of knowledge and experience, as well as enjoying the much closer personal contact and communication this has brought about.

My parents have also visited us at Gorge River several times, and the last time my family all celebrated Christmas together was at Gorge River in 2007. This was the last time I saw my mother alive.

Catherine and I see our role as parents as including that of teachers, so that we know and understand our children and what they have learnt along the way. We were not prepared to relinquish this role to others since we felt this was one of our most important tasks as parents, and a great way to be in tune with Christan and Robin.

In New Zealand, children have to be registered with the Education Department by the age of six, but they can be home-schooled, as long as they are taught as well and as regularly as they would be at a registered school. We home-schooled Christan for his primary education and then switched over to the Correspondence School for most of his secondary schooling. Our daughter Robin was home-schooled for five years, then taught by Correspondence. Catherine has undertaken most of the formal teaching, and is well suited to this role, having a sharp mind and intellect. I have concentrated more on earning the income to support us all, and of course through our daily life our children have learned all sorts of other life skills, including fishing, gardening, tramping, carpentry, goldmining, studying animal and plant life, along with survival skills.

In 2009 Christan decided to complete his final year of secondary school at Mount Aspiring College in Wanaka, specialising in outdoor pursuits along with physics, chemistry and mathematics. In 2010 he began an Outdoor Leadership course at Otago Polytech, going straight into the second year of the course as a result of his achievements at school. He was also awarded a scholarship from Otago Polytech to the tune of $1500 off the fees each year, for up to three years.

While at school in Wanaka Christan would fly in each month along with our supply and mail drop in Roger Monk's Cessna 180. Watching him fly away each time was something else. As the aircraft slowly disappeared in the distance, the wind gusts buffeting my eardrums would meld with the salt of my tears. Our young falcon had flown again. Now, at the dawning of his new life, he is pursuing his own dreams. They may differ from mine, but I have every confidence he will make a success of them.

Robin is also an excellent scholar, and has her own strong beliefs and goals. She intends to study science at Otago University, specialising in ornithology, with the aim of aiding endangered bird species. In 2009 she was involved in counting penguin numbers along the nearby coastline for the NZ Penguin Trust, and she also runs a line of 12 tunnels with stoat traps to protect the local birdlife, penguins and our pet hen, Chooky. (Chooky has been part of our family for the last six years, and travels with us on our tramps, journeys and flights. She has flown across the Southern Alps at least 14 times, and spent eight days tramping with us to Gunn's Camp in the Upper Hollyford Valley. She has also survived three falcon attacks, including one in which she was airlifted off the ground.)

Our children have an intimate knowledge of wildlife. While

Christan and I concentrate on the whereabouts of crayfish and paua, Robin studies the tubeworms and triplefin fish species in the rock pools. Over the years they have both befriended pet seagulls and oystercatchers, as well as deer, penguins, paradise shelducks and trout, and studied the passing whales, dolphins and seals, and the kaka, wood pigeons, blue duck, fernbirds, tui, tomtits and bellbirds that frequent the area.

Christan is a keen trout fly fisherman, and as a 15-year-old guided an American fly fisherman up the Gorge River, where he landed a three-kilogram trout. We often head off fishing together, either off the coastal rocks for blue wrasse, or in the river mouth for kahawai, yellow-eyed mullet and sea-run trout.

When he was younger Christan produced excellent paintings and jade carvings, and he now makes possum-fur products such as cushions and bedspreads which he sews up from locally sourced skins. Robin sets off each day with her camera to photograph birds, waves and sunsets, and she creates beautiful sets of earrings from seashells and local greenstone. She is also adept at embroidery, quilting and poetry.

Although we are isolated in one sense, the children have never been short of companions. Friends and family members fly or tramp in to share time with us, and each year we travel down to Big Bay to holiday and whitebait with our friends the Mitchells. When trampers came through Christan would usually set up his cricket wickets on the airstrip outside the DoC hut, and before too long a game would be in progress.

As a family we feel privileged to live in this beautiful area, and to have enjoyed the opportunity to explore its wonders. Raising a family has made it more difficult for Catherine and me to keep to our ideals. At times our children have drawn us back into the mainstream world, especially as they have become teenagers and interested in the fashions and technology that are a normal part of life for their friends and peers. We have resisted many of the pressures, but there is a gradual influence creeping in. In order to keep our family intact we must compromise our views and learn to adapt.

chapter 24 come fly with me

Over the years I have flown with 56 different pilots and undertaken about 230 flights in light aircraft and helicopters. Some flights were over 500 kilometres, and others just a hop across a river. Flying is part of life in South Westland and Fiordland.

Occasionally I have been invited along if someone happened to be heading in the same direction as me. One time, around 1987, Sax flew me from his hangar at Carter's Beach and dropped me in a paddock opposite the Haast shop and post office. As I crossed the road to withdraw the one dollar left in my Post Office bank account, a bus driver who had seen us land commented, 'You travel in style.'

I could only smile and agree.

Before Christan and Robin were born we had never chartered a flight, although I had already flown with 27 pilots on 93 flights. But before Christan's birth in September 1991, I began clearing the overgrown airstrip at Gorge River, whereupon Roger Monk landed with Lou Brown and offered his services.

We still make a point of walking out to town, either north

to the Cascade and Haast or south to the Hollyford road end. Then, after accomplishing whatever mission we have planned we generally head to Sue and Ian Todd's farm near Arrowtown to make preparations before our flight home across the Southern Alps. We pursue a quick succession of major shopping events at the supermarket, hardware and the Warehouse, visit the bank and tidy up any loose ends before we cut loose for another six months in isolation.

The New Orleans and the Tap in Arrowtown are almost my local pub, since this is where Toddy and I have time to catch up with a few mates and chew the fat while we wait for the weather to break and settle again, providing a safe avenue for us to traverse the passes of the Southern Alps with Roger Monk and Debbie McColl in their Cessna 180. Since the Cessna is a four-seater aircraft, when the whole family is travelling it takes two trips for us all to get home. This part of our journey can be quite intense since everything has to fall into place, including the weather, which is always unpredictable.

Off and away we head into the blue, blue skies and over the tussocky, rocky, snow-covered Alps. Once above the Arrowtown Basin we fly towards the Shotover River catchment, with mountainous scree slopes looming beside us while the river ravines lie far below. We gaze down and see the shadow of the aircraft sliding quickly across the russet schisty mountains. Sometimes, after all the hustle and bustle of the trip to town, I gaze across the Alps in amazement to think that my home lies far away across these snowy peaks. It blows me away to think that here I am actually up here, flying with my family to reach our home. I often wonder how this all evolved.

As we head northwest I see the rainbow mists in the

valleys, Mt Aspiring looming higher on the horizon, a mountainous beacon as we cross Lochnagar at the head of the Shotover and soar out over the expansive Dart Valley, a green carpet beneath us. Robin and I were the second load, heading west with Roger and his pilot, Jess Wilkinson. Catherine and Christan have flown before us and are already at home.

Once through the Bean's Burn and Fohn Saddle, there appears Mt Tutoko and Madeline to the south, their misty valleys aglow. Our shadow continues to slip across a forest wonderland, scree slopes and rocky mountain ridges bathed in brilliant sunlight and pristine snow. I feel a deep empathy with this place as we watch waterfalls plunge off the Olivine ice plateau.

Next we see the meandering, braided Pyke River flowing down shingly gravel flats through swampy river deltas into the depths of Lake Wilmot. This watercourse is choked with logs since the hills are cloaked in trees. We rise gently above turrets of rock, buffeted by thermals. Eventually off to the west lies the Tasman Sea. There is Big Bay with her white rollers streaming in from the blue-green sea.

Many memories adorn this journey, of places where I have wandered on foot or boated by sea. Over to the east stands the Red Mountain's russet scree, barren like a Middle Eastern landscape. Flying through the Pyke Saddle, we are now in the upper reaches of the Jerry as it flows into the Gorge River, a glacial ravine carved through the flattened, ochre hills.

I feel exhilarated as I head home after time away travelling the islands of Aotearoa, back to a place of totally primeval wilderness. The pilot turns the descending aircraft into the Gorge River valley slicing deep between the flattened plateaux. Ahead lie the Tasman Sea, the Gorge River mouth and the islets. We circle out over the ocean to line up with the airstrip running parallel to the coastline. Our home lies nestled among the flaxes beside the river mouth.

Our speed is slowed as we cruise past the Steeples, our wings open like a bird coming back to earth. The green pounamu sea rises up to meet us as we line up with our airstrip. Passing the river mouth we have touchdown, a few shallow bounces, taxiing, and eventually we come safely to rest.

I breathe a sigh of relief. As we unload the aircraft, the smell of salt air and the roar of the wild ocean greets us. The shrill cries of the oystercatchers, the rustling of the flaxes, the rolling waves inside the islands and the overgrown garden welcome us. We have completed our journey. We are home again.

Despite the fact that we have chosen a remote corner of the world to live in, we have been blessed by meeting many wonderful, loving and intelligent people. Along with exploring and living in this awesome place, the highlight of my life here has been the people we have come to know and love. Our friends and contacts extend across the globe.

South Westland and Fiordland attracts independent types out to explore. When they reach these regions their lights are on full beam and their minds and spirits are open to communication. They usually leave their pretences behind them.

Some may have travelled from the far reaches of the world, from densely populated cities, to arrive suddenly in this place. I am amazed by the consistency of the calibre of person who makes the effort to work, live or visit this realm. They are generally on a genuine quest to capture the essence of this wilderness, not in an exploitative way but more as a yearning to reach inside and relate to its spirit. If they only come to take and hold, then their lives and visit will have been wasted, since this place has so much more to offer to those who seek to empathise with this pristine domain.

Unless they seek, they can never find and behold the treasure and sparkle held within. After that they are captured. An umbilical cord continues to nourish them wherever their travels may lead them.

epilogue

There is a place I always go, a place of stillness and serenity. The silence is broken only by the distant grind and boom of the mountains, along with the high-pitched, organ-like sounds coming off the meandering river rapids. The river flats open out to the sun. Tussocks, grasses, flaxes and toetoe have taken to the old river braids. This is an expansive place of no pretences. You are so far away from anywhere that all you see is awesomeness and grandeur, putting you in your place and swallowing up your ego.

Feelings of insignificance are balanced by the energy this area exudes. Breathing in the cool, crisp air invigorates and enriches the soul and spirit. The shores at the head of Lake Alabaster, with its clear, tannin-stained waters, reach upstream through the Pyke River to Lake Wilmot and beyond, surrounded by hanging valleys. The Forgotten and Olivine Rivers are towered over by snow-capped, rocky turrets and glaciers.

This is a place where many others go in spirit when caught in the grind of modern-day life. Somewhere the soul knows it always has a home, a place of indistinct tracks and trails where the legend of the Black Swamp deters many from venturing further. To the south the summits of Mt Madeline and Tutoko pierce the sky and also sit within the depths of the lake. The Darrans are Fiordland's sentinels of diorite, schist and basalt. Places where only the falcons and kea soar or the brave and foolhardy dare to go. This place fills my heart along with the hearts of many others seeking refuge from stress and the storms of everyday life. Many of my friends from near and far come to this place to mingle their spirits with the cleansing waters.

Do you know the feeling when someone arrives out of the blue, literally flies into your living space, lands their aircraft, and invites you along for a look around? So skywards we go into the blue, eyes wide open, terra firma gliding away below. The narrow world of today and tomorrow is suddenly replaced by the wide open spaces of the sky and little else except the whirl of the blades overhead with our space bubble suspended below.

One day in particular lives in my memory: 20 August 2007. Dick Deaker descended out of the blue in his Hughes 500D, after circling around in a whirl of blades, to land in front of our garden. As the jet engine winds down and the blades continue to buzz overhead, Dick's door opens. He steps to the ground with the pilot's careful awareness of overhead danger, then comes across to greet us. After handshakes and greetings he invites me with camera in hand to head up to the Olivines, to his favourite place, the Forgotten River valley. He has mentioned before that he would like me to paint this particular scene with its hanging valley and surrounding glaciers.

In a few short minutes I have grabbed my pack, camera and Swanndri as Dick explains to Catherine that we will be away for a couple of hours. I climb into the machine and buckle up. Dick accelerates to full throttle, applies pitch to the blur of blades and away we go. Christan, Robin and Catherine quickly became miniature people as we climb upwards and over the forest canopy leading up to the coastal ridge and on up towards Mt Malcolm.

As we head south across the upper reaches of Ryan's Creek and the Hacket we can still see the ocean away in the distance. To our left the upper Jerry and Junction Hill stretch away up to the Gorge Plateau, with massive scree slopes descending into the alpine faultline between the Duncan River and Pyke Saddle. Ultramafic red, orange and purple dominate the barren upper reaches of Junction Hill, with the forested canyons of the Gorge and Plateau Creeks slicing into the sloping, flattish moraine.

Glaciers have played a major role in shaping this terrain, leaving tall hills and mountains shaved off to flattened, bare and barren ground. Healthy forest lands ground down and overlaid with marble-shaped boulders, some the size of houses.

But the glaciers have been selective. In some massive valleys such as the Cascade, Big Bay and the Gorge, one side of the valley has the original hills and mountains peaking up, while the other side has been carved off flat. The glacier has curved around a major bend in the valley and reared up and over the hillsides of the outer curve, creating a lateral moraine such as Cascade Plateau, Awarua Point and the area between the Spoon and the Gorge.

Before too long the Red Mountains come into view as we head down the Pyke Valley. As we hover beside a rocky tussock ridge above the Barrier River, a classic view down the Pyke of Lake Alabaster, Mt Madeline and Tutoko, Dick encourages me to take photos. We then head up the Olivine catchment, reaching the hanging valley of the Forgotten River. In the blustery winds Dick does his best to hover while I take a dozen or more shots, taking in both sides of the valley floor, the mountains and the glaciers.

Next we fly through Intervention Saddle below the Tower, north into the Barrier Valley for more classic photos, then on into the Upper Red Pyke, past the old mining huts, and into the head of the Cascade via Simonin Pass. Flying low across the Red Hills, we land on Telescope Hill to admire the view looking out across Big Bay. The journey reminds me of previous travels where I have come across the result of glaciers carving into the heart of the faultlines, exposing the faces of massive seams of pounamu where they were originally formed. The glaciers had deposited the debris all the way out to the coastline.

From Telescope Hill we gaze out across the Gorge and Jerry, then we hop back into the machine and head home for a brew, with enough data to complete a landscape painting of the Forgotten River.

South Westland and Fiordland are the last frontiers. Their people are remnants of the pioneering societies that earlier occupied most of this land.

The land has always taken its toll on its occupants and has allowed only the hardiest to survive, to reap the benefits of a lucky, lively hunt, a successful muster or just a job well done. In doing so it has produced people of knowledge and keen wits along with its characters.

A bushman, hunter or fisherman rises early, as the first rays of sunlight dawn on a new day, with many hopes and prospects to come. 'First up, best dressed' is the old saying.

Those meeting the challenge of the day full on and with enthusiasm enjoy the golden glow of sunset with tales of a day well done.

Hunter-gatherers have been our mainstay since time immemorial and so it is in South Westland. Deer, fish, whitebait and, until recently, forests have succumbed to the hands of men. We are changing our ways, but the true bushman is a man of character, sometimes noble in his bearing and principles and held in high regard. He not only rubs shoulders with his fellow man but also with the elements. He needs to know and understand these forces intimately to be successful in his quest. He may have all the stamina and prowess in the world, but unless his timing is right his exploits will end in disaster as sure as flood follows rain.

The patience of a saint is an attribute we value. It allows us to navigate the cycles, patterns and forecasts that determine our movements. From the outside we may see these people as exploiters of our natural world, but they possess the strengths, stamina and knowledge of a number of people all rolled into one. Many thousands of years of genetic inheritance and skills have passed down from parent to child to ensure survival.

They are people who know and understand the whims and ways of the bush and can live off the land, spending prolonged periods of time immersed within the wilderlands. Many of these principles are in danger of being lost but they are as necessary in today's world as in any other era. When the chips are down one bushman helps another. He drops the task at hand and sets about providing life support for those in need.

The unleashed drive and determination I have seen in some of these men and women never ceases to amaze me. Hopefully the youth will seize the opportunity to do better. Many of the old ways are being reined in, some for good reason. But the spontaneity of the moment shouldn't be softened by paperwork, the banter and barter quashed by the policies of hallowed men in grey suits.

Since I have lived in the south I have come to love and admire the spirit of these people. My idealism has been tempered by my connection with the realities of their existence in a place where the humble are held in high regard but the meek often fall by the wayside. We all have an impact, no matter how aware we are of the concerns of the natural world around us.

As I sit here watching the living ocean roll by, I see the storms come and go. Wind gusts move the sea into a rolling, surging mass, with whitecaps lifting off the crests. The overall power and energy is mind-blowing. It is a living entity all on its own, not needing me or anybody else to enhance its mana.

The awesome energies of the wilderness keep me in my place, one of thanks for the benefits we receive and respect for those aspects we are best to leave alone, so that wild energy can run its own course. I bow my head with tears of emotion, overpowered by the sheer strength of it all. And I raise my eyes to the dawning sun.

I have basically gone back to the stone age and worked my way forward from there, working out what I really need, rather than taking it all for granted or having it forced upon me just because I am part of a particular culture of people. There have been times so hard that today they are difficult to comprehend. During the early 1980s I lived so hard, so isolated, that my essence must have been totally focused on the goal to endure, whatever the cost.

After casting off all the opportunities the world had to offer, I have eked out an existence off my own bat. After looking difficulties in the eye and working out a solution with my own physical, mental and moral strength, I have become a hard man despite my overall compassion and consideration for others. Hard men never weep, they say, but I am pleased to say I do.

Our friends have helped us through, showing us concern and respect. I have been there and back again, scraping the bottom of the barrel, but usually seeing a silver lining whatever the hardship. The idealism of youth still abides within and my compassion is still ready to rise to the surface. But life has to be lived. You yourself have to do it, not someone else. The pipe dreams that we revel in all turn to ashes if we don't act upon them. If you feel dislocated from this society and find it difficult to walk within its expectations, then break away and find yourself at the working face of your convictions. Don't allow family and peer pressure to shackle your true spirit.

Along with hardness comes compassion, and commitment commands respect, whatever the cause. Your inner soul acts as your conscience. No judge needs to preside over your sentence; you already know better than any other the responsibilities that you need to embrace. People will reach out to help you, they can't help but do that, but you alone can save yourself.

I aim to stay healthy so I can watch our children grow, and hopefully live to see our grandchildren. My health is my wealth, enabling me to enjoy the simple pleasures that life has to offer. Most days I feel as young and fit as ever, except when I gaze in the mirror to be reminded of my progression through the stages of life.

I have dealt with many issues along the way, but seek to nourish my body in order to maintain my health. Food is my